Constructional Approaches
to Language 12

Sentence Patterns in English and Hebrew

Ron Kuzar

John Benjamins Publishing Company

Sentence Patterns in English and Hebrew

Constructional Approaches to Language

The series brings together research conducted within different constructional models and makes them available to scholars and students working in this and other related fields.

The topics range from descriptions of grammatical phenomena in different languages to theoretical issues concerning language acquisition, language change, and language use. The foundation of constructional research is provided by the model known as Construction Grammar (including Frame Semantics). The book series publishes studies in which this model is developed in new directions and extended through alternative approaches. Such approaches include cognitive linguistics, conceptual semantics, interaction and discourse, as well as typologically motivated alternatives, with implications both for constructional theories and for their applications in related fields such as communication studies, computational linguistics, AI, neurology, psychology, sociology, and anthropology.

This peer reviewed series is committed to innovative research and will include monographs, thematic collections of articles, and introductory textbooks.

For an overview of all books published in this series, please see
http://benjamins.com/catalog/cal

Editors

Mirjam Fried
Charles University, Prague,
Czech Republic

Jan-Ola Östman
University of Helsinki
Helsinki, Finland

Advisory Board

Peter Auer
University of Freiburg, Germany

Hans C. Boas
University of Texas at Austin, USA

William Croft
University of New Mexico, USA

Charles J. Fillmore
Int. Computer Science Institute, Berkeley, USA

Adele E. Goldberg
Princeton University, USA

Seizi Iwata
Osaka City University, Japan

Paul Kay
University of California, Berkeley, USA

Knud Lambrecht
University of Texas at Austin, USA

Michael Tomasello
Max Planck Institute for Evolutionary Anthropology, Germany

Arnold M. Zwicky
Stanford University, USA

Volume 12

Sentence Patterns in English and Hebrew
by Ron Kuzar

Sentence Patterns
in English and Hebrew

Ron Kuzar
University of Haifa

John Benjamins Publishing Company
Amsterdam / Philadelphia

⊗™ The paper used in this publication meets the minimum requirements of
the American National Standard for Information Sciences – Permanence
of Paper for Printed Library Materials, ANSI z39.48-1984.

Library of Congress Cataloging-in-Publication Data

Kuzar, Ron, 1947-
 Sentence patterns in English and Hebrew / Ron Kuzar.
   p. cm. (Constructional Approaches to Language, ISSN 1573-594X ; v. 12)
Includes bibliographical references and index.
1. English language--Grammar, comparative--Hebrew. 2. Hebrew language--Grammar, comparative--English. I. Title.
PE1099.K89   2012
492.4'5--dc23   2012026056
ISBN 978 90 272 0434 9   (Hb ; alk. paper)
ISBN 978 90 272 7331 4   (Eb)

© 2012 – John Benjamins B.V.
No part of this book may be reproduced in any form, by print, photoprint, microfilm, or any other means, without written permission from the publisher.

John Benjamins Publishing Co. · P.O. Box 36224 · 1020 ME Amsterdam · The Netherlands
John Benjamins North America · P.O. Box 27519 · Philadelphia PA 19118-0519 · USA

To the memory of Haiim. B. Rosén

Table of contents

Acknowledgements — XI
Preface — XIII

CHAPTER 1
Introduction: Justifying sentence patterns — 1
1.1 Preliminary discussion — 1
1.2 In search of an elegant architecture — 4
1.3 Argument structure constructions cannot encode linearization — 5
1.4 A top–down approach to construction analysis — 10
1.5 Sentence patterns — 14
1.6 Argument structure mapped onto sentence patterns — 17
1.7 Categorial affiliation and sentential functional roles — 20
1.8 Unmarked and marked sentence patterns — 22
1.9 Major and minor S-patterns — 25
1.10 The structure of this book — 28
1.11 Summary and conclusion of Chapter 1 — 29

CHAPTER 2
Subject initial sentence patterns — 31
2.1 Preliminary discussion — 31
2.2 Subject initial S-patterns in English — 31
2.3 The verbal S-pattern in English — 31
2.4 The copular S-patterns in English — 34
    2.4.1 The form and function of copular S-patterns in English — 34
    2.4.2 Copular verbs — 41
    2.4.3 Generalizations over the three COP S-patterns — 43
    2.4.4 Predication and patterning in the COP sentence — 45
    2.4.5 The borderline between copular and lexical verbs — 51
    2.4.6 Form and function of the unified COP S-Pattern — 54
2.5 Subject-initial S-patterns in Hebrew — 55
2.6 The verbal S-pattern in Hebrew — 55
2.7 The copular S-patterns in Hebrew — 56
2.8 Summary and conclusion of Chapter 2 — 60

CHAPTER 3
Predicate initial sentence patterns 63
- 3.1 Justifying predicate initial S-patterns 63
- 3.2 Predicate-initial S-patterns in English 65
  - 3.2.1 The existential S-pattern in English 66
  - 3.2.2 The evaluative S-pattern in English 72
    - 3.2.2.1 The cost S-pattern in English 80
  - 3.2.3 The environmental S-pattern in English 83
- 3.3 Predicate-initial S-patterns in Hebrew 86
  - 3.3.1 The existential S-pattern in Hebrew 87
    - 3.3.1.1 Morphologically unique and endemic predicates 87
    - 3.3.1.2 The possessor 87
  - 3.3.2 The existential S-pattern in Hebrew – continued 92
    - 3.3.2.1 The deteriorating-entity S-pattern in Hebrew 102
  - 3.3.3 The evaluative S-pattern in Hebrew 103
    - 3.3.3.1 The cost S-pattern in Hebrew 114
    - 3.3.3.2 The body-part-condition S-pattern in Hebrew 114
    - 3.3.3.3 The animal-induced-condition S-pattern in Hebrew 117
  - 3.3.4 The environmental S-pattern in Hebrew 119
    - 3.2.4.1 The PredP-alone S-pattern in Hebrew 123
- 3.4 Summary and conclusion of Chapter 3 128

CHAPTER 4
A field of sentence patterns 133
- 4.1 Fields 133
- 4.2 The field of S-pattern networks in English and Hebrew 133
- 4.3 Granularity 137
- 4.4 Summary and conclusion of Chapter 4 139

CHAPTER 5
The conceptual category of existence 141
- 5.1 Preliminary discussion 141
- 5.2 Conceptual category 144
- 5.3 Core and periphery of the conceptual category of existence in English 146
  - 5.3.1 The core of the conceptual category of existence in English 146
  - 5.3.2 The first ring of the conceptual category of existence in English 146
  - 5.3.3 The second ring of the conceptual category of existence in English 149
  - 5.3.4 The third ring of the conceptual category of existence in English 151

5.4 Core and periphery of the conceptual category of existence in Hebrew   154
    5.4.1 The core of the conceptual category of existence in Hebrew   155
    5.4.2 Stylistic inversion of S1 versus genuine P1 order   155
    5.4.3 The first ring of the conceptual category of existence in Hebrew   158
    5.4.4 The second ring of the conceptual category of existence in Hebrew   160
    5.4.5 The third ring of the conceptual category of existence in Hebrew   163
5.5 Summary and conclusion of Chapter 5   166

CHAPTER 6
The conceptual category of evaluation   169
6.1 Preliminary discussion   169
6.2 Core and periphery of the conceptual category of evaluation in English   172
    6.2.1 The core of the conceptual category of evaluation in English   172
    6.2.2 The first ring of the conceptual category of evaluation in English   174
    6.2.3 The second ring of the conceptual category of evaluation in English   175
6.3 Core and periphery of the conceptual category of evaluation in Hebrew   177
    6.3.1 The core of the conceptual category of evaluation in Hebrew   177
    6.3.2 The first ring of the conceptual category of evaluation in Hebrew   177
    6.3.3 The second ring of the conceptual category of evaluation in Hebrew   178
6.4 Summary and conclusion of Chapter 6   179

CHAPTER 7
The conceptual category of environmental conditions   181
7.1 Preliminary discussion   181
7.2 The core of the conceptual category of environmental conditions   181
7.3 The first ring of the conceptual category of environmental conditions   182
7.4 The second ring of the conceptual category of environmental conditions   183
7.5 The third ring of the conceptual category of environmental conditions   184
7.6 Summary and conclusion of Chapter 7   185

CHAPTER 8
Situation types and information structure   187
8.1 The non-arbitrary nature of the S1 and P1 word orders   187
8.2 Information structure within and across sentence patterns   196
8.3 Summary and conclusion of Chapter 8   201

CHAPTER 9
Non-canonical expletive behavior 203
9.1 Over- and under-grammaticalization in expletive behavior 203
9.2 Expletive reduction in English 204
9.3 Expletive addition in Hebrew 206
9.4 Summary and conclusion of Chapter 9 209

CHAPTER 10
Patterning revisited 211
10.1 Preliminary discussion 211
10.2 Patterning in the EX S-pattern 212
10.3 Patterning in the EV S-pattern 214
10.4 Patterning in a minor Hebrew S-pattern 215
10.5 Summary and conclusion of Chapter 10 216

CHAPTER 11
Noun incorporation 219
11.1 Preliminary discussion 219
11.2 Incorporation in the EV S-pattern 220
11.3 Incorporation in the possessive EX S-pattern in Biblical Hebrew 225
11.4 Summary and conclusion of Chapter 11 229

CHAPTER 12
Conclusion 231
12.1 Preliminary discussion 231
12.2 Sentence patterns 231
12.3 Patterning 234
12.4 Typological aspects 235
12.5 Finally 236

References 237
Index of constructions 247
Author index 249
Subject index 251

Acknowledgements

I would like to express my thanks to Mira Ariel, Nurit Melnik, and Hillel Taub-Tabib, who have read parts of earlier versions of the manuscript, for their valuable comments. I would also like to extend my gratitude to Hadar Netz, my dear friend and colleague, for her comments, advice, and friendship.

Various chapters and sections of this book have been presented at the following conferences: Workshop on Haiim B. Rosén's Contributions to Israeli Hebrew (Haifa, 2004), German Cognitive Linguistics Association: Second Annual Meeting (Munich, 2006), Fifth International Conference on Construction Grammar (Austin, 2008), Hebrew: A living Language (Tivon, 2010), Israeli Linguistic Society: 26th Annual Meeting (Haifa, 2010).

Various chapters and sections of this book have also been presented at the following colloquia: Department of English Faculty Seminar (Haifa, 2006), Department of Hebrew Faculty Seminar (Tel Aviv, 2006), Linguistic Colloquium (Berkeley, 2008), Department of Linguistics Faculty Seminar (Göttingen, 2008), Linguistic Colloquium (Munich, 2009).

I am grateful for the discussions following these conference presentations and colloquia.

The first draft of this book was written during my half-year Sabbatical at the Department of English and American Studies, Ludwig Maximilians University, Munich, during the Fall Semester of 2008/9. I would like to thank Hans-Jörg Schmid and all other members of the department for the wonderful and very productive time that I spent there. Dick Janney, Elmar Thalhammer, and Daphné Kerremans were all wonderful friends during that semester, and so was Simone Falk, with whom I had daily lunch-time chats on linguistics, food, and life.

Many thanks are due also to the two anonymous reviewers, whose insightful comments helped me correct mistakes and sharpen my arguments.

I am profoundly grateful to the two editors of our book series *Constructional Approaches to Language*, Mirjam Fried and Jan-Ola Östman, whose ongoing advice and encouragement helped me so much to improve the manuscript and complete the book. I thank also Lyn Barzilai, who touched up my style and copy-edited the text.

Preface

Linguistic scholarship is sharply divided nowadays between the more established Chomskyan approach reigning in the field since the late 1950s and various corpus-based, data-based, and usage-based (henceforth *data-rich*) approaches that have been developing during the past two decades.

While Chomskyan linguistics is in many senses still the dominant approach, one should not get the impression that the data-rich approach is a small esoteric trend. It has gained a respectable position in the past decades, and plays a leading role in interdisciplinary enterprises. In its basic orientation, it is well aligned with mainstream empirical research in psychology, psycholinguistics, brain research, and other cognitive domains.

The differences between the formalist Chomskyan and the data-rich enterprises are quite striking. The Chomskyan approach emphasizes theoretical work based on the postulated premise of universal grammar, which is claimed to constitute the core grammars of all languages. The richness of data in individual languages and in constructions that resist universal formulations is thereby rendered peripheral, hence not requiring explanation within the theoretical framework. This is an irrefutable model, and thus lacking scholarly rigor and explanatory power.

Furthermore, the data for research in the Chomskyan approach typically consist of idealized and de-contextualized sentence-forms, often produced as data, tested for grammaticality, and given a formal description – all by the very same scholar.

Data-rich approaches reject universal grammar as a premise. From their perspective, no facts of language are marginal. All facts of language are considered systemic and worthy of research. It is the naturally-occurring spoken and written texts, monologic as well as dialogic, that guide the linguist to theoretical conclusions about the linguistic system rather than the postulated premise of universal grammar.

Where cross-linguistic generalizations can be arrived at, they are best formulated at the level of language typology. In a language typology, similar linguistic factors and sets of factors are shown to be shared by several languages. Language typologies are not presupposed to finally boil down to language universals. Universalism is a possible, yet not a necessary horizon.

In the Chomskyan approach, syntax is viewed as an autonomous system. Grammar at large is viewed as a flowchart with input-output channels connecting the different modules of language. In the data-rich approach, syntax is not viewed as an autonomous system. Rather, different parts of the linguistic system interact in concert at the sentential level.

Within the data-rich approach, *cognitive linguistics* (Lakoff & Johnson 1980; 1999; Lakoff 1987; Fauconnier & Turner 2002; Langacker 1987; 1991; 2000) and *construction grammar* (Lakoff 1987; Fillmore, Kay & O'Connor 1988; Goldberg 1995; 2006; Croft 2001 to name but a few) are two theoretical and methodological frameworks that a large number of linguists share. Neither necessarily implies the other, but they are often coextensive. Both frameworks are actually families of frameworks, rather than tightly knit uniform dogmas. Scholars working in these frameworks cherish this pluralism as a fruitful community spirit and consider it a key ingredient of the linguistic enterprise at large. Cognitive linguistics and construction grammar have become influential also in fields tangential to grammar per se, such as first language acquisition and psycholinguistics (Tomasello 2003). This book has been deeply influenced by the work of the aforementioned scholars, their collaborators, and their followers.

Corpus linguistic research has made great strides in recent years, and in it, the usage-based approach (Bybee 2006; 2007) has been in a fruitful dialog with cognitive and constructional approaches. Due to the heuristic nature of my work in the current volume, a rigorous path of corpus analysis has not been taken. I do, however, hope that such research on issues developed here will be pursued. Here and there in the text, I point out such possibilities.

I spent the formative years of my linguistic education as an undergraduate and PhD student at the Department of Linguistics of the Hebrew University in Jerusalem. The department was established in 1953 by Hans Jacob Polotsky (1905–1991; studied in Berlin and Göttingen). It became one of the centers of European structural linguistics, and quite exceptional among them in its strong proclivity towards research on syntax and information structure.

Polotsky made a monumental contribution to Coptic grammar in his 1944 publication *Étude de syntaxe Copte*, in which he solved the puzzle of the *second tenses*. Coptic has a system of tenses in which each tense has two sets of forms. Polotsky found that their function was parallel to what started to be known in those years as the *cleft sentence* (Jespersen [1937] 1984: 73–74). At the time, constructions were not yet defined as foundational components of syntactic theory, but in the discourse of the teachers of the Department of Linguistics in Jerusalem they were surely felt to be so.

In an attempt to bring the phonological and morphological achievements of structural linguistics into syntax, Polotsky (1960: 1) calls sentence patterns "sentence conjugations". He explains:

> For the purpose of this outline, *conjugation* means the various ways in which a Coptic verb can enter into grammatical construction with actor expressions in such a way as to function either as a main sentence or as a dependent clause. Any such construction is a *conjugation*. We thus have *sentence conjugations* and *clause conjugations*.

Note how the word *construction* is used in passing as a regular word of the English language, while the word *conjugation* is marked for technical use. In current constructional approaches, *construction* is the reserved term. Polotsky's account, then, is an outline of sentential constructions in Coptic.

Haiim Baruch Rosén (1921–1999; PhD from Jerusalem, spent a post-doctoral year in Paris) followed Polotsky in the leadership of the department. In 1966, he published the second edition of *Ivrit Tova* 'Good Hebrew', to which a new, one-hundred-page syntactic supplement was appended, called *digmei mišpat/taxbir ivri* 'Sentence Patterns/Hebrew Syntax'. A shorter but more accessible English version of this chapter appeared later, in his (1977a) book *Contemporary Hebrew*.

Polotsky's *sentence conjugations* (just like Zellig Harris's 1951: 351 *sentence types*) represent a broad view of the sentence, concentrating on the predication relation as the main constitutive factor of sentence form. Hence, he identifies two basic sentence conjugations in Coptic: bipartite and tripartite (Polotsky 1960: 392–395). His treatment of the existential sentence (Polotsky 1960: 392–395), however, is not done within the context of this discussion, and its status in relation to the conjugations is not clear. Rosén's view is different. Besides the *variables* of each sentence pattern, to which the subject and the predicate naturally belong, he identified in some of the patterns also *constants* that are an integral part of the pattern.

In doing this, his work is more similar to Fries's (1952: 158–163) *types of sentences* and to Nida's ([1963] 1966) *sentence types*. Rosén's sentence patterns, however, are different from earlier accounts. On the one hand, Rosén's sentence patterns are much more sensitive to detail than their counterparts in Harris's, Polotsky's and Fries's studies. On the other hand, they are more parsimonious than Nida's detailed account, since Nida's account mixes together argument structure patterns and sentence patterns, whereas Rosén's account, for the first time, makes a distinction between argument structure patterns, which can be described within one single sentence pattern, and sentence patterns. In Rosén's view, the verbal group within the verbal sentence pattern is "subject to valence and case government" (Rosén 1966: 212).

Altogether, Rosén (1966) identified a set of twenty-one sentence patterns in Hebrew (eighteen in the English version of 1977a). These included major as well as minor sentence patterns, without making this distinction. A much later study (Jackson 1981), in which English and German sentence patterns are compared, presents fifty English and seventy German sentence patterns, but in this study, argument structure patterns and sentence patterns are again conflated.

Rosén's detailed, yet economical, view of some twenty sentence patterns stood at that time in diametrical opposition to the transformational-generative universal formula of S → NP VP upheld, in the context of Hebrew linguistics, for example, by Rubinstein (1968: 54). Rosén (1977a: 217) clearly states that "it is vital to emphasize that these patterns are not subject to derivation from one another [...], thus their number cannot be reduced".

Although Rosén did not specifically assign functions to each and every sentence pattern, he clearly stated that sentence patterns have meanings. Furthermore, he said (1966: 198) that "the meaning of a sentence arises from the meanings of the components and the meaning of the pattern". The latter three points, namely the plurality of patterns, their irreducibility, and their independent meanings, are harbingers of accepted tenets of construction grammar.

I started my undergraduate studies in the Department of Linguistics of the Hebrew University in the academic year 1969/70 and finished my Ph.D. (after a long detour) in 1989. During all these years, Polotsky was still active both in teaching and in research, but Rosén was running the department (in full cooperation with Polotsky). Syntax and information structure were predominant not only in the teachings of the latter two, but in the intellectual atmosphere of the whole department.

My dissertation (Kuzar 1989), entitled "Information Structure of the Sentence in Israeli Hebrew", was written under Rosén's supervision. Many of the ideas that are expressed in the current book have their beginning already there. Since then, I have written several articles on Hebrew sentence patterns in general and on predicate-initial sentence patterns in particular (Kuzar 1993; 1996; 2000; 2002; 2006; 2007), moving progressively from a structuralist to a cognitive–constructional scholarly worldview. All these papers are in Hebrew, and their re-working into English and into a more mature cognitive–constructional framework has been a part of the process of writing this book.

One of the effects of the rise to power of Chomskyan linguistics has been a collective amnesia of linguistic work done before Chomsky (1957). Everything done earlier was deemed descriptive and non-explanatory, hence also not a part of theoretical linguistics. Current cognitive, constructional, and psycholinguistic research is making an effort to find pathways to reconnect to valuable work done before 1957. For me, this has been a most natural course of thought and action, and I hope I have made some contribution towards this worthy tendency.

The reintroduction of the *sentence pattern* as a vital and useful theoretical construct, namely as a *construction*, alongside *argument structure* and other sentential constructions (primarily *information structure* constructions), is one of the main objectives of this book.

The justification for the introduction of the sentence pattern as a construction comes from two perspectives: (1) the shortcomings of the argument structure framework alone in accounting for syntactic generalizations and (2) the inability of argument structure constructions to account for sentences that do not have a clear predicate. The view that "describing the various types of simple clauses is tantamount to describing the various types of verbs, or *predications*, used in language" (Givón 2001a: 105) is strongly challenged here. This is done by the introduction of *patterning* as a complementary, and sometimes alternative, path for sentence formation, alongside *predication*.

The recognition that despite its Semitic origins, Hebrew is very similar to English in the sentence patterns that it maintains, has led me to view the two languages as belonging to the same typological group. A detailed analysis of the syntactic and semantic behavior of sentential constructions in the two languages has resulted in placing English and Hebrew at two poles of this typology. The position of other languages in this typology has not been pursued; it is just an educated guess (so I hope), based on my knowledge of other European languages and on literature about their sentential constructions. Hopefully, similar treatments of other languages within this typology will follow.

Another continuity between structuralism and current data-rich models is the recognition of the importance of naturally occurring language samples for linguistic research. All the examples in this book (save some schematic or speculative sentences) are real-life examples, taken primarily from the Internet (marked by "(I)"); "searching the web for specific morpho-syntactic patterns and novel uses of verbs is by now an established method for data collection" (Boas 2008: 13, and see references there). I have made a serious attempt to use only sources that show clear signs of being produced by native speakers of English and Hebrew. Sites on the Internet have been scanned and some active searches have been conducted, but no corpus (in a rigorous sense) has been defined, hence no statistical tendencies have been observed. Rigorous corpus-based verification would be a desired outcome of the current study.

In the spirit of reconnecting and re-familiarizing ourselves, as a community of scholars, with less known precursors of the constructional view on grammar, this book – in some of it more significant parts – constitutes a re-working and systematization of Rosén's work on sentence patterns in current constructional terms.

CHAPTER 1

Introduction

Justifying sentence patterns

1.1 Preliminary discussion

Construction Grammar made its first strides showing how supposedly peripheral constructions, such as the deictic *there* construction (Lakoff 1987: Case Study 3), the *let alone* construction, and the Comparative–Correlative construction (*the X-er, the Y-er*) (Fillmore, Kay & O'Connor 1988), as well as fully idiomatic expressions, can all be incorporated in a full constructional account of a language. This insistence on minor constructions came to demonstrate how forms that went unexplained in Transformational-Generative Grammar fared much better in Construction Grammar. Eventually, however, it is expected of a maturing school of thought to cover also the central mechanisms of language. Goldberg's (1995) book is one of these turning points, offering an account of the connection between the two most central mechanisms of language, namely verbal behavior and sentential encoding.

Peripheral or minor sentences do not always have a predicate whose role is to launch their structure. Yet sentences they are. It is the pattern alone that determines their form. This is true for a sentence such as *so far, so good* as well as for the Hebrew sentence *otxa l-a-mora* you.acc.m.sg to-the-teacher '(I am going to tell on) you to the teacher'. This way of sentence formation will be called here *patterning* as distinct from *predication*, since in such cases, it is the pattern – not some predicate – that gives life to the sentence. It will be shown, however, that patterning goes much beyond minor sentence constructions. In some of the following chapters, patterning will figure prominently also in major sentence constructions, either as a total replacement of predication or in some interplay with it. Fried & Östman's (2004: 78: n.4) note comes to mind here: "While marking the phrasal head is relevant and appropriate in some patterns, it is far from clear that all constructions in a language require a separate statement about head-dependent relations. We prefer to leave the theoretical issue open now".

There is, of course, nothing new in the recognition that some sentence forms have no predicate, but the common behavior of both minor and major sentence patterns has not been stated and has not been generalized as a device of sentence formation on a par with predication.

In the canonical verbal sentence itself, Goldberg's (1995) argument-structure approach has been problematized in different ways. Some scholars have gone in the direction of requiring more detailed semantics in event structure (Kay 2005) and in frame semantics (mini-constructions in Boas 2003, detailed verbal polysemy in Nemoto 2005). Others have suggested adding discourse and context factors to constructions, in addition to the traditional form and function pairings ("form" being read here as "argument structure"). The articles in Bergs & Diewald (2009) point in that direction, as do some of the presentations offered at ICCG–6 (Nikiforidou 2010; Östman 2010; Traugott 2010).

A central part in my own critique of Goldberg (1995) will come from the perspective of word order (linearization). Word order issues are not new, and have figured prominently in many schools of linguistics. Notably, tree diagrams in the Chomskyan tradition encode linear order through the tree-building principle of precedence (Carnie 2002: 72–75). In European functional Grammar à-la Dik,

> The cross-linguistic factors underlying the word order patterns found in natural languages are expressed in Functional Grammar by nine general principles of order which are supplemented by more specific principles reflecting the type of choices that languages tend to make from among the available options. Linear patterns in individual languages that comply with the general principles are not specified independently, but are handled with reference to the word order predictions encapsulated in the body of preferences and tendencies stated for the grammar as a whole. Language-specific aspects of order, on the other hand, are dealt with by a set of placement rules which locate constituents in predetermined, language-specific functional patterns. These functional patterns, in the case of clausal constituents, are based on the language-independent schema in (i), where S, O and V stand for subject, object and verb respectively, and the P positions designate special positions, as discussed in §6.2.

(i) $P_2, P_1 (V) S (V) O (V), P_3$ (Siewierska 1991: 201)

Neither the formal nor the functional views on linearization are construction specific. They presuppose the operation of universal or "language independent" (Siewierska 1991: 201) factors, and are consequently of no use in constructional approaches. In other formal approaches that are partly compatible with certain varieties of construction grammar, issues of word order are built into the syntactic mechanisms, as in Van Valin and LaPolla's Role & Reference Grammar (1997), in Head-driven Phrase Structure Grammar, and in Sign Based Construction Grammar (Sag 2010), but linearization considerations have not been discussed in a *generalized* way and have not triggered major discussions in the constructional literature.

The one exception is marked word order that is motivated by considerations of Information Structure. However, left dislocation or object fronting are mechanisms that apply to sentences whose unmarked linear form might be of different kinds, e.g. verbal sentences (SVO), existential sentences (*there* V(O)X), or evaluative ("extraposition") sentences (*it* V(O) *that.../to...*). Precisely these *unmarked* word orders of various sentential constructions are targeted in this book (more will be said on the multi-dimensional nature of markedness in the context of sentential word order in Section 1.8). Specifically, it is suggested here that while argument structure constructions play an important role in the formation of a verbal sentence, they need a complementary linearization mechanism, namely the *sentence pattern*, to linearize them.

But sentence patterns do not only linearize. They also specify the form and function of sentence components that do not belong to the predicate–argument set, but are present in the sentence pattern. Furthermore, each sentence pattern has a function that is stated in conjunction with the pattern.

Goldberg's (1995) book is a constructional answer to a lexicalist approach, in which lexical entries get directly mapped onto sentences. Such an approach does not properly account for a wide variety of sentences. The sentence *Pat kicked Bob the football* cannot come to life as a sentence out of the semantic nature of the verb *kick*. The verb *kick* requires a "kicker" and a "kicked thing", but it does not have a participant role reserved for the extra component *Bob*.

Argument structure constructions, then, mediate between the individual verb and its syntactic encoding. The ditransitive construction, for example, has three argument roles: agent, recipient, and patient. While the individual verbal roles "kicker" and "kicked thing" get comfortably mapped onto the constructional roles of agent and patient, accounting for *Pat kicked the football*, the recipient role realized by *Bob* does not come from the semantic frame (participant roles) of the verb, but from the semantic frame (argument roles) of the argument structure construction.

Argument structure constructions, however, are intended by Goldberg (1995) to perform two tasks: they map (and sometimes enrich or reduce) the individual participant roles of verbs onto the generalized slots of the argument structure construction, but they also map the generalized argument structure roles onto syntactic roles, such as subject and object. "Sentence types are viewed as argument structure constructions", says Goldberg (1995: 24), thereby reducing syntactic representation to a mere reflection of argument structure constructions.

The first part of Goldberg's model, namely the mapping of participant roles to argument structure roles, elegantly solves the problems Goldberg identified in lexicalist models, in that it is able to account for both semi-conventionalized and ad hoc uses of a verb in an argument configuration that is not prototypically its own. The mapping of argument structure roles to syntactic roles, however, raises problems, to be discussed in more detail in Section 1.3. Most acutely, Goldberg's argument structure constructions are not designed to account for linearization facts and indeed do not linearize them into their sentential form. In this introductory chapter, the second mapping in Goldberg's model will be critiqued in some detail, and it will be suggested that argument structure constructions should be limited to the mapping of the verb's participant roles onto generalized argument role slots, but that the mapping of argument structure roles onto sentential syntactic roles is better handled by a separate mechanism, a sentential construction called *sentence pattern* (S-pattern).

This is a general introductory chapter, so its argumentation will be interlaced with some preliminary pronouncements of theoretical orientation. I will start with a declaration of my preferred style of modeling in Section 1.2. In Section 1.3, a critique of Goldberg's argument structure constructions will be presented. Section 1.4 is another methodological section, in which I will align myself with Croft's (2001) concept of the construction as the primitive unit of syntax and with his top–down methodology of analyzing constructions. In Section 1.5, the *sentence pattern* will be presented in more detail as a construction. The mapping of argument structure constructions onto sentence patterns will be elaborated in Section 1.6. Categorial and functional terms will be discussed in Section 1.7. The issue of markedness will be discussed in Section 1.8. Major and minor S-patterns will be teased apart in Section 1.9. Finally, a general outline of the chapters of the book will be given in 1.10.

1.2 In search of an elegant architecture

A construction is an abstract entity that is extracted out of actual instances of language samples. It is a theoretical construct, or in Saussure's ([1916] 1959: 111) terms *form*, while the actual instances of language are *substance*. Substance does not determine form. In deriving form from substance, much depends on one's point of view. Various forms may arise from the same substance. It is part of its raw nature, that substance does not come classified and categorized. Form always has pre-existing organizing principles. As organized matter, form often has an elegant appearance. But elegance in science is an elusive term. Watson's famous statement at the moment of the discovery of the double helix "We knew it was right because it was so beautiful" does not necessarily apply in all cases. The journalist Jim Holt has this to say about the beauty of modeling in contemporary physics:

> Looking back through the history of science, it is plain that beauty is a harbinger of probability only in retrospect. Most aesthetic convictions held by scientists – like the Aristotelian notion that uniform circular motion is the loveliest of all – ended up impeding the advance of knowledge. Innovations like Kepler's ellipses or quantum mechanics usually come surrounded by an aura of ugliness, which predictive success replaces with the splendor of truth. The great exception is Einstein's relativity theory, a singularly heroic discovery that set the tone for the rest of the century. Today's physicists have returned to the classical Greek project of understanding the cosmos by thought alone. The beautiful Final Theory will be the true one, not because it accords with the empirical evidence, but because it reflects the mind of God – a God who geometrizes or arithmetizes, depending on your taste (Holt 1996).

Indeed it is geometry, or in our case perhaps architecture, that is so fascinating. Rather than viewing constructions as being chaotically jumbled in an unordered *constructicon* (Jurafsky 1992), Fillmore (2006; Forthcoming) conceives of the constructicon as containing organized frame-to-frame relations. Goldberg (1995: 5) views argument structure constructions as members of one large network, interconnected by links. Constructions may, however, have more than one kind of organizing principles. Trying to force unrelated constructions into one network may at times be no less inelegant than leaving them in chaos. In the approach developed in the current study, the architectural representation of constructions will prove to be both ordered and unordered at different parts of the model, with no a priori commitment to a fully inter-linked system (see specifically the discussion of fields in Chapter 4).

1.3 Argument structure constructions cannot encode linearization

Goldberg (1995) has taken a strong position against a purely lexicalist approach to sentence formation (contra e.g Rappaport Hovav & Levin 1998.), a view that is shared in the current study as well. In addition to the lexicon, there are phrasal formations onto which lexical formations are mapped, providing the sentence with its syntactic roles and linear arrangement. In Goldberg's view, this happens in one fell swoop in the argument structure construction, where the individual participant roles of a verb are matched with the generalized argument structure roles of the construction, the latter being defined in terms of semantic roles such as *agent, cause, patient, theme, goal,* etc. These are concomitantly mapped onto the syntactic roles *subject, object,* and *oblique (object)*.

Postponing for the moment the questionable universality (or even globality, regarding English) of all these semantic and syntactic roles, let them be presumed

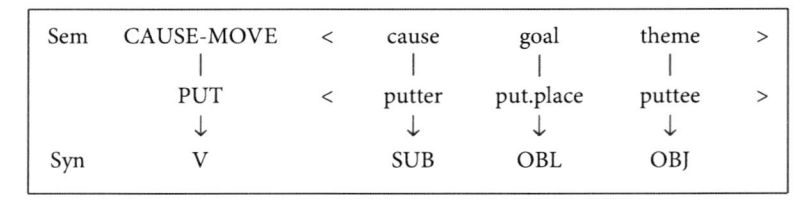

Sem	CAUSE-MOVE	<	cause	goal	theme	>
	|		|	|	|	
	PUT	<	putter	put.place	puttee	>
	↓		↓	↓	↓	
Syn	V		SUB	OBL	OBJ	

Figure 1. The Caused-Motion construction (Goldberg 1995: 52)

to be unproblematic for the sake of the present discussion. One of Goldberg's argument structure constructions is given in Figure 1, as an example. This one depicts the Caused-Motion construction (some minor details have been omitted). The top and bottom lines, tagged on the left as Sem(antics) and Syn(tax), represent generalized semantic and syntactic roles respectively. The middle line is reserved for the individual verb and its participant roles.

This diagram says that verbs with the semantics labeled *cause-move* have the argument structure that appears on the top line between the angular brackets, namely they will have three arguments, semantically characterized as *cause*, *goal*, and *theme*. These are mapped (via the arrows) onto syntax (bottom line) such that each is associated with a unique syntactic role, namely SUBJ, OBL, and OBJ. The individual verb selected here happens to be *put*. The verb has its own specific profile of participant roles labeled in verb-specific terms, such as *putter*, *put.place*, and *puttee*. These fall into the appropriate argument roles (in Goldberg's terms "get fused" with them) by virtue of their being in an "instance of" relation with the generalized argument roles. This mapping is "determined by general categorization principles" (Goldberg 1995: 50).

There is a whole array of argument structure constructions that are constituted in the same manner. Each of these constructions is routinely associated with verbs whose participant roles get unproblematically fused with their respective argument roles by general categorization principles.

However, a speaker may, and in fact quite often does, select a verb whose participant roles do not fit the argument roles of the construction. In this case, the speaker takes advantage of the unfilled slots of the constructions and supplies additional arguments, thus creating a new meaning for that verb on the fly. Some of these meanings have been conventionalized to a certain degree; others may be entirely ad hoc and creative. Goldberg's stock example is the intransitive verb *sneeze*, which may be transitivized, by being inserted into the caused-motion construction, resulting in the sentence *Sam sneezed the napkin off the table* (Goldberg 1995: 29).

Along with the first move, in which the participant roles of the verb have been enriched by the creative speaker and the fusion with the argument roles of the construction has been accomplished, a second move takes place. Via the association of the argument roles with syntactic roles, the participant roles are indirectly mapped onto syntactic roles. The mapping onto syntax is blind to the original source profile of the verb.

The mapping onto syntax, however, has two disparate aspects: syntactic role assignment and linearization. The syntactic role assignment is carried out in each argument structure construction by the one-to-one arrow relation shown in Figure 1. Yet, the word order of the sentence is not specified there. In the argument structure construction, as may be seen in Figure 1, the verb appears on the left side, outside the angular brackets of the argument frame. The order of components inside this frame is also not necessarily – and indeed is not in this case – the order of arguments in the actual sentence.

To understand how word order is determined in Goldberg's model, we have to expand our field of vision and look at the way all argument structure constructions are related to one another. This is done through a hierarchical network of constructions, the top parts of which are represented (with minor omissions) in Figure 2 (Goldberg 1995: 109).

The network is inter-connected by arrows indicating the top–down inheritance relation between the constructions. Whatever is not specifically stated in a certain daughter construction is inherited from the mother construction in the hierarchy. In Goldberg's words:

> Generalizations across constructions concerning word order facts, case-marking properties, and links between semantics and grammatical relations can all be captured by stating these generalizations at a sufficiently high node in an inheritance hierarchy of constructions. Thus, such generalizations are inherited through dominated constructions, unless a particular construction prevents such inheritance by having a conflicting specification (Goldberg 1995: 108).

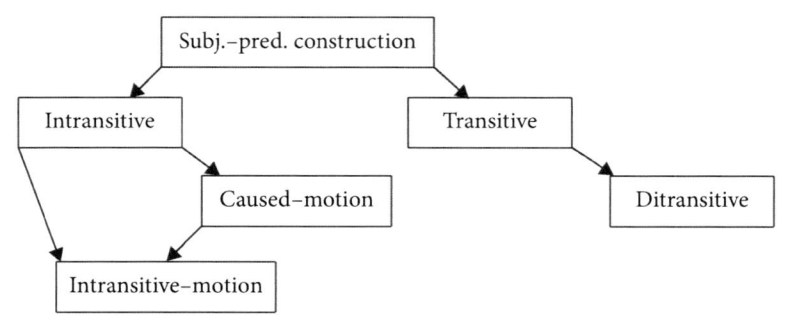

Figure 2. The network of argument structure constructions (partial)

Further down Goldberg suggests:

> The fact that English is an SVO language can be captured by specifying a word-order constraint on the top node of the diagram, at the level of the subject–predicate construction. Certain constructions further down the inheritance hierarchy, such as the topicalization construction or the locative *there* construction (not shown), can override the word order constraint with construction specific constraints. Thus generalizations about word order can be captured while at the same time other constructions with exceptional word order are permitted (Goldberg 1995: 110).

Goldberg, however, leaves all the parts of the model that have to do with word order unspecified. A careful examination of her proposal reveals a number of gaps. First of all, we do not know what the top node might look like. The top node is an abstract node that remains a black box: it does not show internal structure nor actual instantiation. There are no sentences that are subject–predicate alone, without being something more specific down the hierarchy.

Even if the top node were somehow specified, it could not capture the SVO order, but only the SV order, since the inclusion of an object only occurs at the first bifurcation, where intransitive and transitive argument structure constructions are differentiated. In fact, it is not at all clear that such a construction is necessary. Indeed, in the "thumbnail sketch" of Construction Grammar by Fried & Östman (2004), such a construction is not suggested. Rather, the need for this construction seems to arise from the theory-internal requirement in Goldberg's theory to have all argument structure constructions belong to a single network.

The fact that the top node is not specified is not an oversight. In Goldberg's (1995) model, there are genuine difficulties that must have prevented Goldberg from doing so. At the heart of the argument structure construction stands the mapping of semantic to syntactic roles. But at that presumed high level of abstraction, there is no semantic generalization that would hold for the whole network. The only safe assumption is that on the *Syn* line there would be a subject. But the identity of the argument role that would be mapped onto it is unclear, most probably unassessable. The SVO order could not be stated there, unless the frame is filled with more informative matter not directly related to the concept of argument structure. Even if Goldberg's statement is modified so that the SVO order would be separately stated at the level of the immediate daughters of the top node, namely the SV order for the intransitive construction and the SVO order for the transitive construction, the methodological tools for carrying this out are not supplied.

There are some places in Goldberg (1995) where a discussion of word order is unavoidable, for instance when the difference between the Ditransitive and the Transfer-Caused-Motion construction is elaborated. The Ditransitive construction is exemplified in (1a), the Transfer-Caused-Motion construction in (1b).

(1) a. John gave Mary an apple.
    b. John gave an apple to Mary.

The difference between the two constructions is presented by Goldberg as involving a separate focus structure, which is incorporated into the diagrams, as can be seen in Figures 3 and 4.

However, here too, the order of arguments does not represent the linearized order. Even if an SVO generalization were inserted somewhere up the hierarchy, the issue here is not SVO, but the relative order $OBJ_1 - OBJ_2$ or OBJ – OBL. Hence, a linearization mechanism is needed, *external to the argument structure construction*, which could place the focused OBL element representing the *recipient* in final position.

The multiplicity of verbal argument structure constructions is a necessity compelled by the facts of language. But their number is their strength as well as their weakness. It is their strength, because all the verbs of the lexicon fit into a relatively small and elegant taxonomy of constructions. It is, however, also their weakness, because there are too many argument structure constructions than needed to make word order generalizations (see discussion on granularity, Section 4.3). If linearization cannot be stated at the top of the hierarchy, as has hopefully been demonstrated here, then it would have to be stated repeatedly across the lower level elements of the hierarchy. Even if we knew how to represent it on the

Sem	CAUSE-RECEIVE	<	agt	rec	pat	>
	|		|	|	|	
	PRED	<				>
	↓		↓	↓	↓	
					focus	
Syn	V		SUB	OBJ	OBJ_2	

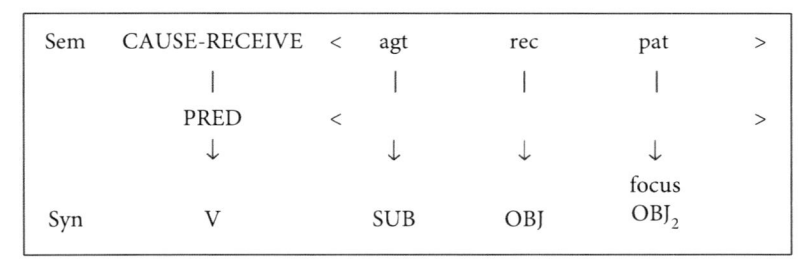

Figure 3. The Ditransitive construction (Goldberg 1995: 93)

Sem	CAUSE-RECEIVE	<	agt	rec	pat	>
	|		|	|	|	
	PRED	<				>
	↓		↓	↓	↓	
				focus		
Syn	V		SUB	OBL	OBJ	

Figure 4. The Transfer-Caused-Motion construction (Goldberg 1995: 93)

argument structure construction, we would be left with an inelegant atomization of syntactic information.

The simplest way to avoid this atomization is to postulate the existence of a sentential syntactic construction, called here *sentence pattern* (S-pattern), which consists of linearized slots that are labeled in such a way that argument structure constructions are unproblematically mapped on them.

It should be noted, in passing, that in later work, Goldberg addresses issues of word order (Goldberg & Del Giudice 2005; Goldberg 2006: Ch. 8; Goldberg, Casenhiser & White 2007); however, these are all cases of marked word order alternants of the Verbal (V) S-pattern, and no treatment of the unmarked word order of the V S-pattern or of the non-SVO S-patterns is offered there.

Marked word order is easy to motivate, precisely because it is marked; namely, it is employed to achieve a particular function. Hence, different linearizations within the *same* S-pattern may be accounted for through an "ordering construction". This is what is done by Kuningas & Leino (2006: 303–306) in their treatment of the Left-Topic Construction in Kabyle. The postulation of an ordering construction in this case is premised by the existence of a "basic word order" (Kuningas & Leino 2006: 301).

Such cases of simple motivation are a far cry from what happens in languages such as English and Hebrew, which maintain two major "basic" word orders, subject initial and predicate initial, and the S-patterns are multiply motivated by a host of factors, some of which merely suggest cognitive inclinations to be manifested as either subject initial or predicate initial. This will be described in detail in Chapter 8. It is therefore suggested here that subject initial and predicate initial S-patterns may not be viewed as each other's basic and non-basic counterparts. The postulation of separate S-patterns with *separate* basic (unmarked) word orders is unavoidable. This does not exclude the possibility, which is hardly discussed in this book, that more simply motivated word order variations *within* each S-pattern may be accounted for through ordering constructions of the kind discussed by Kuningas & Leino (2006).

Before discussing S-patterns as linearizing constructions in the context of the verbal sentence (in Section 1.5), another methodological clarification is necessary, regarding the question of the basic units of our analysis. This will be done in the next section (1.4).

1.4 A top–down approach to construction analysis

Sentences are linguistic signs in the Saussurean sense. They are Janus-faced: they have a signifier and a signified, or in current constructional terms, they display a pairing of form and meaning/function.

In modern linguistics, it has been customary to use a bottom-up procedure in the analysis of linguistic structure. It has been assumed that the small linguistic signs are atomic primitives (Croft 2001: 45–49), and that the larger signs are arrived at by putting together smaller building blocks (Langacker 2000: 151) to form a structured ensemble. In other words, sentences are complex units, made out of smaller primitive units.

A minority position in the structuralist school was held by Hjelmslev, who suggested using a top–down motion to discover the building blocks, from which, in turn, larger structures, his *units*, are arrived at in a bottom-up motion. For Hjelmslev the starting point is the whole synchronic body of texts of the language: "all that is written and said in Danish" (Hjelmslev 1961 [1943]: 98).

> After a syntagmatic deduction of the textual analysis is brought to an end, a paradigmatic deduction is undertaken. Here the language is articulated into *categories*, into which the highest-degree taxeme categories of the textual analysis are distributed, and from which, through a synthesis, can be deduced the possible *units* of the language (Hjelmslev 1961 [1943]: 100–101).

In Hjelmslev's view, the small elements are global to the whole language, and they serve as the building blocks of higher-order constructions. Hjelmslev's model suffers from circularity. It is supposedly based on discovery procedures, but no detailed methodology has ever been suggested or actually rigorously used in his framework.

Inspired, inter alia, by Cognitive Grammar (Langacker 1987; 1991), Croft (2001: 5) put forward the proposition that syntactic constructions are the primitives of syntactic theory, and that the constituents of the constructions are arrived at through a top–down motion. This is a more rigorous top–down model, which does not take the whole corpus of a language as its starting point, but the syntactic construction itself. Hjelmslev assumed no primitives. Croft takes the construction as the primitive of language. At least for sentential syntax this allows actual implementation.

In a top-down analysis of the syntactic pattern, under these theoretical premises, there is no guarantee, nor indeed any expectation, that the subparts resulting from the analysis of one construction would be identical to those of another. They might do so, but this has to be established empirically, and not assumed in advance. There are, then, no global building blocks, only parts of specific constructions. For example, the comparability of the "subject" of an SVO sentence and the "notional subject" of an existential sentence is far from being obvious.

As primitives, syntactic constructions are not arrived at by discovery procedures. In structuralism, the discovery of a phoneme was an almost technical issue of testing sounds distributionally and assessing whether two sounds are in pertinent opposition, hence phonemes, in complementary distribution, hence allophones, or in free variation, hence free variants. Morphological units have also been subjected to the same kind of testing. The achievement of structuralism in applying discovery procedures to the smaller units of language is a well known fact. It was syntax and sentence structure that resisted these procedures. "The full sentence as a product of the linguistic laboratory was that stubborn nut on which all [structuralist] wrenches broke" (Kuzar 1997: 252).

Sentences, then, are sliced out of the substance of language by observation, and by applying general principles of categorization onto heretofore unstructured substance. Categorization is very different from testing. It is based on general cognitive principles of sameness and difference, of identifying distinctive and non-distinctive difference, etc. As such, categorization is subject to yielding different results, relative to different objectives in making the categorization and perhaps also relative to other determinative factors. This is not by itself a disadvantage, but it should be recognized.

"The identification of constructions is essentially a *categorization* problem" says Croft (2001: 52; also Croft 2007: 646), and indeed a problem it is. There are several levels of abstraction at which a pattern may be identified by categorization, and it may take some trial and error before the optimal constructional form of a particular pattern is established in order to then be analyzed into its parts.

We might, for example, find an initial recurrent pattern such as *it is good to see you, it is so nice to be here, it is quite sad to witness all this*, etc. All sentences in this pattern share some features of form: they start with the expletive *it*, followed by the copula *be*, by an adjective, and finally by an infinitive phrase (InfP). This set of sentences also shares the same function, namely these sentences express the speaker's subjective evaluation (expressed by the APs *good/so nice/quite sad*) of an event (expressed by the InfP *to see you/to be here/to witness all this*). By saying that, we have extracted a pairing of form and function, we have in fact postulated the existence of a construction. But are we done now?

Not quite, because as we continue observing the substance of language, we find that sentences such as *it is fun to see you, it is a great honor to be here, it is a tragedy to witness all this*, also display a similar pairing of form and function. In this new set, *fun, a great honor*, and *a tragedy* are NPs, hence they differ in form from the APs *good, so nice*, and *quite sad*. Yet they share with the first set the same function, namely these sentences express the speaker's subjective evaluation (expressed by the NPs *fun, a great honor*, and *a tragedy*) of an event (expressed by the InfP *to see you/to be here/to witness all this*). Based on the data from these two sets, we may conclude that we either have two constructions paired with the same function, or one construction with a bivariate slot, which may host either APs or NPs.

However, this is not where the story ends. Soon enough we realize that sentences such as *it sucks to see you/it surely pays to be here/it makes me sad to witness all this* differ from the first two sets only in that they have a VP (*sucks, surely pays*, and *makes me sad*). We further conclude that VPs may also appear in that position. Based on the data from these three sets, we have to conclude now that we either have three constructions paired with the same function, or one construction with a trivariate slot, which may host APs, NPs or VP. A sentence such as *it is out of the question to be here*, adds to this multivariate slot also PPs such as *out of the question*.

The options are tripled, as we observe that the InfP may be substituted by a *that*-clause, as in *it is good* or *it makes me sad that you came*, or by a gerund phrase (GrdP), as in *it is fun having you with us*. The form–function relation is still the same, in the sense that the *that*-clause or the GrdP represents the event being evaluated by the speaker just as the InfP does. There are, of course, differences between the encoding of an event as an InfP, GrdP, or *that*-clause, but these differences do not invalidate the shared function of all these sentences. The number of options is doubled again, when we realize that there is also an optional slot for an affectee in these sentences (the PP *for her* in the sentence *it is good for her that you came*). The combination of four possible predicates, with three possible nominalizations of events, with a binary option of having or not having an affectee, culminates in twenty four possible constructions, which all share the same function.

Two questions arise now. First, to what extent and for what purposes are these patterns to be viewed as different constructions or one construction? Second, what is the appropriate descriptive tool to account for the many-to-one relation between the many forms and the one function?

On the one hand, it is clear that for certain purposes, individual treatment of the constructions is needed. For example, when the predicate is a verb, we might have six mini-constructions (one verb, three nominalizations, with or without an affectee). These constructions are subject to verb morphology and will enter verb complexes specific to verb morphology. All other constructions, which have an NP, AP, or PP as a predicate, enter verb complexes specific to the copula *be*. So for these purposes, the group of twenty four constructions discussed above may be divided into two groups, to handle verb and copula morphology and syntax. Other divisions may be needed as well.

What is common to all of them, though, is (a) the definition of their major sub-parts (expletive *it*, evaluative predicate, optional affectee, and nominalized event), (b) their linearization (in the order just mentioned), and (c) their function (subjective evaluation of an event). Since linearizations have to be formulated in terms specific to the subparts of each construction, a generalization over these twenty four constructions is justified.

The many-to-one mapping of twenty four forms to one function may be carried out through a network. Doing this takes up redundant descriptive machinery and is less elegant than the tool of S-patterns suggested here, which enumerates the components of the construction in terms of multivariate slots listed in their linearized form. The S-pattern is associated with one generalized function, which is spelled out in this book in a verbal way, but may of course be formalized as a feature of the construction.

The construction that has been discussed here is the evaluative sentence pattern (EV S-pattern) to be described in detail in Sections 3.2.2 for English and 3.3.3 for Hebrew.

To summarize the top–down procedure advocated here, it is based on the assumption that constructions are form extracted from substance; namely, a construction is not an entity pre-existing its assessment. Rather, it is a form that is extracted by way of categorization from the substance of language for particular descriptive purposes, using relevant conceptual tools.

The various possible levels of generalization display the issue of granularity. If we consider each variant as a separate construction, we get a fine-grained perspective, which is useful for certain purposes. Having all variant constructions contained in one construction represents a coarse-grained point of view, which is useful for other purposes. If we wish to include in one construction all the forms that share (a) functionally similar subparts, (b) the same linearization, and (c) the same function, we need to allow for inner variability in form, namely to have multivariate slots.

In the upcoming discussion of S-patterns, a coarse-grained perspective will be taken, which is well suited to making generalizations over as many formal variants as possible, so long as the generalized function is the same. This does not preclude a further fine-grained categorization of each of these constructions for other types of investigation.

In Section 1.5, the concept of S-pattern is presented in detail.

1.5 Sentence patterns

A sentence pattern (S-pattern) is a specific kind of a sentential construction. The term *pattern* echoes traditional practices, but at the same time it also constitutes a proper name that distinguishes it from other kinds of sentential constructions with which it interacts. The use of *pattern* as a specific kind of *construction* is similar to the use of *object* as the name of a specific kind of *complement*.

S-patterns constitute a linearized list of components defined in terms of their categorial affiliation (form) and their functional role (function). It is predominantly in the verbal sentence that the number and identity of components correspond to the predicate and its arguments. Indeed in the V S-pattern only these components are present. But in other sentence types, there are other components – constants as well as variables – which have nothing to do with the predicate and its arguments. Still, they do need to be specified and defined in terms of their form and function, and they need to be assigned their position in the linearized S-pattern. The copula in the copular sentence, the expletives *it* and *there* in the evaluative and existential sentences, are examples of grammatical components that are independent of argument structure. However, also lexical components, such as adjuncts, may be central to certain sentence types. For example, the locative adjunct in locative-inversion sentences (the PP *on the table* in the sentence *on the table stood a strange looking vase*) has to be defined and assigned a place in the sequence. In all these cases, the formation of a sentence involves not only predication but also patterning. The S-pattern, then, is the place where all the components of the sentence are specified, defined, and linearized.

Every S-pattern has a default form. In its default form, all other constructional dimensions of the sentence (such as sentence mood, polarity, modality, and information structure), are unmarked. A sentence, then, is unmarked when it is declarative, positive, non-modal, and has the word order and information structure prototypical of the S-pattern that it instantiates. Different languages may have a different ensemble of sentential dimensions. In French, for example, different word order variants will need to be stated for lexical and pronominal objects, while this is not the case in English or Hebrew.

The S-pattern is postulated in terms of the maximal number of slots possible in any sentence instantiating that pattern. Taking the V S-pattern (verbal sentence pattern) as an example, this information is extracted from generalizing over all the argument structures of verbs participating in this S-pattern. In English, for example, we end up with SV, SVO, and SVOO. The maximal form, therefore, is SVOO. Each verb will make use of the slots appropriate for its argument structure. Incidentally, the term *oblique* has been eliminated in the proposed S-patterns, since it is a hybrid that marks both function as object and form as PP. Categorial affiliation (parts of speech, phrasal categories) are separately marked in each S-pattern, thus NP and PP complements are equally seen as objects. In other words, both NP V NP NP and NP V NP PP are viewed as SVO_1O_2.

In the case of the verbal sentence, the unordered output of the fusion between participant roles and argument structure roles gets mapped onto the linear S-pattern. In the S-pattern, the different positions are defined not only in terms of functional roles but also in terms of their categorial affiliation (part of speech). Goldberg's model marks categorial affiliation only implicitly (subject and object are presumed to be NPs, oblique is PP). But Goldberg's model does not address sentences with nominalized participants, such as InfPs, GrdPs, and *That*-clauses, which appear in existential or evaluative sentences. In the model of S-patterns proposed here, such nominals will be central categories in some of the S-patterns, thus the dual marking is mandatory.

All the cases that Goldberg (1995) and others discuss in the literature on argument structure fall under the Verbal (V) S-pattern. Naturally, The V S-pattern uses verbs as predicates, determining the number and nature of the arguments. There are, however, two additional kinds of sentences that are not covered in Goldberg's framework. One includes S-patterns that employ verbs as predicates, but are not SVO, such as existential sentences (*there is a mouse in the kitchen*) and evaluative (extraposition) sentences (*it annoys her to do this*). The other kind includes S-patterns that use non-verbal predicates, such as copular sentences (*this wine is sour*) and again evaluative sentences (*it is good/fun to be here*). These kinds of sentences will concern us later. Notably, the copular S-pattern is presented in Section 2.4.4 as a case of patterning rather than predication. Patterning does not require predicates, let alone arguments, hence argument structure constructions are irrelevant altogether in this case.

Going back to the V S-pattern, English has five basic syntactic formations in this pattern. (Excluded from our discussion are *environmental* verbs, such as *rain, snow, freeze*, for reasons that will become clear in Section 3.2.3.) The five formations of the V S-pattern are shown in (2). In addition, NPs may be substituted under certain constrains by infinitive phrases (InfP), gerund phrases (GrdP), and *that*-clauses. The latter three are referred to by the superordinate term *nominal*. Nominals, however, are not primary members, but only substitutes in the V S-pattern. They will feature prominently in the evaluative S-pattern, where they are the primary constituents of the construction. Consequently, only NPs (but not nominals) appear in the formulas of the possible formations of the V S-pattern in (2).

(2) a. NP V
    b. NP V NP
    c. NP V PP
    d. NP V NP NP
    e. NP V NP PP

These five formations are lower-level constructions. Note that these formations are not argument structure constructions. Each could accommodate more than one argument structure construction. The highest generalization over the list in (2) is given in the V S-pattern formula shown in Figure 5.

A quick comparison between the formations in (2) and the V S-pattern formula in Figure 5 discloses the fact that not all theoretically possible combinations

NP	[vp	V	NP/PP	NP/PP	]
Subj		Pred	Obj₁	Obj₂	

Figure 5. V S-pattern in English

of NPs and PPs are materialized in the V S-pattern. For example NP V PP PP is not an option in English. This is a direct result of the fact that the S-pattern is a generalization of its constituting argument structures, and not an independently postulated structure.

The V S-pattern exemplifies the way S-patterns will be encoded in diagrams throughout this book. The diagrams consist of two rows, the top row representing categorial affiliation and the bottom row representing functional roles. In the V S-pattern, the argument structure constructions get linearized by being mapped onto the S-pattern. The details of this mapping are discussed in the next section.

1.6 Argument structure mapped onto sentence patterns

In this section, a model will be proposed in which argument structure construction are mapped onto S-patterns. In this model, the S-pattern adds linearization to the unordered argument structure construction.

Let us take Goldberg's (1995: 63) Conative Construction (*Ethel shot at Fred*) as a starting point. In Figure 6, the upper box is the argument structure construction, and the lower box is the S-pattern, which serves here as the linearization construction. Within the argument structure construction, the generalized argument structure roles *agt* (agent) and *theme* are mapped onto the syntactic roles Subj and Obj$_{\text{"at"}}$ (Goldberg's Obl$_{\text{"at"}}$ has been changed to Obj$_{\text{"at"}}$ in line with the separation between categorial and functional terms discussed in Section 1.5).

The lower box represents the S-pattern. The bottom row of the S-pattern lists the sentential functional (syntactic) roles in the appropriate linear order. Now, between the two constructions a simple process of label matching takes place, mapping the unordered arguments onto their linearized slots. The v of the argument structure construction gets mapped onto the V of the S-pattern, Subj onto Subj, and Obj$_{\text{"at"}}$ onto Obj$_1$. The subject is by default an NP. The mark "at" indicates that Obj$_1$ will be a PP. These facts are shown in the lower row of the S-pattern. The slot Obj$_2$ remains unfilled, which is in line with the fact that not all slots in the S-pattern have to be filled, since the S-pattern has been defined as the *maximal* representations of its potential instantiations.

```
Sem  DIRECT-ACTION-AT   <    agt      theme    >
         |                    |         |
       PRED SHOOT          shooter   shot.one   >
         ↓                    ↓         ↓
Syn      V                  SUBJ      OBJ"at"
```

```
[  NP        [vp   V      NP/PP    NP/PP    ]
   Subj            Pred   Obj₁     Obj₂

   Ethel           shoot  at Fred
```

Label matching

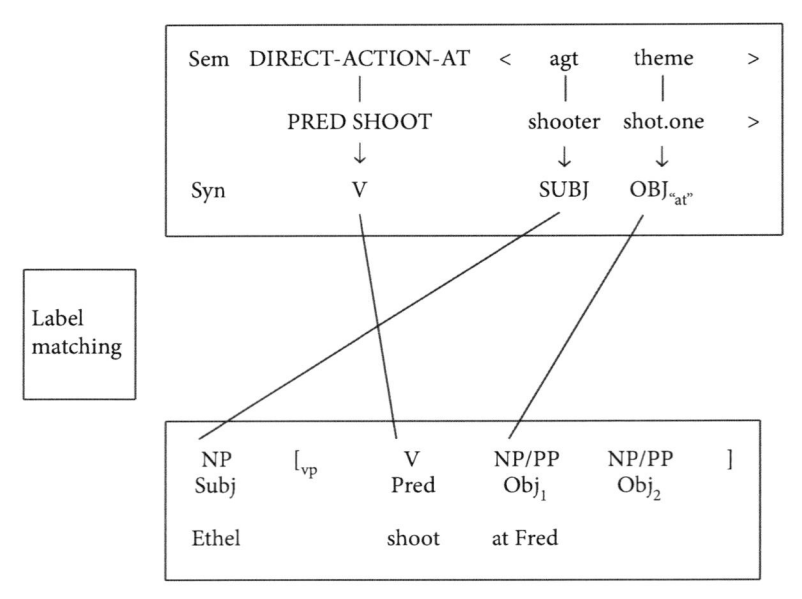

Figure 6. Argument structure construction mapped onto S-pattern via label matching

As can be seen from the "sentence" incorporated in the S-pattern (*Ethel shoot at Fred*), this is not yet a sentence. It is missing the finite tense dimensions and a slot for a modal. This is, then, not a full sentence yet, but a sentential *syntactic expression* (Goldberg 1995: 108). The missing dimensions of verb morphology and sentence modality will be supplied to the sentence by their own designated constructions and need not concern us here.

Note that in this model, the sentential functional roles are simply postulated, i.e. they are taken to be stored (rather than computed) matter. Indeed, Goldberg proposes that "Dowty's linking generalizations are naturally accounted for in the present framework" (Goldberg 1995: 117), but such generalizations are not actively used in order to *select* the sentential functional roles. Computation is, of course, more elegant than postulation. Indeed, in the argument structure construction, where participant roles are mapped onto argument roles, computation is used: the participant role is an "instance of" the argument role, a calculus which leads to the correct categorization: a "shooter" is an instance of an agent, and a "shot.one" is an instance of a theme.

The question arises, therefore, whether the argument roles could not be mapped onto sentential functional roles by computation, through a calculus of argument selection principles. Dowty's (1991) seminal work on proto roles sparked a lively debate over argument selection principles. Moore & Ackerman (2001) translated Dowty's principles into a comprehensive account of argument selection in Finnish and other languages. Givón (2001a: 108) briefly discussed what he called "mapping from semantic roles to grammatical relations". In Fillmore & Kay (1993: 8.16), the first argument in the list of an argument structure is the distinguished argument (DA), which stands out as such due to a hierarchy of semantic properties, and is eventually assigned the subject role (in active sentences). Levin & Rappaport Hovav (2005: Chapters 5–7) have a detailed discussion of various possibilities proposed in several approaches.

Two arguments in favor of the idea of postulation over the idea of computation come to mind here. First, the number of argument structure constructions is by definition relatively small, compared to the list of verbs in the lexicon, over which they constitute generalizations. The relationship of these constructions with the S-patterns that linearize them is conventionalized and routinized. Such routinized procedures often belong to the stored, not to the computed, repertoire.

Second, argument selection rules run into problems when faced with "non-standard lexicalizations" (*receive, inherit, undergo, sustain (an injury), suffer (from), submit to, succumb to,* and *tolerate*) (Dowty 1991: 581). "These are in fact exceptions", says Dowty (1991: 581), "but they are few in number, so the selection principle is not an absolute rule but is nevertheless a strong tendency". In a network of argument structure constructions, these exceptional verbs do not constitute a problem. They would be encoded in a daughter construction linked to the one that encodes similar verbs of standard behavior (*give, bequeath, subject, inflict,* etc.) in standard argument structure constructions. The assignment of sentential functional roles that contradict the semantic relations of canonical argument structure construction will then override (via postulation) these tendencies.

The question of postulation or calculation of syntactic roles cannot be resolved here. It should, however, be clear that the linearization of the syntactic expressions encoding the arguments is a separate issue, independent of the question of postulation or calculation of syntactic roles. It is the issue of linearization that justifies the S-pattern.

The term *mapping* used in the current discussion may imply an asymmetrical, directional relation, since A gets mapped onto B, not B onto A. Two events of mapping have been described above. Participant roles are mapped onto argument structure constructions, which get mapped onto S-patterns.

Goldberg uses the term *fusion*, which is similar to *unification*, the technical term used in the more formal varieties of Construction Grammar. The latter are symmetrical terms that do not imply directionality. It should be noted, however, that despite the use of the more traditional term *mapping*, no directionality needs to be assumed, unless one wishes to develop separate models sensitive to the production and comprehension of speech. The simultaneity of the two mappings rests on the routinized and therefore automatic nature of the linearization, once the argument structure construction has been selected for a given verb.

The term *categorial affiliation* (*part of speech, phrasal category*) and its counterpart *sentential functional role* have been used above under the assumption that they are non-problematic. A more careful consideration of these terms is undertaken in the next section.

1.7 Categorial affiliation and sentential functional roles

The use of the two sets of terms *categorial affiliation* (including word level *parts of speech* and *phrasal categories*) and *sentential functional role* (*part of the sentence*) calls for explanation. Parts of speech and syntactic categories such as subject and object have usually been employed in a global (language-wide), or even universal sense. This practice contradicts the premise of the current study (briefly stated in Section 1.4) that the sentence is our relevant syntactic primitive, and that categories and functional roles are *not* global, but rather carved out of the sentential constructions in a construction specific manner.

The easier case is categorial affiliation. Let us forget for a second that we know what nouns, verbs, and other parts of speech are and how they form phrases. In a top–down methodology, the categorial classes of a sentence will first have to be established construction-specifically. The initial phrasal expression of the V S-pattern may, at this point, be temporarily named, say, the "Preverbal-Phrase-of-the-V-S-pattern". The phrasal expression following the verb may then be named the "Postverbal-Phrase-of-the-V-S-pattern". A similar procedure on the Copular (COP) S-pattern would yield a "Pre-Copular-Phrase-of-the-Copular-S-pattern", and in the case of the Nominal Copular (N COP) S-pattern, also a "Post-Copular-Phrase-of-the-N-COP-S-pattern" would be identified, and so on.

Then a distribution test would be conducted, and if a domain could be found in which the same phrase may be used in several positions of one S-pattern, or across S-patterns, the local terms might then be generalized and upgraded. Within the domain of the V S-pattern and the COP S-pattern, these phrasal expressions turn out to be indeed mutually replaceable, yielding what we all know as a standard NP in English. The English NP has thus been established as a shared constituent of several constructions, not as a global constituent of English (let alone a constituent of Universal Grammar).

The same goes for the other parts of speech. It turns out that any NP, PP, InfP, or GrdP that is licensed in one S-pattern may be used also in the others, if a similar slot exists in that S-pattern. Furthermore, the meaning of such forms is semantically and pragmatically the same within the scope of these S-patterns.

This generalization applies to what is termed here *major* S-patterns, to the exclusion of *minor* S-patterns, such as the one instantiated by the sentence *the sooner, the better*, in which *the sooner* is a puzzling phrasal expression (a comparative adjective preceded by the definite article), specific to its S-pattern, and not licensed anywhere else. (Major and minor S-patterns are discussed in Section 1.9 and again in Section 4.2). Odd PPs, consisting of P + AP, are another case in point and will be discussed in Section 2.4.3.

The case of the sentential functional roles is very different from that of categorial affiliation. Croft's view that the partition of a construction into functional parts should be based on a meronomic (part–whole) relation (Croft 2001: 20), is upheld here. In the discussion of Goldberg's model, the term *syntactic roles* has sometimes been employed, since Goldberg uses labels such as Subject and Object as global primitives. In the model proposed here, the term *(sentential) functional roles* is employed instead. As the discussion unfolds, we will see that more often than not, these functional roles are construction specific, and that the broad terms *subject* and *object* are used sparingly, and only where representation in broad categories is justified.

To give a simple example, the "notional subject" of the Existential (EX) S-pattern (the expression *warm water* in the sentence *there is warm water*) will not be referred to here as "subject", but as the *existent* (Halliday 1994: 142), namely that part of the sentence, an NP in its categorial affiliation, *whose referent is asserted to exist* when the sentence is uttered. EX sentences have no argument that would deservedly be called subject. The same goes for the evaluative (EV) S-pattern (*it is good to see you*). Here, there is no subject argument either. The phrase *to see you* is an InfP by categorial affiliation, and its functional role is *evaluee*, representing the situation (event, state, process, etc.) being evaluated by the predicate. Similarly, the predicates in the different constructions are not just predicates at large. They are, for example, *existential* or *evaluative* predicates specific to their S-pattern. This practice is in line with the fact that the group of predicates that may fill the predicate slot in each construction is semantically and pragmatically constrained.

On the other hand, in the V S-patterns, the parts of the construction are less specific semantically. The unmarked nature of the V S-pattern defies any attempt to attribute a functional common denominator to its pre-verbal or post-verbal NPs. Hence, the broad terms *subject* and *object* are used. As for the COP S-pattern, since the pre-copular phrase shows great uniformity in form and function throughout the three sub-patterns (nominal, adjectival, and prepositional), it deserves a common name. In this case, the term *basis subject* is used, to capture both its partial similarity to the subject of the V S-pattern, but to indicate also its narrower semantic role as the basis to the three functional assignments in the three types of COP sentences: equivalence in the N COP S-pattern, attribution of a property in the A COP S-pattern, and a relation between entities in the P COP S-pattern.

Given the centrality of the V S-pattern in the linguistic literature, it is not surprising that the terms subject and object have been generalized beyond their deserved realm of felicitous applicability. The parsimonious use of the widely accepted terms *subject* and *object* here, should therefore not be misconstrued as an endorsement of these terms as universal terms, but rather should be construed as a recognition of their unmarked generality within one language or cross-linguistically within a typological group.

1.8 Unmarked and marked sentence patterns

It is suggested here that the V S-pattern is the unmarked S-pattern among all S-patterns. In order to evaluate this suggestion, the term *(un)markedness* calls for a clarification.

Markedness is a term that has been current in linguistic literature since the 1920s. An extensive discussion of its different uses may be found in Battistella (1990; 1996). Notably, markedness has been adopted by the Chomskyan school as a characterization of grammatical phenomena that are not covered by Universal Grammar, or, in terms of language acquisition, do not represent the initial setting of parameters. This is *not* how the term markedness is used here. Rather, the older notion of markedness in structuralism is embraced. Jakobson's ([1932] 1984) observation about the two seemingly contradictory facets of unmarkedness are of great value. Two examples will serve as reminders of Jakobson's view.

In some cases, the unmarked term of a category simply signifies "all the meanings of the category other than the meaning of the marked term". For example, in the English category of person–number, the suffix -*s* means III.Sg., namely it is marked for this meaning, while Ø means "all other person–number options", hence it is the unmarked term. This relatively simple notion of unmarkedness is not the one relevant to our discussion of S-patterns.

At other times, in Jakobson's view, the unmarked term has a more complex relation with the marked term. In the case of the pair *horse* and *mare*, for example, the word *horse* has two distinct meanings. In certain contexts, it signifies the male counterpart of *mare*, namely it is marked as masculine in the category gender, while in others contexts, it is the gender-neutral term, namely it is unmarked for gender.

The unmarkedness of the V S-pattern among all other S-patterns is of the *horse–mare* kind. On one hand, the V S-pattern is the primary vehicle for expressing *agentive events*. Generally, events belong to a prototype-based category. The best instances of events are *actions* carried out volitionally by human agents, as exemplified in (3a). Non-human causes, such as animals and forces of nature, are very close to the prototype and their actions are also encoded through verbs, as in

(3b–c). Instruments are further away from the prototype, but their actions can also be encoded in the V S-pattern, as in (3d). Finally, inanimate objects may accidentally carry out actions, as in (3e).

(3) a. Sam opened the door.
    b. The cat opened the door.
    c. The wind opened the door.
    d. The key opened the door.
    e. Mrs. Blazzer was closing a window and her dress accidentally caught a revolver which was on a bureau, and threw it to the floor, causing it to discharge. (I)

While agentive events get encoded in English (and other languages) in the V S-pattern, other kinds of events, such as spontaneous happenings, differ in the way they are encoded, both in the same language and cross-linguistically. For example, "getting sick" and "getting healthy" are encoded in English in two different ways: "getting sick" is encoded in a resultative A COP sentence, using a dynamic copular verbs (*become*, *get*, etc.), as in (4ai), while "getting healthy" may be encoded in a similar way, as in (4aii) but also via a sentence in the V S-pattern, as in (4aiii). In Hebrew, they are encoded in the V S-pattern, as in (4bi–ii).

(4) a. (i)   Mary became/got/fell sick.
       (ii) Mary became/got healthy
       (iii) Mary recovered.
    b. (i)   *rina xalta*
             Rina "sickened"
       (ii) *Rina Hivri'a.*
             Rina recovered.

So, on one hand, the V S-pattern is marked for agentive events, since no other S-pattern may express them. On the other hand, the V S-pattern is unmarked in the sense that it may convey functions that are specifically assigned to the other (marked) S-pattern. In the English examples of (5), sentence (5a) is existential (EX) and (5b) adjectival copular (A COP).

(5) a. There appeared on my window sill a large green bird.
    b. Jeffrey was ecstatic.
    c. A large green bird appeared on my window sill.
    d. Jeffrey rejoiced.

The EX and COP S-patterns have marked functions. The EX S-pattern presents an entity (the existent) as being in existence and the A COP S-pattern attributes a property to an entity encoded as the Basis Subject. At the same time, the V sentences in (5c–d), convey similar contents respectively. The difference between (5a–b) and (5c–d) is that the latter do so *without the special edge* of the constructional meanings of the EX and A COP S-patterns. The V S-pattern is *unmarked*, in the sense that it is capable of expressing situation types other than agentive events, but they do so without the constructional support that is evoked when the marked S-patterns are used.

There are many situation types that may be differently encoded in different languages. English is extremely anthropocentric. Almost any situation type that involves a human being is phrased in English with the human being serving as the subject of a V sentence. Dowty's (1991: 572) sentience criterion ranks high in present-day English, even where volition or causation are not at work. Compare (i) and (ii) in each of the pairs of (6), representing various situation types in English and Hebrew.

(6) a. (i) I am sorry that....
    (ii) *car l-i še...*
       Sorry to me that...
       'I am sorry that...' ('*Es tut mir leid dass*' in German)

  b. (i) I have an idea.
    (ii) *yeš l-i ra'ayon.* (Hebrew)
       EXIST to me an.idea

  c. (i) I feel like getting out of here.
    (ii) *ba l-i la'uf mi-po.* (Hebrew)
       comes to me to.fly from here

  d. (i) I care about them.
    (ii) *ixpat l-i me-hem.* (Hebrew)
       matters to me from them

  e. (i) I happened to take the exam yesterday.
    (ii) *yaca l-i la'asot et ha-bxina etmol.* (Hebrew)
       came.out to me to do ACC the exam yesterday.

In these (and many other) non-agentive situation types, English encodes humans as subjects, while Hebrew does not (see also Kidron & Kuzar 2002). Mathesius (1928; 1929: 203–204) has more examples of this tendency in English, such as what he calls the *possessive passive* (7a) and the *perceptive passive* (7b).

(7) a. Even lords and ladies have their mouths sometimes stopped.
  b. Upon examination of these, I found a certain boldness of temper growing in me.

To summarize this point: the V S-pattern has a dual function. On the one hand, it is marked for agentive events, and in English also for many other types of human-centered events. On the other hand, the V S-pattern is the unmarked S-pattern, in that it houses verbs that could have been encoded, or are indeed alternatively encoded, in English as well as in other languages, in some other marked S-patterns.

It was suggested at the beginning of this section that "the V S-pattern is the primary vehicle for expressing *agentive events*". The word *primary* is used to provide for the fact that agentive verbs may get peripherally employed in the existential (EX) and evaluative (EV) S-patterns as well, as shown in (8).

(8) a. At the last stroke of the bell [...], there marched into the room from out of the Egyptian darkness a long file of knights [...] (Allsopp 1992: 313)
   b. It destroys me that you think this way. (I)

The sense in which the use of such predicates is primary, or central, in the V S-pattern, but peripheral in the EX and EV S-patterns, will be developed in Chapters 5 and 6. I want to stress, however, that the use of the word "peripheral" here is not intended in the Chomskyan sense but rather in the sense of prototype effects.

1.9 Major and minor S-patterns

The terms *major* and *minor* in describing S-patterns in English grammars dates back to Nida's dissertation of 1943, of which Nida ([1963] 1966) is the second printed edition. However, Nida does not provide a criterion for distinguishing between his major and minor "sentence types". It is suggested here that the distinction between the two types of S-patterns is a matter of susceptibility to other sentential constructions.

Every sentence instantiates an interaction between many sentence-level constructions. Constructions, in turn, may be viewed either as randomly jumbled in an unordered *constructicon* (Jurafsky 1992), or alternatively, as hierarchically connected by inheritance links (see Lakoff 1987: Case Study III; Goldberg 1995: 72–81; Fillmore 1999 for discussions). Some aspects of the interaction between constructions may be best captured in a multi-dimensional model. To bring the point home, a reduced model of this idea is presented in the following passages.

Suppose we have a set of three S-patterns only: the V S-pattern, the EX S-pattern, and the EV S-pattern. Now, sentences in these patterns may be declarative or interrogative. In other words, their S-patterns interact with clausal mood constructions, yielding six resultant forms. Furthermore, these resultant forms interact with information structure constructions such as Topic–Comment, Thetic, Left Dislocation, *it*-clefts, and *wh*-clefts, multiplying the resultant forms fivefold.

In our reduced model, then, we have a three dimensional cube, the three dimensions of it being (a) S-patterns, (b) Clausal Mood constructions, and (c) Information Structure constructions. Each cubicle in this cube represents an instance of the intersection of the three dimensions. Some examples are given in (9).

(9) a. (i) They could easily find this book in the library.
V S-pattern, Declarative, Topic–Comment

(ii) Could they easily find this book in the library?
V S-pattern, Interrogative, Topic–Comment

(iii) This book – they could easily find it in the library.
V S-pattern, Declarative, Left-Dislocation

(iv) This book – could they easily find it in the library?
V S-pattern, Interrogative, Left-Dislocation

b. (i) It leaves me cold to see them dance together.
EV S-pattern, Declarative, Thetic

(ii) Does it leave me cold to see them dance together?
EV S-pattern, Interrogative, Thetic

(iii) What leaves me cold is to see them dance together.
EV sentence, Declarative, *wh*-cleft

This cube does not have to have a perfect shape. Some forms may be well entrenched in usage, some barely used, and others ungrammatical altogether (an empty cubicle).

This is not a multistratal view. It is *monostratal* as far as this term indicates lack of transformations. It is not literally monostratal, though, in as much as it is not flat. It assumes an architectural design of different *categories of phenomena* (the *dimensions* of the cube–cubicles metaphor) interacting with one another simultaneously. If brain research or psycholinguistic experiments shows one day that these processes are sequential, the multi-dimensional model can then also be reformulated in terms of sequential input–output modules. But it does not *have* to be.

A reduced model with three dimensions has been used here to make it perceptually accessible. But there are more than three dimensions interacting in the world of sentential constructions. Prosody, for example, also interacts with the dimensions already described, as do predicate expansion constructions (verb raising, verb concatenation, etc.), and others.

Each sentence, then, is an instance embodying the interaction of several sentential constructions, and each sentence has one fully unmarked form, in which all the dimensions of that sentence are unmarked. However, markedness is not global to the entire stock of sentences in a language. Rather, markedness is sensitive to the S-pattern. The two sentences in (10), for example, are instantiations of the V S-pattern and the two sentences in (11) of the EX S-pattern.

(10) a. They sell this book.
 b. It is this book that they should sell.
(11) a. There are mice in the pantry.
 b. Have there been mice in the pantry?

In each pair, the (a) option is the unmarked case. This means that in (10a), the linearization is unmarked, namely it matches the S-pattern as postulated in its formula. Its information structure is that of Topic–Comment and its focus is in the comment. This is the unmarked option for the V S-pattern, where modality is also unmarked, namely the sentence is non-modal (as are other dimensions, such as polarity). In (10b), on the other hand, information structure is marked, since the cleft sentence construction is used, and the modality of the sentence is marked in that the modal *should* is used. Naturally, the linearization is also marked, since it now differs from that of the S-pattern as postulated in its formula.

Sentence (11a) instantiates the EX S-pattern in its unmarked form. In the ensemble of constructions associated with this S-pattern, the unmarked information structure construction is not topic–comment, but rather the thetic construction. Hence, the unmarked linearization is very different from that of the V S-pattern. Other dimensions of (11a), such as polarity, aspect, and modality, are unmarked as well. In (11b), on the other hand, two of these dimensions are marked in that the sentence represents a polar interrogative and a perfect form.

Much more may be said on the interaction between different sentential constructions, but in this book, only one dimension is explored in detail: that of the S-patterns itself, as a linearized construction of pattern components, their internal functions, and the generalized function of the entire S-pattern in discourse.

S-patterns that are susceptible to participating in the multi-dimensional interaction of sentential constructions constitute the group of *major S-patterns*. By contrast, *minor S-patterns* have fixed dimensions. The sentences *like father -like son*, *down with the occupation,* or *me worry?*, may not be subject to clausal mood alternations, polarity alternations, information structure alternations, prosodic alternations, etc. (In Chapter 4, it will also be shown that major S-patterns come in networks, while minor S-patterns often stand alone.)

Nida ([1963] 1966: 168) lists the sentences of (12) (inter alia) as "minor sentence types".

(12) a. Well begun, half done.
　　 b. Old saint, young sinner.
　　 c. No pains, no gains.
　　 d. Like father, like son.
　　 e. So far, so good.
　　 f. First come, first served.
　　 g. Love me, love my dog.
　　 h. Better untaught than ill taught.
　　 i. Least said, soonest mended.

Indeed, none of these sentences may be susceptible to any change in their dimensions. They are fixed in their patterning.

It should, however, be clear that major and minor S-patterns are not coterminous with predication and patterning. The copular S-pattern is argued (in Section 2.4.4) to be better presented as a case of patterning than as a case of predication, yet it is a major S-pattern. Conversely, the Existential–modal S-pattern in Hebrew (discussed in Section 10.4) is a minor S-pattern formed canonically through predication. The two issues, then, are only loosely related.

The two kinds of S-patterns – major and minor – may well be a continuum rather than a dichotomy. The Locative Inversion (LI) S-pattern might be a case in point. It has not been included in this study as a major S-pattern, but this question will deserve more consideration in future research. Major or minor, it is, nevertheless, maintained here that LI is an independent construction exhibiting a non-compositional pairing of form and meaning, contrary to the view that it is "a 'pure' argument alternation" that shares "the same truth conditional meaning as its non-inverted counterpart" (Levin & Rappaport Hovav 2005: 195).

1.10 The structure of this book

This book has twelve chapters. In Chapter 2, the form and the function of subject initial sentence patterns is addressed. Chapter 3 has a similar discussion of predicate initial sentence patterns. Chapter 4 undertakes the question of whether and how the sentence patterns are linked with each other in one *field*. Chapter 5 elaborates on the conceptual category of existence, Chapter 6 – on the conceptual category of evaluation, and Chapter 7 – on the conceptual category of environmental conditions. Chapter 8 examines the relationship between sentence patterns and information structure. Chapter 9 presents non-canonical expletive behavior in the predicate initial sentence patterns. Chapter 10 revisits the issue of patterning developed in earlier chapters. Chapter 11 views certain syntactic behaviors from the point of view of noun incorporation. The book is summarized and concluded in Chapter 12.

1.11 Summary and conclusion of Chapter 1

This chapter starts with a general expression of preference for architectural elegance in model building. It is then suggested that syntactic description is best served in viewing sentential constructions as primitives of syntactic analysis (Croft 2001), supporting the idea that the categorial as well as functional components of a construction are to be arrived at in a top–down analytic procedure, resulting in construction specific parts, which are not universal or global in nature, even though they may turn out ex post facto to be shared by more than one construction.

Then Goldberg's (1995) view of argument structure constructions is presented and critiqued. It has been suggested that while Goldberg's model does well at accounting for argument structure variations that could not be accounted for in a lexicalist model, it is an inadequate tool for capturing facts of syntactic linearization. It has been suggested that this may be remedied by the addition of a phrasal module of S-patterns.

Argument structure is a very fine-grained mechanism. As such it is well designed to capture details. But it also atomizes the field, making it hard to make higher level generalizations. Word order is such a generalization, and so is information structure, and narrative function. S-patterns are coarser grained constructions which are able to support these generalizations at the appropriate level (see the discussion of narrative function in Section 2.3 and of granularity in Section 4.3).

It has finally been suggested that S-patterns are only one dimension in a multi-dimensional architecture of sentential constructions, such as sentence mood, modality, information structure, polarity, etc., which interact simultaneously in the formation of every concrete sentence. The susceptibility of S-patterns to this multiple interaction defines the group of major S-patterns, while the minor S-patterns have mostly fixed dimensions.

One of the issues that has been mentioned only in passing in this chapter is the concept of patterning as a mechanism of sentence formation parallel to predication. This concept will be further developed in several places in the upcoming chapters.

CHAPTER 2

Subject initial sentence patterns

2.1 Preliminary discussion

The major S-patterns of English and Hebrew fall into two groups: subject initial (S1) and predicate initial (P1). The rationale for this division and terminology will unfold in the discussions to come. This chapter is devoted to the S1 S-patterns, which include the verbal (V) S-pattern and the three copular (COP) S-patterns, namely the nominal copular (N COP), adjectival copular (A COP) and prepositional copular (P COP) S-patterns. Sections 2.2–2.4 addresses S1 S-patterns in English. Their Hebrew counterparts are discussed in Sections 2.5–2.7.

2.2 Subject initial S-patterns in English

The V sentence in English (and in many other languages) has been extensively discussed in the constructional literature. Due to its unmarked nature, it is the home of many situation types, which are best captured through argument structure constructions. The need for a linearization device for all the verbal argument structure constructions has been discussed already at some length in Chapter 1. A detailed repetition of this discussion is not necessary. For the sake of completeness, it will be briefly recapitulated here in Section 2.3, with a more complete and systematic presentation of examples, and a discussion of its narrative function. The COP S-patterns in English are discussed in Section 2.4. The verbal S-pattern in Hebrew is discussed in Section 2.6, and the Hebrew COP S-pattern in Section 2.7.

2.3 The verbal S-pattern in English

The formula of the V S-pattern in English (Figure 5 above), is repeated in Figure 7. The top line supplies the categorial affiliation of each slot, the bottom line its sentential functional role.

The terms Subj and Obj are used, we may recall, as superordinate functional labels for positions that defy specific semantic characterization, due to the unmarked nature of this construction.

NP	[$_{vp}$	V	NP/PP	NP/PP	]
Subj		Pred	Obj$_1$	OBJ$_2$	

Figure 7. V S-pattern in English (repeated)

The different formations that occur in the English V S-pattern are repeated in (1). Nominals (GrdPs, InfPs, and *that*-clauses) may substitute NPs, but they are not shown here as primary constituents.

(1) a. NP V
 b. NP V NP
 c. NP V PP
 d. NP V NP NP
 e. NP V NP PP

The formations are instantiated respectively in (2). The representation is exhaustive in terms of the formations, but not in terms of the argument structures instantiated.

(2) a. Naomi laughed.
 b. John finished the book.
 c. Steve relies on Hannah.
 d. Lidia gave Oz an apple.
 e. Marilynn sent a letter to Jack.
 f. Talia agreed to come home early.
 g. Noam told Joey that the party was over.
 h. Elad explained to Yonatan and Rotem that the batteries ran out.

Each syntactic formation may accommodate more than one type of argument structure construction. The sentences of (3), for example, share the form of formation (1e), but they clearly do not share their semantic makeup, since they belong to two different argument structure constructions.

(3) a. Our farm cat battered it [the shrew] to death. (I)
 b. They delivered it to the wrong house. (I)

The sentential functional roles do not by themselves reveal how sentences of this S-pattern are used in discourse. *Discourse* is a very broad term that covers the way constructions are actually used. Actual usage involves a whole array of factors surrounding the linguistic expression. The same sentence, then, may be used for different communicative purposes in different settings, such as monolog and dialog, written and spoken text, and within the four "modes of discourse", namely narration, description, exposition, and argument (Bain 1871), or any other classification thereof (see Smith's 2003: 8 more recent five discourse modes). To cover the whole array of such usages would go beyond the scope of this book. I have chosen one such environment, the narrative discourse mode, to exemplify the usage of the various major S-patterns in it.

Since the V S-pattern is the home of all agentive and many non-agentive events (Section 1.8 above), it constitutes much of the *foreground* of the narrative (Hopper 1979: 214–215), or its *storyline* (Longacre 1987).

> It presents actions and events, which are (a) sequential, (b) punctiliar, (c) at least in part causally connected. Since a discourse is not a story unless it is so characterized, it follows then that the structurally most important part of the story is its *storyline*, i.e. the sequence of sequential, punctiliar, and (at least partially) causally connected actions and events which are represented in the narrative. A storyline reports not simply events but actions, i.e. voluntary doings of animate (usually human) agents (Longacre 1987: 51).

Due to its unmarked nature, the V S-pattern does not *mark* the sentence as part of the storyline. This would be an overstatement of its narrative function. Some languages can actually perform such a marking. For example, in Biblical Hebrew, the use of the *waw*-consecutive (a variant of the connective morpheme *wə-* 'and'), followed by a verb with sequential tenses, marks the sentence as belonging to the storyline. Thus, while *wə-yēLḖX* 'and goes/will go' is not marked as part of the storyline, *wa-YYḖlex.* is marked as such by *wa-* (a variant of *wə-*) and by the jussive form (a sequential tense) of the verb with a retracted accent. But such a device does not exist in English or in Israeli Hebrew.

The dual nature of the narrative function of the V S-pattern as both marked and unmarked is given in (4).

(4) The V S-pattern hosts all actions and events constituting the storyline of a narrative. At the same time, it is the unmarked S-pattern, which may be used for the designated functions of other S-patterns.

The use of the V S-pattern in the storyline is related to its word order and goes hand in hand with its information structure. As an S1 S-pattern, it has the unmarked information structure of topic–comment. The intra-sentential structure of topic–comment is reflected inter-sententially by the cumulative formation of a chain of topics, serving as the aboutness skeleton of the storyline. Furthermore, each sentence in this sequence has focus in the predicate phrase, thereby facilitating the gradual and cumulative addition of new information to the topical chain of the storyline.

The second S1 S-pattern is the COP S-pattern. Its three sub-patterns in English will be discussed in the next section.

2.4 The copular S-patterns in English

The type of sentence in which an NP is associated with a non-verbal phrasal expression, serving as its predicate, is widespread cross-linguistically. Some languages express the connection between these two parts through word order (and case) alone, while others use a special word for this purpose: the copula (Lat. *co* + *ap* + *ula* together + bind + diminutive). Finally, some languages employ both strategies, utilizing the two for some functional distinction. The difference between using or not using a copula is merely technical. This technical difference should not deter us from comparing and contrasting these two types of forms. Strictly speaking, the term copular (COP) sentence might refer only to S-patterns that contain a copula, but by extension, it may also be used as a cover term for sentences in which an NP is "coupled" in a predication relation with a non-verbal phrase.

Some of the problems in analyzing copular sentences are connected to the copula itself. Others arise from other factors, not the least of them being the question of the functional roles of the different parts of the sentence.

In this section two approaches to the COP S-patterns will be presented. One is based on the traditional view, in which there are three types of COP sentences, in which the head of the non-verbal phrasal expression – being Noun (N), Adjective (A), or Preposition (P) – is viewed as the predicate of the sentence. This is then the traditional view of *predication*. An alternative view will then be presented, which suggests that COP sentences may be better described as being formed by *patterning* rather than by *predication*. Under this view, only one S-pattern needs to be postulated.

2.4.1 The form and function of copular S-patterns in English

The three copular S-patterns in English, N COP, A COP, and P COP, contain a copula. The copula is a constituent of the construction, not of the argument structure. The copula is not the predicate of the sentence. It is not a lexical component and it does not determine the argument structure of the sentence. The predicate is the component that is the head of the post-copular phrase. This is the element that will determine the number and nature of the participants in the sentence.

At first sight this looks simple enough. If we take the A COP S-pattern as an example, then the choice between the adjectives *green* and *replete* will determine whether the sentence will only have one argument (*The house is green*) or two (*The *poem is replete with winter imagery*) and will also impose some semantic restrictions on the participants (**The poem is green/*The house is replete with winter imagery/*Winter imagery is replete with the house*).

In recent reference grammars, the post-copular phrase is called *subject predicative* (Biber, Johansson, Leech, Conrad & Finegan 1999: 101) or *predicative complement* (Huddleston & Pullum 2002: 53). The latter is indicative of the hesitation that linguists have encountered when faced with the COP S-pattern. On the one hand, we are used to having verbs as predicates, so the verb *be* is a candidate for being the predicate. Indeed, in one of these grammars, the copula *be* is said to fill the "verbal predicator position" (Huddleston & Pullum 2002: 218). Position – but not character. The verbal predicator has a "complement", whose task is to supply the predicative nature, hence "predicative complement".

To be faithful to the top–down construction-internal procedure professed above, it should be emphasized that the copula needs to be established separately in each of the three constructions. This methodology indeed yields fruitful results. Although the three constructions share the use of the verb *be* as the unmarked copula, they do not share the same list of copular (linking) verbs. Each COP S-pattern has its own specific set of copular verbs. Strictly speaking, then, this set should first be referred to as Copula-of-N-COP, Copula-of-A-COP, and Copula-of-P-COP S-patterns. The higher-order generalization as "copula" at large, especially when only the unmarked *be* copula is concerned, may be useful at times, but it becomes blind to these differences, and should be used with awareness of potential gains and losses. Copular verbs besides *be* will be discussed in Section 2.4.2.

The form and function of the three COP S-patterns will now be presented in some detail. As stated above, this division into three COP S-patterns, based on predication, will be challenged and modified later on.

The formula of the N COP S-pattern is shown in Figure 8. Following the notational conventions used in the V S-pattern above, the top line indicates the categorial affiliation of the slot, the bottom line its sentential functional role.

The symbol XP{-YP} indicates that the appearance of XP is contingent on the absence of YP. This captures the complementary distribution of the complement (Comp) of a head noun as either a post-modifying PP (*player of football*) or a pre-modifying NP (*football player*). Somewhat redundantly, this is also captured by the

NP	COP	[$_{NP}$	NP{-PP}	N	PP{-NP}	]
Basis	Assigner of		Comp$_1$	Entity	Comp$_1$	
Subject	Equivalence			Pred		

Figure 8. N COP S-pattern in English

fact that both are indexed as Comp$_1$. Determiners of the NPs and possible modals and auxiliaries have been left out of the formula. Recall that this formula represents a "syntactic expression" (Section 1.6) rather than a full sentence.

The term *Subj* captures the commonality between the subject of the V S-pattern and the subject of the COP S-patterns. Both are Subject Initial (S1) S-patterns, hence they are prototypical subjects, whose default information structure construction is topic–comment and predicate focus. In the COP S-patterns, however, the subject is more narrowly characterized as *Basis Subj* to capture the fact that the subject is the basis on which the assignments of equivalence is made.

The function of the N COP S-pattern is stated in (5).

(5) The N COP S-pattern assigns an equivalence between a basis subject and the predicate entity.

In the N COP S-pattern there inheres a paradox. On the one hand, the function of the S-pattern is defined as equivalence, which implies symmetry. On the other hand, language is not a logical system, and syntax makes a distinction between the comparandum (the basis) and the comparatum (the predicate entity). This is, then, an asymmetrical equivalence.

As for complements, a full account of complementation within the NP headed by the predicate is beyond the scope of our discussion. In general, nouns have a different type of argument structure than verbs. Typically, they do not have obligatory complements, only optional ones. Occasionally, de-verbal nouns may have an obligatory complement, such as *reliance on/upon X* (Huddleston 2001: 93–94). The complement, whether obligatory or optional, adds specificity to the head noun. The NPs in the sentences of example (6) contain nouns with obligatory complements.

(6) a. A major flaw in this approach is reliance on the honor system. (I)
    b. The third strategy is commitment to continued good governance. (I)
    c. A weak state is prey to external military threats. (I)

Note that these NPs can be freely expanded, e.g. *our full reliance on...*, *a resolute commitment to...*, and *easy prey to...*.

The second COP S-pattern is the A COP S-pattern. Its formula, based on the same principles as that of the N COP formula, appears in Figure 9.

NP	COP	[$_{AP}$	A	PP	]
Basis	Assigner of		Property	Comp	
Subj	Attribution		Pred		

Figure 9. A COP S-pattern in English

The function of the A COP S-pattern is stated in (7).

(7) The A COP S-pattern assigns the attribution of the property expressed through the property predicate to the basis subject.

Similarly to nouns, most adjectives have either no complement or an optional one, but some have obligatory complements, as in (8).

(8) a. Human culture is subject to natural selection. (I)
    b. Women are prone to hair loss after pregnancy. (I)
    c. God is willing to answer some prayers. (I)

Third in the list of COP S-patterns is the P COP S-pattern. Its formula appears in Figure 10. The term PNP in the formula of Figure 10 represents composite prepositions, to be discussed later in this section.

The function of the P COP S-pattern is stated in (9). The term *relation predicate* applies to both P and PNP.

(9) The P COP S-pattern assigns the relation expressed in the relation predicate between the basis subject and the complement.

Within the predication framework, the P COP S-pattern is most problematic, primarily because we expect predicates to have distinctive semantic content. Yet prepositions are relatively poor in semantic content. This limits their ability to serve as predicates. A small number of prepositions express a very wide range of relations. The specific meaning of the preposition is therefore contingent on the semantic nature of its complement. The meaning of *on* is different if some entity is physically *on* some surface, if a written message is *on* a certain page, or if an event is *on* a certain date, as is shown in (10a–c). Similarly, the meaning of *at* is different if a person is *at* some event or an event is *at* some hour of the day, as in (10d–e).

(10) a. The book is on the table.
     b. The note you're looking for is on page 97.
     c. My birthday is on Monday.
     d. The assistant director is at a meeting.
     e. The reception is at five o'clock.

NP	COP	[$_{PP}$	P/PNP	NP/PP	]
Basis	Assigner of		Relation	Comp	
Subj	Relation		Pred		

Figure 10. P COP S-pattern in English

This state of affairs may be demonstrated on many other prepositions. Technically, then, in all these cases, the P itself is supposed to be the predicate, but it works in tandem with its arguments to establish the meaning of the relation between the Basis Subject NP and the NP inside the PP.

A complete description of the PP in the P COP S-pattern must also include the group of pro-forms that may replace PPs. These are deictic expressions such as *here, there, upstairs, downstairs, inside, outside, home, away, now, then, tomorrow, yesterday*, etc., as shown in (11).

(11) a. The children are downstairs.
　　 b. The demonstration is tomorrow.
　　 c. The dentist is away.

These expressions have intrigued linguists. Traditionally, they have been treated as adverbs. Jespersen ([1937] 1984: 135) calls the word *here* in *John is here* a tertiary, thereby implying it is an adverb. Quirk et al. (1985: 865) call *then, here*, and *there* "definite adverbs of time and place". They are discussed under the heading "pro-forms used for coreference". Huddleston and Pullum, however, call these expressions "prepositions" that "cannot take NP complements" but may serve as "complement[s] of *be*" (Huddleston & Pullum 2002: 614), in other words, they may be used as predicates in the P COP S-pattern.

Quirk et al. are right in calling these expressions pro-forms, but they are wrong in the double assignment of "adverb" and "pro-form". The term *pro-form* indicates categorial affiliation, thus a pro-form cannot at the same time be an adverb, which is also a term of categorial affiliation. Pro-forms are holistic phrasal morphemes representing a head + all its modifiers. For example, *she* is a pro-NP, representing, say, *the mayor of Jerusalem*, even though it is not analyzable into head + modifiers. In the same way, *upstairs* and *yesterday* are pro-PPs, despite their unanalyzability.

These expressions are *deictic* pro-forms that substitute non-deictic PPs. In other words, every time a deictic expression such as *downstairs* or *tomorrow* is used, it stands for some non-deictic expression such as *in the basement* or *on Monday* that would spell it out in concrete terms. Hence, there is no need for a fourth COP S-pattern with an "adverb" as its predicate. Real adverbs cannot be predicates in COP sentences, as is clear from the ungrammaticality of (12).

(12) *The party is happily/slowly/inadvertently.

Functionally, the deictic pro-PPs in the P COP S-pattern express a relation, as do regular PPs. Since the list of these expressions is finite, they can be comfortably treated within the predication model of the P COP S-pattern, i.e. pro-PPs are holistic phrasal predicate expressions, even though no head P predicate is in sight.

Another group of deictic expressions is itself phrasal. NPs such as *next week*, *last month*, *next door*, *the day after*, etc., are often used in the predicate position of COP sentences, as exemplified in (13).

(13) a. The party was last week.
 b. Her office is next door.

These expressions are NPs by form, but unlike non-deictic NPs, which express equivalence in the N COP S-pattern, these deictic NPs do not express equivalence. Rather, they express a relation. If a non-deictic expression were to replace the NP, it would be a PP. No mistakes are made by the hearer of (13) in the interpretation of such sentences, namely, it is not the case that *the party* is equivalent to *last week* or that *her office* is equivalent to *next door*, but rather it is the case that *the party* is in a deictically marked temporal relation with *last week* and *her office* is in a deictically marked locational relation with *next door*. The deictic NP *last week* may be replaced by a PP such as *during the third week of April*. Similarly, the deictic NP *next door* may be replaced by the non-deictic PP *in room 1412*.

Unlike the single word deictic expressions discussed before, which constitute a finite set, the deictic NPs of the kind *next week* are harder to define. They start with modifiers such as *this*, *that*, *next*, or *last*, and the Ns are temporal and locative words. However, certain combinations seem to be conventionalized in the predicate position of COP sentences and grammaticalized (*her office is next door*), others less so (?*the party is next semester*), and others yet totally ungrammatical (**her office is next building*). Whether these forms can be captured lexically remains an open question at this point, as does the level of challenge that it poses to the predication model of sentence formation.

A more serious challenge to the predication model comes from *composite prepositions* such as *on account of* (Jespersen [1937] 1984: 6). The small number of prepositions in English and many other languages carries with it semantic vagueness. Preposition are polysemous, as is evident in Lakoff's study of the preposition *over* (Lakoff 1987: Case Study 2). Composite prepositions have a much more specific meaning compared to a single preposition, whose meaning arises in conjunction with its surrounding arguments.

Typically, composite prepositions have a relatively fixed PNP form. In most cases the N between the two Ps is a bare noun, not a full NP. Occasionally it is accompanied by a definite article, in which case the bare form is either a free variant or non-existent (*in spite of*/*in the spite of, *on the verge of*/?*on verge of*, *under the auspices of*/?*under auspices of*). The whole PNP sequence forms a chunk. Chunking refers to a string of components stored in memory and accessed as a single unit (exemplified in detail on the composite preposition *in spite of* in Beckner & Bybee 2009). A partial list of English PNPs, initially based on Om Grammar

(Om Grammar 2008) but further expanded from several Internet sources, appears in (14). Whether all of them may actually be used as predicates in a P COP sentence remains to be assessed in corpus work.

(14) Akin to, at ease with, at the end of, at home with, at odds with, at the side of, at variance with, because of, by dint of, by force of, by means of, by reason of, by the side of, by virtue of, by way of, for fear of, for the purpose of, for the sake of, for want of, in accordance with, in case of, in charge of, in common with, in conjunction with, in consequence of, in the course of, in defiance of, in evidence of, in favor of, in front of, in honor of, in the hope of, in lieu of, in light of, in line with, in love with, in place of, in prospect of, in response to, in search of, in spite of, instead of, in sync with, in tune with, in view of, in the event of, in the face of, in the name of, in the rear of, in the sight of, in support of, in the teeth of, in proportion to, in regard to, in relation to, in connection with, in harmony with, in keeping with, on account of, on behalf of, on the brink of, on the eve of, on the face of, on the ground of, on the part of, on the point of, on the verge of, out of harmony with, out of keeping with, out of proportion with, out of sync with, under the auspices of, under the name of, under the pains of, with an eye to, with the help of, with the hope of, with the intention of, with reference to, with regard to, with respect to, with a view to.

The large amount of composite prepositions is evidence for the strong need felt by speakers to flesh out the single preposition with added lexical material. Once a preposition is bolstered in this way, its meaning is much more independent of its complement.

Some composite prepositions undergo reduction. They may have allegro forms, as is the case when the independent P *by* becomes *be-* in *because of* (from *by cause of*). They may display orthographic fusion, as in *because of* and *instead of* (from *by cause of* and *in stead of*). They may use obsolete nouns (*stead, spite, behalf, auspices*). All these properties testify to the accelerated univerbation of these chunks. On the other hand, the use of the articles *a/the* in tandem with some of the Ns (*in the course of*), as well as the ability of some of them to have modifiers (*at great variance with*), shows that they do not all share the same level of fusion.

The composite prepositions in the P COP S-pattern also act as a single element functionally. If the PNP had been considered as P NP P in (15), then the P would presumably assign a relation between the subjects of these sentences and the NPs *sync with national goals* and *defiance of biblical ethics*. But such NPs are not at all intended. The real relation in (15) is between the basis subject NPs *regional leadership* and *the policy enforced* on the one hand and the NPs *national goal* and *biblical ethics* on the other.

(15) a. Regional leadership is in sync with national goals. (I)
    b. The policy enforced is in defiance of biblical ethics. (I)

The whole PNP expression, then, functions as a single preposition, expressing the specific semantic content of the relation between the two entities. In sum, the formal as well as the functional properties of the PNP sequence render it a single lexicalized unit, a composite preposition.

The composite prepositions pose a challenge to the predication approach when applied to the P COP S-pattern. The predication model would only be tenable if PNPs can be clearly identified as composite Ps in the mental lexicon. Yet the grammaticalization of these prepositions has been shown to be a slow and gradual process historically (Hoffmann 2005: Ch. 5–6), resulting in uneven grammaticalization synchronically.

Up to this point, only COP sentences with the copula *be* have been discussed. In the next section other copular verbs will be discussed.

2.4.2 Copular verbs

Copular verbs other than *be* (link/linking verbs) occupy the same slot in the COP S-pattern as the verb *be* and have a similar function. However, since they are semantically richer, they convey additional information beyond the mere assignment of equivalence, attribution, or relation.

The copular verbs are only partly grammaticalized in their role as copulas. This partial grammaticalization is evident, for example, in the fact that unlike *be*, the other copular verbs do not participate in subject–auxiliary inversion, as can be seen in (16).

(16) a. (i)   The tools are dirty.
        (ii) Are the tools dirty?
    b. (i)   The tools seem/become dirty.
        (ii) *Seem/become the tools dirty?

Copular verbs fall into two major groups: depictive (stative) and resultative (dynamic). The verb *be* itself is neutral between a depictive and a resultative reading. The specific reading of *be* as depictive or resultative is determined in each case by the context. For example, the sentence *everybody was very happy* is depictive in (17a), since it is construed as describing the mental state of the participants *during* the workshop. The reading is resultative in (17b), due to the presence of the adverb *suddenly*, which indicates a change in the mental state of the observers.

(17) a. Thank you for organising everything so well for the SPACH Workshop last week at the University Club. Everybody was very happy with everything. (I)
b. He plunged into the dancing party, seized a young woman and kissed her. Suddenly everybody was very happy. (I)

The other copular verbs are more specific and usually have a typical behavior as either depictive or resultative. In (18) and (19), lists of copular verbs are provided, amassed from several sources (Leech & Svartvik 1975: 297–299; Greenbaum & Quirk 1990: 343–344; Richards, Platt & Platt 1992: 88; Byrd 1997, among others). List (18) has depictive and list (19) resultative copular verbs. The lists show that although many copular verbs are shared among all three or between two of the COP S-patterns, nevertheless each COP S-pattern has its own idiosyncratic set.

(18) a. Depictive copular verbs shared by N COP, A COP, and P COP sentences:
seem, appear, remain, stay.
b. Depictive copular verbs shared by A COP and P COP sentences:
look, sound. feel.
c. Depictive copular verbs used in A COP sentences only:
smell, taste.

(19) a. Resultative copular verb shared by N COP, A COP, and P COP sentences:
become.
b. Resultative copular verb shared by N COP and A COP:
turn.
c. Resultative copular verb shared by A COP and P COP:
get.

Besides the copular verbs of (18) and (19), there are many idiomatic copular verbs (*stand corrected, ring familiar*) or collocational copular verbs with a limited number of variables (*fall silent/sick/asleep; run wild/amuck*, etc).

The boundaries between copular and regular intransitive verbs can usually be clearly delineated. Compare, for example, (20a) and (20b).

(20) a. 19-year-old girl went crazy after drinking and smashed a KTV room. (I)
b. I grew up in a world where children went barefoot. (I)

In its copular use, the meaning of the verb is often bleached enough, so that only a trace of its original meaning – usually a metaphorical extension (Goldberg 1991)

– survives. You can *go crazy* while seated in your armchair, but you cannot *go barefoot* sitting there. In (20a), *go* is a copular verb and *crazy* the adjectival predicate of an A COP sentence. In (20b), *go* is a lexical intransitive verb, the predicate of a V sentence, and *barefoot* is a circumstantial adjective, performing a non-finite secondary predication. The difference between the lexical and the copular behavior of *run* is evident in the different sets of adjective that they may co-occur with. With *run* as a full lexical verb we find a wide range of circumstances, such as the runner's mood, clothing, ordinal placement, etc., (*happy, angry, preoccupied, exhausted, naked, fully dressed, barefoot, third* etc.), commensurate with a running person. On the other hand, in the copular use, *run* is restricted to a few semantically similar adjectives, such as *wild* and *amuck*.

It is now time to ask whether the separate forms and functions of the three COP S-patterns have to remain distinct, or perhaps it is possible to extract from them generalizations that will allow us to unite them in one COP S-pattern. This will be done in the next section.

2.4.3 Generalizations over the three COP S-patterns

Two kinds of generalizations may now be made over the COP S-patterns, one with regard to their subjects, the other concerning their functions.

In keeping with a top–down analysis, the pre-copular-phrases of the three COP S-patterns have first been established separately for each COP S-pattern. They may, however, be subjected to successive generalizations, first within the realm of the unified category of the COP S-pattern, as subject-of-COP-S-pattern in general, and then at the higher level of the S1 S-patterns as the subject of COP as well as V S-patterns, i.e. as the subject of all S1 S-patterns.

The detailed procedure is saved here from the reader. Suffice it to mention some well known facts about the subject NPs of all S1 S-patterns. Firstly, they are freely interchangeable; no structural property of the NP in one is barred in any of the others. Secondly, these subject NPs share many structural dimensions such as subject–auxiliary inversion, appearance of subjects in tag-questions, subject raising, subject–verb agreement (Lakoff 1987: Case Study III), and so on. Finally, all S1 S-patterns have the two unmarked complementary information structure constructions Topic–Comment and Predicate Focus. The subject, if not otherwise marked, is the sentential topic, serving as the shared point of departure. It is pronominal in its unmarked contextual form (Lambrecht 1994: 172–184).

In the narrative discourse mode, the V S-pattern and the COP S-pattern have different functions. While the prototypical V sentence represents an agentive event, the COP sentence prototypically breaks the storyline, presenting the temporal, spatial, or other circumstances (i.e. states), at the background of which the storyline unfolds. In both S-patterns, however, the subject serves a similar role. When an action/event is asserted in the V S-pattern, the subject is the topic to which a newsworthy action is attributed in the unfolding storyline. In the case of the COP sentence, when a circumstance is stated, the subject is the topic to which a newsworthy property is attributed as background information for the storyline.

This explanation is, in fact, in line with the traditional view that in S1 sentences the subject is to various degrees prototypical. In the P1 S-patterns, to which we will turn in later chapters, the notion *subject* has often been problematically forced upon the final, post-predicate, component, due to the accepted belief that Subject is a universal or at least a global category. Even where this traditional view is challenged, it may be covertly upheld (as is the case in the title of Lambrecht 2000 "When subjects behave like objects"; not so in Ziv 1976, who talks about "reanalysis of grammatical terms"). In the treatment of the P1 S-patterns in Chapter 3, it will be argued that a construction specific top–down characterization of the final component of the P1 constructions will lend itself to higher generalizations *within* the P1 S-patterns. Such generalizations, however, will not go beyond the P1 S-patterns; hence the final component of the P1 S-patterns will not be conflated with the subject of the S1 S-patterns. The formal and functional properties of the subject of S1 sentences and the final component of P1 sentences are too different to allow their conflation.

The three COP S-patterns also share functional generalizations, involving both constructional functions and discourse functions. The three constructional functions of equivalence, attribution, and relation expressed in the COP S-patterns fall under the category of states. Hence, the COP S-pattern is a superordinate category marked for the expression of states.

As for the discourse functions of the COP S-pattern, it should be noted that unlike some languages that are capable of *directly* encoding discourse functions, English and Hebrew are not. In Biblical Hebrew, for example, which uses a P1 VSO word order in the narrative text, there is a *circumstantial clause* (Driver 1874: Appendix I; Kautsch & Cowley 1910: 489), which has the S1 SVO order, usually preceded by the connective *wə-* 'and' (akin to Israeli Hebrew *ve-* 'and'). In terms of narrative function, such clauses are said to be "subordinate to the main course of the narrative" and "qualify the main action by assigning the *concomitant conditions* under which it took place" (Driver 1874: 200–201). For example, in the story of Noah and the flood, as shown in (21), the sentence in (21a) is a narrative sentence, while the one in (21b) is circumstantial, giving Noah's age at the time the flood was taking place. The latter sentence starts with *wə-* 'and' and is followed by an S1 SVO sentence.

(21) a. *wa-yyaʕas nōaḥ kə-xōl ăšer ciwwāhū YHWH.*
and did Noah as all that commanded.him the.Lord
'Noah followed all of the Lord's orders'

b. *wə-nōaḥ ben šēš mēʕōt šānā.* (Genesis 7, 5–6)
and Noah son.of six hundreds years
'being at the time six hundred years old.'

Very similar syntactic behavior may also be found in Classical Arabic, where a circumstantial clause beginning with *wa-* 'and' followed by an SVO sentence is marked as circumstantial (Wright 1933: II: 330–331). English and (Israeli) Hebrew are not languages of this type. In their case, the narrative functions are *indirectly* encoded through the constructional functions of the S-patterns. Since COP sentences are designated to express states, they are, by extension, mostly used in the narrative to provide "supportive material", i.e. "background information" (Hopper 1979: 214–215), or in the terminology of Semitists, the "circumstances".

V sentences may also convey states, since the V S-pattern is unmarked, but depictive COP sentences are *designated* to do so. As such, their distribution among background materials is high. Resultative COP sentences may go either way, namely they can belong to the foregrounded part of the storyline, due to their more dynamic nature, or to the background.

In the next section, the theoretical grounds of viewing the COP S-patterns as a case of *predication* is re-examined. Instead, *patterning* is proposed as a better way of capturing their structure.

2.4.4 Predication and patterning in the COP sentence

In this section, an alternative model of the form of COP S-patterns is proposed. Rather than viewing N, A, and P as predicates, a view which has been termed here *predication*, it is rather suggested that *patterning* is at work. In Patterning, a linearized string of components serves as a mold for sentence components, without privileging one of the slots as the predicate, namely the "life-giving element" (Jespersen [1937] 1984: 121) of the sentence. It is the pattern itself, not the predicate, that gives life to the sentence. But before patterning is discussed, a problematization of the model of predication as applied to COP S-patterns will be undertaken.

There is a certain asymmetry between the N and A COP S-patterns on the one hand and the P COP S-pattern on the other. This asymmetry calls for some attention. All three COP S-patterns share two structural properties: (a) they involve two terms, a Basis Subject and an NP/AP that is assigned to it. In the N COP and A COP S-patterns, the assignment of the Assigned Term to the Basis Subject is carried out by the very placement of the N or A as direct counterparts of the Basis

Subject. The copula might be there, or might be absent (as is the case in many languages, among them Hebrew), but even if it is present, equivalence and attribution are not differentiated by the copula *be*. Rather, it is the actual act of using N or A that results in the construal of the form as equivalence in the case of N and attribution in the case of A. In these two cases, the Assigned Term (i.e. N or A) has been traditionally called *predicate*.

In the case of the P COP sentence, the situation is different. In addition to the copula, if one is present, there is the preposition P, which specifies the relation between the Basis Subject and the Assigned Term. In the predication view used above, this P has been taken to be the predicate. The PP as a whole cannot, strictly speaking, be seen as the predicate, since predicates are word-level constituents. Under this interpretation, then, the Assigned Term is not the predicate, but rather the complement of the predicate P, namely the NP following it. This asymmetry is shown in (22). In the case of the N and A COP S-patterns presented in (22a), the Assigned Term is the predicate, whereas in the case of the P COP S-pattern presented in (22b), the Assigned Term is not the predicate.

(22) a. N and A COP S-patterns:
     Basis Subject ——COP——Assigned Term$_{[predicate]}$

  b. P COP S-pattern:
     Basis Subject——COP——P$_{[predicate]}$——Assigned Term

In terms of their function, however, the Basis Subject and the Assigned Term are analogous in all three S-patterns, a fact that is also visible in our naming strategy (which is not based on universals but on a construction-local meronomic taxonomy). It should be possible, then, to express the analogy between the two sets of terms, the Basis Subject and the Assigned Term of the three COP sentences, in a formal manner.

One suggestion to solve this discrepancy is to acknowledge that prepositions are not at the center of the lexicon, but tend towards the grammatical end of the grammar–lexicon continuum. If this is so, we may then say that the preposition is merely a morphological dimension of the NP. In Givón's (2001a: 116) view, "PP is not a valid syntactic node", since prepositions are case markers in the realm of morphology, not words in the realm of syntax. Under this view, the NP following the P will be the predicate, hence all Assigned Terms will be predicates.

It should be noted, however, that prepositions also prevail in languages that have case, where their function is often similar to that of composite prepositions in English; namely, they nuance the relatively limited range of meanings of the case system. In languages that have no case, prepositions are not uniform in their location on the grammar–lexicon continuum. They are located on this continuum between fully grammatical forms at one end of the scale, where they do resemble case, through partly motivated forms in the middle of the scale, further through prepositions fully motivated semantically, all the way to PNPs that are lexical words at the other end of the scale.

Thus, the P *by* in *abide by the law*, or *of* in *dispose of the can*, are not semantically motivated and therefore fully grammatical, but the P *to* in *close to* and *from* in *far from* are partly motivated by a journey metaphor, in which a person moving from A to B is getting farther away from A and progressively closer to B. Fully motivated semantically is the P *on* in *the bowl is on the fridge*, and even more so are composite prepositions such as *on top of* in sentences such as *the bowl is on top of the fridge*. In conclusion, the identification of prepositions as case markers, a view that could have been useful in rendering the Assigned Term in a P COP sentence as the predicate, seems untenable.

To enrich the problematization of the predication framework, let us look at more data. Consider (23).

(23) a. (i) Before she had finished it, she turned teacher, and settled down in Boston. (I)
 (ii) I think she turned into a frog. (I)
 b. (i) Everyone turned sweaty and dirty from playing ball. (I)
 (ii) Something that was cool and funny a couple years ago has turned into boring and uninteresting. (I)

In the sentences of (23a), the Assigned Term is a noun, in (23b) an adjective. In (23ai) the copular verb *turn* is used without a preposition, while in (23aii) the preposition *into* is added. Despite minor stylistic differences between them, the two pairs (23ai–aii) and (23bi–bii) are functionally identical. In light of this identity, it seems quite awkward to say that in (23ai) the predicate is *teacher*, i.e. the Assigned Term, whereas in (23aii) the predicate is the preposition *into*, leaving *frog*, namely the Assigned Term, merely as a complement. But this is precisely what the methodology of the model of predication would predict.

The peculiarity of the A COP sentences in (23bii) is striking from the perspective of phrasal syntax. The coordinate AP *boring and uninteresting* is preceded by the preposition *into*. But *into boring*, a phrase with a head P and an AP complement, is not a canonical PP in English. Saying that *turn* is not a copula but a regular verb that calls for a PP in its argument structure would not remedy the problem of the awkward PP.

Some examples from Hebrew will be presented now, even though the systematic presentation of the Hebrew data only comes after this discussion. Consider the Hebrew examples in (24). The verbal past form *haya* 'was' is a variant of the nominal present copula *hu* 'he'. (Note: *hu* 'he' happens to be the subject of (24a). It should not be confused with the copula, which is expressed here in the past verbal form *haya* 'was').

(24) a. (i) *hu haya xaver miflaga, ve-lo yoter mi-ze.* (I)
he was member.of party, and not more than this
'He was a party member, not anything beyond that.'

   (ii) *hu haya le-xaver ha-miflaga ha-komunistit be-1936.* (I)
he was to member.of the party the communist in 1936
'He became a member of the Communist Party in 1936.'

b. (i) *arkadi haya ha-me'ušar mi-kulam.* (I)
Arkadi was the happy from everybody
'Arkadi was the happiest of all.'

   (ii) *im šmi'at xadašot elu ezra haya l-a-me'ušar be-ovdey elbit.* (I)
with hearing.of news these Ezra was to the happy in the.workers.of Elbit
'Upon hearing this news, Ezra became the happiest of all Elbit workers.'

The Hebrew sentences of (24) are similar to the English sentences of (23); namely, both the N and the A COP sentences have a variant with the preposition *le* 'to'. Here, however, this happens with the verb *haya* 'be', which is not just *some* copular verb but an allomorph of the *main* copula. In other words, the copula is followed by a P, which in turn is complemented (in the case of 24bii) by an AP. Here, it is harder to suggest what might be speculated for the English sentences of (23); namely, that perhaps this is a regular verb with its own argument structure. It *is* after all the past form of the copula itself.

This state of affairs may look puzzling at first, because we are so used to looking for globally (or universally) uniform phrasal categories. But in fact, under a top–down analysis that takes the construction as primitive and parses it into its *distributionally relevant* parts, the discovery of "deviant" phrasal constituents should not be a problem. A top–down procedure of analysis of the group of sentences (ii) in (23) and (24) reveals two construction-specific strings, which are not familiar from other syntactic constructions.

One is a P AP string; the other might look like a verbal complex which consists of a copula or a copular verb and a directional preposition. This verbal complex is neither a prepositional nor a phrasal verb. It is not a phrasal verb, since in English, for example, the regular word order variation that is sanctioned with phrasal verbs is not sanctioned here, as can be seen in (25).

(25) a. She turned into a frog.
     b. *She turned a frog into.

Hebrew does not have phrasal verbs at all, so this is not even an option. Neither is it, though, a regular verb requiring prepositional complementation. If it were a regular verb requiring prepositional complementation, the sentence would be a P COP sentence. However, in P COP sentences, the Basis Subject and the Assigned Term represent two different referents, between which a certain relation prevails (*[she]$_i$ is in [school]$_j$*). But here, the referents behind the Basis Subject and the Assigned Term are two manifestations of the *same* entity (*[hu]$_i$ haya le-[xaver mifla-ga]$_i$*, literally '[he]$_i$ was to [a party member]$_i$'; *was to* = 'became'). In fact, this sentence behaves functionally like an N COP sentence, assigning equivalence between the two terms "he" and "party member", not like a P COP sentence assigning a relation between them.

Seeing some of the problems presented here, Croft (2001) suggested making a distinction in COP sentences between a functional head and a semantic head. He explains:

> A copula occurring with a predicative noun or adjective appears to be the profile equivalent, because the overall clause profiles the assertion classifying the subject as belonging to the category of the predicate nominal, or possessing the property of the predicate nominal. However, the copula verb is of minimal semantic content, adding only a predicative function to a maximally schematic categorization of the referent of the S [=Subject] argument. The profile of the whole [N or A COP] clause is determined partly by the copula and partly by the predicate noun/adjective – categorization of the S referent as being of the type profiled by the predicate noun, or ascription of the property profiled by the predicate adjective (Croft 2001: 266).

The exclusion of the P COP sentence from Croft's discussion is unfortunate, because much of the problematic nature of COP sentences is revealed in it. For some reason, this exclusion is systematic (see the extra-systemic status of *location predication* in Croft 2001: 92). Croft's suggestion to view the COP sentence as having two heads is, nevertheless, a substantial step in the direction of refuting the reign of predication as the sole source of sentence formation.

All the expectations of phrasal constituency and of a neat pairing of the three forms of the COP S-patterns with three distinct functions are related to the expectation to find a clear predicate–argument structure in the three COP S-patterns. Yet, with the data at hand, this is an unrealistic expectation. The centrality of predicate–argument structure in the formation of sentences is a result of the centrality of the V S-pattern in syntactic research. "The verb is the chief life-giving element in the most usual type of sentence" – says Jespersen ([1937] 1984: 121). But there is another path to sentence formation, within which the above problems disappear. The COP sentences may be viewed as based not on *predication* (or not on predication alone) but (exclusively or additionally) on *patterning*.

Patterning has long been tacitly recognized as a principle of sentence formation in minor S-patterns, such as the Comparative–correlative S-pattern, (*the X-er, the Y-er*) (Fillmore, Kay & O'Connor 1988). All one needs to do is list the constants and the obligatory and optional variables. Patterning can be similarly used also in major S-patterns, such as the COP S-pattern at hand.

The COP S-pattern, then, has two primary and obligatory slots: the Basis Subject and the Assigned Term. In addition, a device is needed to specify the assignment of the Assigned Term to the Basis Subject. In some languages, the mere juxtaposition of the two suffices. Other languages have a copula that assigns equivalence and attribution. A relation is assigned by combination of the copula with a P or PNP. Finally, a resultative state of affairs may be symbolized metaphorically by a copula followed by a directional P (*to, into*, etc.) followed by the Assigned Term (NP or AP).

The parsing of the sequence COP P AP is problematic, if phrasal constituency is expected in advance to be "well formed". However, if we look at this string from a local constructional point of view, it may simply be stated as a flat sequence in the formula of the S-patterns without hierarchical arrangement as either [[COP P] AP] or [COP [P AP]].

The constituency in a situation of patterning could be mixed, with some elements showing more canonical constituency and others being laid out flat as part of the S-pattern itself. The Basis Subject is a canonical NP and the Assigned Term a canonical NP or AP. The middle area between them is filled by a number of optional sequences, some of which have canonical constituency, such as the Affectee (NP or PP), while other sequences are flat and local to this construction.

Predication and patterning are not necessarily in all-out competition. It has been suggested at the beginning of this section that some minor S-patterns, such as the Comparative–correlative S-pattern, (*the X-er, the Y-er*), are produced by patterning alone. The COP sentence, so it seems, is a playground for both mechanisms of sentence formation. In those cases where a clear argument structure construction may be recognized, the predicate is mapped onto the slot of the Assigned Term. This happens with most N and A predicates in the so-called N COP and A COP S-patterns (save the deictic ones, such as *next week* in *the party is next week*). At times however, particularly in the P COP S-pattern and in the cases of the resultative copular verbs with an NP or AP as the Assigned Term, a predication-alone perspective lacks descriptive and explanatory power. Here, patterning is at work.

Other cases of patterning will be discussed in Chapter 10, which targets this issue specifically. In the next section the borderline between copular and regular lexical verbs will be discussed. This discussion will have consequences with regard to the borderline between the V S-pattern, where lexical verbs are predicates, and the COP S-pattern, where grammatical verbs, namely copulas, are non-predicates, i.e. grammatical (or grammaticalized) elements inserted into pattern-slots.

2.4.5 The borderline between copular and lexical verbs

In the argument structure of a lexical verb, the arguments refer to distinct entities. In the Chomskyan framework, this follows from the theta-criterion (Chomsky [1981] 1993: 36), which postulates a bi-unique relation between theta-roles and arguments. As a normal consequence of this principle, the subject and the object do not refer to the same entity (unless a reflexive pronoun reverses this default).

In this sense, the verbs of (26) constitute a problem:

(26) a. Clint acts his age. (I)
 b. Willie's railway career spans almost 50 years. (I)
 c. Star striker Ronaldo Nazario weighs 90.5 kilos. (I)
 d. Italy earthquake reconstruction will cost billions. (I)
 e. By 2000, no single race or ethnic group constituted a majority of California's population. (I)

In all the sentences of (26), the post-verbal NP refers to an aspect of the subject referent which is presented as being equivalent to it in some sense. Indeed, COP sentences with the copula *be* may often replace these verbs, resulting in the same meaning (*Nazario* is *95.5 kilos*, *this ethnic group* is *a majority* etc.). Similarly, if the earthquake reconstruction will cost billions, we may say that it will *be* billions, or ask how much it will *be*. There exists an equivalence between the two terms: the man and his weight or the commodity and its price. In functional terms, then, the post-verbal NP behaves like an Assigned Term of a COP sentence rather than an object of a V sentence. Hence, the verbs of (26) are in fact copular verbs. A similar state of affairs may be recognized in (27).

(27) My cat acts very tired and dizzy. (I)

Here, the post-verbal expression is an AP. By definition, canonical APs may not be objects. The sentence may be quite accurately rephrased with the copula *be* (*my cat is tired*). Here too, the AP represents a property attributed to the subject, in other words it is an Assigned Term of a COP sentence rather than an object of a V sentence. In (27), then, the verb *act* is a copular verb as well.

The literature on the semantics of verbs is hesitant and inconsistent in its treatment of such verbs. Levin (1993) classifies *act* in the group of *masquerade* verbs (183), *span* in *verbs of contiguous location* (257), *weigh* in the *register* subgroup of *measure verbs* (272), and *cost* in *cost verbs* (272). The verb *constitute* is not discussed in Levin (1993).

The nature of these verbs as copular verbs is only occasionally acknowledged. With regard to the *masquerade* group, Levin comments that "the verbs in this class take a predicative complement predicated of their subject. They require *as* to introduce this complement" (Levin 1993: 184). The verb *act*, which belongs to this group, does not use *as* in (26a), but its copular nature is indirectly acknowledged by Levin. On the other hand, *span* appears in a group that otherwise contains lexical verbs, such as *border* and *cap* (*Italy borders France*, *Snow caps the mountain*). Clearly, *Italy* and *France* are two separate entities, as are *snow* and *mountain*. This is why the two post-verbal NPs *France* and *the mountain* are objects of the lexical verbs *border* and *cap*. On the other hand, as we have noted already, there is a clear referential equivalence between *Willie's railway career* and *50 years* in (26b). Hence, the verb *span*, which in Levin's treatment belongs to the same group, is in fact a copular verb, with the NP *50 years* being an Assigned Term, not an object.

Another example: *Register* verbs, of which the verb *weigh* (26c) is a member, are described by Levin in the following way: "These verbs can be used intransitively with a postverbal noun phrase expressing the measurement. The noun phrase does not show the properties of a direct object" (Levin 1993: 272). Levin says the same about *cost* verbs. She does not, however, say that these are predicative complements, as she does in the case of the *masquerade* group, an assertion which would have better represented the fact that these are copular verbs than the circumlocution "does not show the properties of a direct object".

Some verbs display double behavior, which clearly testifies to their path of grammaticalization from lexical to copular verbs. Compare sentences (i) and (ii) in (28a–b).

(28) a. (i) The OSI constituted a committee to study the issue. (I)
      (ii) By 2000, no single race or ethnic group constituted a majority of California's population. (I)
  b. (i) Adam formed a hypothesis on the genetics of bakers' yeast. (I)
      (ii) More than one thousand people formed a line that snaked from the platform back into the parking garage. (I)

The verb *constitute* in (28aii) is a depictive copular verb, substitutable by *be*, and the verb *form* in (28bii) is a resultative copular verb conveying the meaning of *become*. A trace of their lexical origin points to some peripheral aspects of their meaning: there is some formality in *constitute* that is lacking in *be*, and there is some trace of agentivity in *form* that is lacking in *become*. In this sense, they behave just like the copular verbs of the senses (*look*, *sound*, etc.), whose meaning amounts to "*is* (judging by its look/sound)"

Some copular verbs share other behaviors with lexical verbs. The copular verbs of the senses, along with the verb *cost*, may be accompanied by an affectee, in the form of a direct or an oblique object, as can be seen in (29). Other copular verbs cannot do that, as is evident in (30).

(29) a. EU red tape cost us £100bn in 10 years. (I)
 b. So much of modern fiction just sounds to me so self-conscious. (I)
 c. Your water Koi fish painting looks to me very artistically performed. (I)
 d. War feels to me an oblique place. (Title of book by Emily Dickinson)

(30) a. *Clint acts to me his age.
 b. *Willie's railway career spans to me almost 50 years.
 c. *Star striker Ronaldo Nazario weighs to me 90.5 kilos.

The ability of copular verbs to co-occur with an affectee should not surprise us, if we keep in mind that *be* and *become* may do so as well, as is evident in (31).

(31) a. He was to me a Dostoiesvkian figure. (I)
 b. Statistics, thus, became to me a study that is intimately related with the workings of nature. (I)

Another behavior of some of these verbs, which may give them the appearance of lexical verbs, is their being followed by the preposition *like*. One might object to the characterization of *like* as a preposition. But no better suggestions have been made. (Matushansky 2002: 227 calls such a phrase a "*like*-DP or a *like*-CP".) With lexical verbs, *like*-phrases are adjuncts, as in (32).

(32) If it walks like a duck and quacks like a duck, it's a duck.

But some variants of this saying also contain the sentence *and looks like a duck*. The external similarity in behavior between the lexical verbs *walk* and *quack* and the copular verb *sound* points to the thin borderline between them. In the vicinity of the lexical verbs *walk* and *quack*, the copular verb *look* loses its usually bleached meaning as a copular verb and gains the power of expressing physical appearance as the main component of its meaning, on a par with its walking and quacking, even though *look* does not have a canonical middle alternation.

The fact that there is a PP-like entity in the sentence does not mean that we have a *relation* here rather than *equivalence*. As noted in Section 2.4.2, pragmatics overrides the formal dimensions of the COP S-patterns.

Based on the discussion above, we might summarize the question of the borderline between lexical and copular verbs, and consequently between the V S-pattern and the COP S-pattern, in the following points. (a) There is no formal way to fully tease apart lexical and copular verbs. What counts is the functional perspective. (b) From this perspective, if the post-verbal phrase represents an entity separate from the referent of the subject, this phrase is an object and the sentence belongs to the V S-pattern. If, on the other hand, the post-verbal phrase is an NP representing an entity rendered equivalent to the referent of the subject, or an AP representing a property attributed to referent of the subject, then the post-verbal phrase is an Assigned Term, the verb is a copular verb, and the sentence belongs to the COP S-pattern.

This said, we have seen that some verbs have double behavior, and that under certain discourse conditions, the borderline between lexical and copular verbs may be blurred, due to the creativity and playfulness of language usage.

This section ends the problematization of the form and the function of the COP S-pattern. The formula and the function of the unified COP S-pattern under the model of patterning will be undertaken in the next section.

2.4.6 Form and function of the unified COP S-Pattern

Keeping in mind the similarity between the three COP S-patterns and the great variation they may display in form, a corrected formula of the COP S-pattern as a single unified construction is suggested in Figure 11. As has been the case before, the S-pattern formula maximally represents the syntactic options.

The Basis Subject NP and the Assigned Term NP or AP are the obligatory slots of the formula. Between them, from right to left, we find the COP slot, filled by a copula or a copular verb, or absent altogether in languages that allow this behavior. The slot of Affectee may be filled by NP or PP, and then there may be a slot of relation, filled by a P, by a composite preposition PNP, or by some other preposition-like element (*as*, *like*). Based on the concept of patterning, then, there is no single element, a predicate, that selects the other participants. Rather, the construction as a whole is chosen by the speaker for statements in which the Assigned Term is assigned to a Basis Subject in one of three ways – equivalence, attribution, relation

NP	COP	NP/PP	P/PNP	NP/AP
Basis Subj	Assigner	Affectee	Relation	Assigned Term

Figure 11. COP S-pattern in English (unified)

– and the other slots of this formula get filled by several sets of conventionalized combinations. These combinations have their distinctive meanings, just like any phrasal chunk.

The three functions of equivalence, attribution, and relation are partly suggested by formal features, such as the part of speech of the Assigned Term and the occurrence or non-occurrence of a preposition. In the final analysis, however, it is the construed meaning in context that either upholds or overrides the formal suggestion.

The function of the unified COP S-pattern is formulated in (33).

(33) The COP sentence expresses a state in which an Assigned Term is assigned to a Basis Subject as being its equivalent, its attribute, or in a relation with it. The choice between the three is based on a combination of formal and pragmatic factors.

This concludes the discussion of the S1 S-patterns in English. Let us now turn to the Hebrew data.

2.5 Subject-initial S-patterns in Hebrew

Hebrew, just like English, has two S1 S-patterns: a V S-pattern and a COP S-patterns, the latter having the same predicate classes – N, A, and P – if one takes the traditional perspective of predication. Little will be said about the V sentence beyond what has been said about English. The COP S-pattern requires additional attention, due to the nature of the copula and the copular elements in it.

2.6 The verbal S-pattern in Hebrew

The formula of the V sentence in Hebrew is identical to that of English. The argument structure constructions that feed this S-pattern show both similarities and differences to the English ones, but this investigation goes beyond the scope of this book.

The formula of the V S-pattern is repeated in Figure 12.

NP	[$_{vp}$	V	NP/PP	NP/PP	]
Subj		Pred	Obj$_1$	OBJ$_2$	

Figure 12. V S-pattern in Hebrew

Some examples, with common argument structures, are given in (34).

(34) a. *talya caxaka.*
　　 Talia laughed

　b. *No'am siyem et ha-sefer.*
　　 Noam finished ACC the book

　c. *ǧo'i somex al ma'ayan.*
　　 Joey relies on Ma'ayan

　d. *ilana natna le-rafi tapuz.*
　　 Ilana gave to Rafi an.orange

　e. *lidia šalxa et ha-xešbon le-oz.*
　　 Lidia sent ACC the bill to Oz

　f. *yonatan he'exil et rotem tapuz..*
　　 Yonatan fed ACC Rotem an.orange

The function of the Hebrew V S-pattern is the same as the English one. The V S-pattern is home to all agentive events expressed by its prototypical predicates. As such, this S-pattern forms the backbone of the storyline. But it is also the unmarked S-pattern, hence it hosts also functions that could be markedly expressed by other S-patterns. All this is summarized in (35).

(35) The V S-pattern hosts all actions and events constituting the storyline of a narrative. At the same time, it is the unmarked S-pattern, which may be used for the designated functions of other S-patterns.

But as will become evident in several of the following chapters, Hebrew makes more extensive use of the P1 S-patterns for various non-agentive situation types, hence the less prototypical periphery of the unmarked Hebrew V S-pattern is significantly narrower than that of the unmarked English V S-pattern.

2.7 The copular S-patterns in Hebrew

In principle, the COP S-pattern in Hebrew is similar to the English one. Hebrew differs from English in two details. First of all, the main Hebrew copula in the present tense is non-verbal. Its forms are identical to the personal pronouns: *hu* 'he', *hi* 'she', *hem* 'they.m.', and *hen* 'they.f.'. The past and future allomorphs are regular verb forms of *haya* 'be'. Secondly, the COP S-pattern has a zero variant of the present tense copula, a topic which raises the question: to what extent are the English and Hebrew forms of the COP S-patterns comparable? Is it at all justified to name the Hebrew construction as COP S-pattern, if it lacks a copula?

Along with other Semitic languages, Hebrew has traditionally been described, both in grammars that are modeled on Biblical Hebrew and in prescriptive school grammars in Israel, as having a bipartite "nominal sentence" with no copula. While this is a valid claim with regard to Biblical Hebrew (Goldenberg [1985] 1998: 164–167; Zewi 2000), it is no longer true for Israeli Hebrew (Rosén 1977b: 213; Glinert 1989: 168–177; Amir Coffin & Bolozky 2005: 318–321), since the zero copula is now in pertinent opposition with the copula *hu*.

The use of a personal pronoun *hu* 'he' as a copula probably emerged out of a re-analysis of the resumptive pronoun in a left-dislocated nominal sentence as the copula of a simplex sentence. This is exemplified in (36).

(36) a. *ha-šaʾar patuax.*
   The gate open

   b. *ha-šaʾar hu patuax.*
   The gate he open

   c. The gate is open

   d. The gate – it is open.

In (36a–b), two Israeli Hebrew sentences are given: (36a) has no copula, while (36b) has one. In Israeli Hebrew, both are simplex sentence forms, and both roughly have the meaning of the English sentence (36c). (For a debate on the meaning difference between the various copulas in Israeli Hebrew, see for example Rosén 1977b: 212 contra Rubinstein 1968: 60, but all agree that both sentences are simplex forms in Israeli Hebrew). If these two sentences had been in Biblical Hebrew, then only (36a) could be considered a simplex sentence, translated as the English sentence (36c). On the other hand, (36b) would have been a Left-Dislocation sentence, whose translation would have been the English sentence (36d).

Irrespective of the exact difference in meaning between the various copulas – still a controversial issue – the absence of the copula in Israeli Hebrew has to be viewed in the context of the presence of other copulas. The "absence of an otherwise necessary sign to the contrary" (Whitney 1875: 214) is in itself a sign.

In the early twentieth century, there was a debate on the question whether "nominal sentences" without a copula should be viewed as having zero or nothing. Bally (1922) supported the view of zero and Benveniste ([1950] 1971) the view of nothing. This debate, however, took place in the context of languages *without* other copulas. In that context, Benveniste was right. But Israeli Hebrew has *hu* and Ø (and other copulas) within the category of copulas. It is, therefore, fully justified to say that the Ø is a copula, and to refer to a sentence with Ø copula as a *copular* sentence, rather than using the classical term *nominal* sentence. This practice underscores the similarity between COP sentences in English and Hebrew as members of the same typological group.

As for the form of the various copulas, the depictive copulas in Hebrew are both non-verbal and verbal, while the resultative ones – only verbal. Here are some examples, just to get a sense of the richness of this category. The past and future allomorphs of the pronominal copula *hu* 'he' are regular conjugated forms of the verb *haya* 'be'. Example (37a) has the past plural form *hayu* 'were'. Another depictive copula is formed from the deictic interjection *hine* 'here.is'/'voilà'. As a copula, this grammatically tamed interjection is obligatorily accompanied by the bound pronominal third-person possessive suffix agreeing in number and gender with the subject, namely *hin-o* here.is-him, *hin-a* here.is-her, *hin-am* here.is-them.m, *hin-an* here.is-them.f. These forms have lost much of their deictic force, but they preserve it to the extent that they have no past or future forms. Deixis is weakly preserved in their meaning, as these forms are often used for authoritative or legal performative speech acts. The disclaimer pronounced in (37b) is such a statement. The use of deixis for performative statements is somewhat reminiscent of the English performative particle *hereby*, which similarly contains the deictic element *here-*. Another depictive copula is the indeclinable *ze* 'this'. Its function is still controversial: Rubinstein (1968: 136) saw it as a stylistic variant of *hu*, while Rosén (1966: 245–247) suggested it served as a copula in a "commenting" sentence, comparing it to French *c'est*. Example (37c) supports the latter view.

(37) a. *ha-cipiyot šeli me-ha-xevra hayu gvohot.* (I)
the expectations of.mine from the company were high
'My expectations from the company were high.'

b. *ha-xomarim ha-mefursamim b-a-atar hinam be-axrayut kotveyhem.* (I)
the materials the published in the site are in the.resposibility.of their.writers
'The materials posted on the site are under their writers' responsibility.'

c. *ha-medina ze ani.* (King Louis XIV)
the state is me
'L'état c'est Moi.'

Among the resultative copulas we find two kinds. One is the verb *hafax* 'turn', the other two are V + P sequences, *hafax* 'turn' or *haya* 'be' followed by the preposition *le* 'to'. This brings us back to the discussion on patterning (see Section 2.4.4 above and Chapter 10 below). These V + P sequences fill the two slots of COP and P/PNP in the unified formula of the COP S-pattern, repeated here in Figure 13.

The directional preposition *le-* 'to' metaphorically signifies the movement from one state to another. The copula *hafax* without the preposition *le* is nowadays mostly obsolete in the spoken language but is well attested in written texts. Example (38a) has the verb alone, while (38b) has the added preposition *le-* 'to'.

NP	COP	NP/PP	P/PNP	NP/AP
Basis Subj	Assigner	Affectee	Relation	Assigned Term

Figure 13. COP S-pattern in Hebrew (unified)

(38) a. *moše hafax manhig be-xoax išiyuto.* (I)
Moses turned leader in power.of his.personality
'Moses became leader by the power of his personality.'

b. *moše haya/hafax le-manhig be-xoax išiyuto.*
Moses was/turned to leader in power.of his.personality
'Moses became leader by the power of his personality.'

The examples with an adjectival Assigned Term are repeated here in (39).

(39) a. *arkadi haya ha-me'ušar mi-kulam.* (I)
Arkadi was the happy from everybody
Arkadi was the happiest of all.

b. *im šmi'at xadašot elu ezra haya l-a-me'ušar be-ovdey elbit.* (I)
with hearing.of news these Ezra was to the happy in the.workers.of Elbit
'Upon hearing this news, Ezra became the happiest of the Elbit workers.'

Like English, Hebrew also has composite prepositions. Some come from the classical stock: *al pney* 'on the.face.of' from Biblical Hebrew, *be-emca'ut* 'by means.of' from Medieval Hebrew, while others have been newly formed in Israeli Hebrew, such as *al saf* 'on the.threshold.of' 'on the verge of'. Hence, the appearance of PNP in the P slot of the formula of the unified COP S-pattern is justified for Hebrew as it is for English.

The existence of composite prepositions, along with the prevalence of sequences such as COP P AP (see Sections 2.4.1 and 2.4.3 above), show that Hebrew is very similar to English with regard to the materials that may mediate between the Basis Subject and the Assigned Term in the formula of the COP S-pattern.

The unified function of the COP S-pattern in Hebrew is identical to that in English. It is repeated in (40).

(40) The COP sentence expresses a state in which an Assigned Term is assigned to a Basis Subject as being its equivalent, its attribute, or in a relation with it. The choice between the three is based on a combination of formal and pragmatic factors.

As for its narrative function, the COP S-pattern, like its English counterpart, does not have a directly designated narrative function, but based on its constructional function, namely the expression of states, it is often used to supply the background and the circumstances pertaining to the storyline.

2.8 Summary and conclusion of Chapter 2

In this chapter, the S1 S-patterns in English and Hebrew have been presented and discussed. The discussion of the V S-pattern in English (Section 2.1) and in Hebrew (Section 2.5) has been limited to a skeletal presentation and exemplification of its different formations. Due to the rich system of argument structures associated with the V sentence, every serious discussion of this pattern must also include an analysis of argument structures, an enterprise that has been going on in the cognitive constructional literature for a while and is not taken up in the current work.

In Section 1.4 it has already been suggested that the argument-structure-only approach atomizes the field in a way that makes it impossible to make higher level word order generalizations within the argument structure network itself. In the framework of S-patterns developed here, the V S-pattern is precisely the place where such generalizations are natural. Word order, information structure, and narrative function all apply much more elegantly to the level of S-patterns than to individual argument structure constructions.

The copular sentences have suffered from atomization as well, and have merited little attention in cognitive constructional literature, probably due to the difficulties associated with identifying their predicates within the predication paradigm. Under these conditions, the tools of argument structure analysis could not be easily applied to them. On the other hand, copular verbs other than *be* have been viewed in the literature as regular verbs, and discussed in the context of regular verbal behavior, sometimes leading to awkward circumlocutions.

In the lexicalist literature, e.g. in Levin (1993), the copular verbs show up in a host of verb groups. In Goldberg & Jackendoff (2004) (based on earlier articles by the two authors), where the resultative construction is analyzed, the analysis comprises constructions in which the verbs are copular, or in the authors' words "intransitive resultatives", such as *the lake froze solid*, which is in my view a resultative COP sentence, but also – and mostly so – "transitive resultative" verbs (e.g. *The gardener watered the flowers flat*) in which a COP sentence inheres in secondary predication.

Nowhere in Goldberg and Jackendoff's discussion are copular sentences mentioned, and the fact that these verbs have AP "arguments" goes unmentioned. In fact, sometimes they are referred to as "predicates", which they are indeed in secondary predication. PP resultative phrases are treated differently, and are not referred to as predicates, although they *are* in secondary predication. The difference can only be attributed to the fact that PPs as arguments are supposedly normal, whereas APs are not.

In the view developed here, the sentences of (41) (parallel Hebrew examples can be provided as well) represent a set that belongs to one S-pattern, namely the COP S-pattern.

(41) a. The lake was solid. (I)
      b. The lake becomes solid. (I)
      c. The lake froze solid. (I)
      d. The lake turned into a swamp. (I)
      e. The lake froze into an ice skating rink. (I)

The existence of a zero copula in Hebrew, of PNP alongside P forms, of NPs that masquerade as PPs, and of non-hierarchical sequences such as COP P NP/AP, have all served as the grounds for an alternative view of the three COP S-patterns as being constructed not (or not only) in an act of predication but (also) in an act of patterning. In this view, the unified COP S-pattern has two obligatory slots, the Basis Subject and the Assigned Term, which are canonical phrasal constituents. Between them there are additional slots, some with canonical hierarchical phrases and others with a flat structure, whose constituency and ordering are local to this construction and defy universal or global hierarchical constituent structure.

Patterning has featured prominently in this chapter. It will be shown to operate also in other syntactic environments in Chapter 10. The rest of this book is concerned mostly with Predicate Initial (P1) S-patterns.

CHAPTER 3

Predicate initial sentence patterns

3.1 Justifying predicate initial S-patterns

Predicate Initial (P1) S-patterns are sentential constructions in which the predicate appears first among the members of the predicate–argument set. Under this calculus of first position, expletives and other grammatical elements are counted out. An expletive or a grammatical verb may indeed precede the predicate, but such a sentence would still count as belonging to a P1 S-pattern. All canonical P1 sentences in English are obligatorily preceded by an expletive (*there* or *it*) followed optionally by modals and auxiliaries, as can be seen in (1).

(1) | Expletive | Mod + AUX | Predicate + the rest of the sentence |
    | It | would be | wonderful to see you again. |
    | There | has been | looming on the horizon the possibility of [...] |

In the Introduction, the need for S-patterns has been discussed in the context of the Subject Initial (S1) S-patterns. Now a similar justification is due with regard to the P1 S-patterns.

One foundational discussion of a P1 S-pattern in the cognitive–constructional literature is Lakoff (1987: Case Study III), in which the existential (EX) S-pattern with the expletive *there* is accounted for in the context of the locative *there* construction (*there is Derek again* and similar sentences with a locative *there*). Lakoff suggests viewing the locative *there* construction as a radial family of constructions. In the center is the locative *there* construction. In its periphery – the EX S-pattern, which Lakoff calls the "expletive *there* construction". As noted in the Introduction above, Goldberg treats the whole family of *there* constructions as a sub-network, in her network of predicate argument constructions. The basic orientation of Goldberg's network is S1 (SVO), but an override instruction will change the linearization of the argument structure to P1 in the relevant part of the network.

Yet, the same problem that has been shown to plague this design in the S1 word order persists here as well. Argument structure constructions are non-linear structures, and Goldberg does not elaborate on how word order facts can be stated in them.

Additional problems arise, which are specifically related to the different nature of P1 constructions. First of all, Goldberg's design requires the use of global terms such as Subject and Object, but Subject is an inappropriate term for the final component of the P1 S-patterns, since the entity whose existence is declared, to be called here the *existent*, is not a "good" subject. It is not initial, not agentive, not necessarily nominative, not necessarily agreeing grammatically with the predicate, it does not participate in subject auxiliary inversion, and it cannot be made covert by passivization, etc.

A further difficulty for the incorporation of P1 constructions under a single network headed by S1 constructions comes from parallel bifurcations in the S1 and the P1 subsystems. In the S1 argument structure constructions, transitive and intransitive verbs belong to *different* branches of the network. Would, then, transitive and intransitive P1 constructions all be linked to one P1 node, the one that also reverses the linearization, or perhaps there would be two such nodes, one under Goldberg's intransitive S1 construction, the other under her transitive one? In the latter case, the reversal of linearization will have to be stated twice. Either way, redundancy will show up: either the redundancy of an intransitive–transitive bifurcation or the redundancy of two separate word-order override statement.

In the model suggested here, the set of all S-patterns is not seen as belonging to a single network. Further below in Chapter 4, all major S-patterns in English and Hebrew will be shown to belong to two separate networks of S1 and P1 S-patterns respectively, not linked to one another. The S1 network contains the Verbal (V) and Copular (COP) S-patterns and the P1 network contains the Existential (EX), Evaluative (EV), and Environmental (ENV) S-patterns.

Unlike argument structure constructions, S-patterns are linearized phrasal entities. Word order is fixed in each construction, and not all constructions are linked, hence there is no need for the mechanism of override. Furthermore, since the formula of the S-pattern is maximal, transitivity variation is built into the formula and does not require bifurcation. Let us finally remember that Goldberg's model has not been developed for predicates other than verbs. The P1 S-patterns will be shown to be able to host a whole array of non-verbal parts of speech as predicates in each construction.

As such, S-patterns are constructions at the appropriate grain size to enable the observer on the one hand to ignore the differences between the parts of speech of predicates and the diversified argument realizations across one construction, and on the other hand to have a clear view of the relations between these constructions both in one language and across a typological group.

The multiplicity of parts of speech in the predicate position of the P1 S-patterns is *not* accompanied by a multiplicity of functions. Verbs, adjectives, and prepositions all have the existential function in the sentences instantiating the EX S-pattern in (2)

(2) a. There exist at least four different editions of this work. (I)
    b. There are extant only two sources for the Dramatic Text. (I)
    c. There are in existence more than 14000 Old Testament manuscripts. (I)

Similarly, verbs, nouns, adjectives, and prepositions all have an evaluative function in the sentences instantiating the EV S-pattern in (3)

(3) a. It moves me to glimpse in you the life I abandoned. (I)
    b. It's a drag to roll into the new year feeling fat and hung over. (I)
    c. It is hilarious to see her get excited jumping up and down singing it. (I)
    d. It is in order to leave a small tip. (I)

Finally, verbs, nouns and adjectives all have the function of presenting environmental conditions in the sentences instantiating the ENV S-pattern in (4).

(4) a. It is raining.
    b. It is summer.
    c. It is cold.

In the rest of this chapter, these three groups of P1 S-patterns will be presented, first in English then in Hebrew. The predication perspective is central in the formation of many P1 sentences, but patterning is concomitantly at work since these constructions also have additional constants and variables that have to be declared and linearized.

In this chapter, the form and function of the EX, EV, and ENV S-patterns is addressed. The semantics of the predicates participating in these S-patterns is separately discussed in Chapters 5, 6, and 7 respectively.

3.2 Predicate-initial S-patterns in English

The predicate initial S-patterns in English show some asymmetries that do not apply in the case of Hebrew P1 S-patterns. This is so, since English does not make full use of all potential slots, while Hebrew does. In English, for instance, only the EV S-pattern has a slot for a (direct or oblique) affectee, as is evident from the phrases *me* and *to me* in (5a–b). On the other hand, the EX and ENV S-patterns do not allow such objects, as can be seen in (5c–d).

(5) a. It moves me to glimpse in you the life I abandoned. (I)
    b. It really matters to me that honesty and integrity are recognized. (I)
    c. *There is me a book/*there is to me a book/*there is a book to me.
    d. *It is me cold/*it is to me cold/*it is cold to me.

The formulas of these S-patterns will be presented here language-specifically. Hence, the English EX and ENV S-patterns will lack this slot, whereas the Hebrew ones will have them. In a broader typological perspective, such a position should be viewed as an option that is differently materialized in different languages.

A similar asymmetry of English is evident in the categorial affiliation of the final component of the EX and EV S-patterns. In English, the final component of the EX S-pattern, the *existent*, may be an NP, but not a nominal (InfP, GrdP, etc.), as is evident in (6a). Conversely, the final component of the EV S-pattern may only be a nominal, but not an NP, as is evident in (6b). In Hebrew, as will be demonstrated below, all these slots may be filled.

(6) a. (i) There was a long pause.
      (ii) *there was to write an essay/writing an essay.
   b. (i) It is worthwhile to buy a new computer.
      (ii) *It is worthwhile a new computer.

The detailed discussion of P1 S-patterns begins with the EX S-pattern in English in the next section.

3.2.1 The existential S-pattern in English

In the English EX S-pattern, the verb *be* is prominent. In fact, in many varieties of spoken English, only *be* is used, excluding other verbs. Hence, we find doublets of style/register. The more literary style has a semantically rich existential verb, as in (7a–b), the spoken variety has only the verb *be*, and the semantic contents of the literary counterpart are expressed by secondary predication (here in the form of active or passive participles) following the EX sentence, as exemplified in (7c–d).

(7) a. There rang a bell.
   b. There parked a car.
   c. There was a bell ringing.
   d. There was a car parking/parked.

Clearly, then, the discussion of all existential verbs other than *be* only applies to the higher, more formal, more literary varieties of English. The higher the style, the richer the diversity. This is also true for diachronic depth. Texts from the nineteenth century show a far more diversified set of predicates in the EX S-pattern than contemporary texts. Hence, an archaicizing text will display a larger variety.

The verb *be*, then, is "the existential verb par excellence" (Breivik 1999). Milsark called only the *be* EX sentence *existential*, referring to those with other verbs as *verbal*, further distinguishing between *inside* versus *outside* verbal EX sentences.

The inside verbal EX sentence has the existent immediately following the verb, as in Milsark's example in (8a), while the outside type has the existent at the end, following an intervening phrase, as in his example in (8b) (Milsark 1979: 152–154).

(8) a. There arose many trivial objections during the meeting.
    b. There walked into the room a fierce-looking tomcat.

According to Milsark, (a) the verbs that may appear in inside EX sentences are more restricted than those in the outside variant, and (b) the definiteness restriction applies only to inside verbal EX sentences. Following Erdmann's (1990: 71–73) convincing textual evidence against both claims, they are not maintained here. In some sense, Chapter 5 elaborates the intuition behind claim (a), but it is not tenable the way it was presented by Milsark.

The formula in Figure 14 provides the form and function of the slots of the EX S-pattern.

The terms Ex Pred (Existential Predicate) and Existent (in Figure 14) are in line with the practice of parsing the construction into construction-specific components and preferring – where feasible – semantically meaningful function tags over general functional terms such as subject and object.

Figure 14 ignores minor details of form. A more differentiating look at the predicate phrase will reveal some variation between V versus COP behavior, namely, when the predicates are A or P, the copula *be* is used, as in all COP sentences. This is, of course, not the case with the V predicate. A more distinctive representation of the formula would need to have two separate lines for V and A/P behavior, as is done in Figure 15.

there	[PredP	V/A/P	NP/PP	]	NP
Expletive		Ex Pred	Obj		Existent

Figure 14. EX S-pattern in English

there	[VP		V	NP/PP	]	NP
	[AP/PP	*be*	A/P	PP	]	
Expletive		COP	Ex Pred	Obj		Existent

Figure 15. EX S-pattern in English (detailed version)

A similar distinction between verbal and copular varieties will also apply to the other two P1 S-patterns, EV and ENV, and could be spelled out in the upcoming tables as well, but since we are not interested here in these morpho-syntactic details, this distinctive presentation will not be repeated in subsequent figures.

Note further that the COP behavior is residual, allowing just the verb *be*, not other copular verbs found elsewhere in the COP sentences, as is evident in (9), where the adjectival predicate *needed* is used.

(9) a. There are needed new civil and criminal laws addressing... (I)
    b. *There seem/sound/look needed new civil and criminal laws addressing...

In the translation of the Scriptures, the copular verb *become* is sometimes used (10a–b). In Modern English, such behavior might occur, see (10c), but it is quite unusual. It is perhaps not completely accidental that this sentence originates in the Bible Belt of the US and addresses a question of faith in an archaicizing style.

(10) a. And there became light. (Gen. 1.3)
     b. And there became a great calm. (Matt. 8.26)
     c. In Texas, there was a case called Tilden v. Moyer, where Mr. Tilden was an evangelist and ran a church and there became a dispute over whether his claims of healing were accurate claims. (I)

The term *existent* is used in Figure 14 as shorthand for *the entity whose existence is asserted in the sentence*. Its semantic role is evident, and the naming merely sums it up. Of course, it is not only existence per se that is pronounced in the EX S-pattern, but also occurrence in place or time, appearance on the scene, introduction into the discourse, etc. All these meanings are extensions of the basic existential meaning. The existent is a post-verbal NP, which displays other object-like properties as well, such as showing lack of agreement with the copula in the spoken language (*there's many possibilities*). For these reasons, the existent cannot be conceptually conflated with the subject of S1 sentences. Unlike the existent, the subject of S1 sentences lacks a single semantic role. It displays syntactic properties, such as passivization, subject-auxiliary inversion, topicality, which are prototypical of subjects. The traditional term *notional subject* is therefore rejected here, and is replaced by *existent*..

The function of the EX S-pattern is stated in (11).

(11) Through the use of the existential predicate, the EX S-pattern announces the existence of the existent.

Additional functions of the EX S-pattern ensue from this function under certain contextual and pragmatic circumstances. For example, the EX S-pattern has often been assigned a narrative role. In Jespersen's view, the EX sentence "generally indicates (vaguely) the existence of something on which fuller information is to follow" (Jespersen [1937] 1984: 130). Hetzron similarly suggested that the function of the EX S-pattern is to call "special attention to one element of the sentence for recall in the subsequent discourse" (Hetzron 1975: 347). Lambrecht (1994: 180–181) talks about a bi-clausal construction, in which a referent is first presented and then used as topic in the next sentence. One of the bi-clausal constructions he discusses has the EX S-pattern as its first clause. Due to the scarcity of ontological existential statements and the prominence of the presentative function, Lambrecht finds the term *existential* inappropriate, and calls these sentences *presentational clauses*.

If the existential sentence establishes a topic to be used later, it should "persist" (Givón 1983) in the subsequent discourse. Introduction for subsequent use, however, is not a direct narrative function of the EX S-pattern. Not all existents represent entities introduced for subsequent use (Sasaki 1991; Martinez Insua 2001). Furthermore, the EX S-pattern may have other pragmatic functions as well. An EX sentence may be used for modal evaluation, as is the case in (12a–b), where *there is a good chance that...* is paraphrasable as *it is quite likely that...* and *there is no necessity to assume...* is a variant of *it is not necessary to assume...* These EX sentences do not introduce *good chance* and the lack of *necessity* as topics to be used in subsequent discourse. Besides, EX sentences may also be used for expressing environmental conditions, which form the background of future narration, as is the case of the *huge storm* in (12c). The storm is presented as background, in order to become presupposed in the following sentence, but it is not rementioned as topic in the subsequent discourse. An EX sentences may even appear at the end of a text, serving as its final conclusion. The referent of *nothing else* in (12d) has no subsequent discourse to be rementioned in.

(12) a. There is a good chance that my female cat is pregnant. How can I tell if she is, and if so when will she deliver? Is there anything that I should do to help her if she is? (I)
b. There is no necessity to assume a special distribution density. (I)
c. I loved the zoo and Sentosa Island even though there was a huge storm and we didn't get to see the pink dolphins. (I)
d. I would get tired, my hands would begin to shake, I would grow tired of it all, and believe that it was useless. But there was nothing else I could do. [End of text] (I)

It is important, therefore, to draw a clear distinction between the basic function of the EX S-pattern to assert the existence of an entity, and the different pragmatic applications of this function in different contexts and situation types. It is definitely possible to point out that a certain function prevails over the others, or that it is highly significant in a certain discourse mode. But any attempt to formulate the function of the EX S-pattern beyond its designated constructional function will turn out to be an overstatement. Mathesius ([1961] 1975: 118–119) makes this distinction already in 1961. He first says that the EX S-pattern "states the existence of something", and then he proceeds to talk about the different *uses* of the construction, including some that have not been discussed here.

Last in this section I would like to discuss negation in the EX S-pattern. Grammatical negation (with *not, never*, etc.) is felicitous in EX sentences, as can be observed in the sentences of (13).

(13) a. There is not enough space in the mouth for the wisdom tooth. (I)
 b. There does not exist a Diophantine quadruple with the property D(n). (I)
 c. There did not happen so much on this page during the last weeks. (I)
 d. There is never jealousy where there is not strong regard. (I)

EX sentences with the predicate *be* and a lexically negative secondary predication, such as Hannay's (1985: 8, 60) examples in (14), are also unproblematic. In these, an entity is first presented, and only then is its existence negated.

(14) a. There were two soldiers shot dead in Belfast last night.
 b. There are two pupils absent today.

Despite the seeming logical fallacy in a predication of existence followed by a secondary predication of non-existence, such sentences are fully felicitous, and do not sound odd.

The problem is with predicates that *lexically* express non-existence in primary predication, such as those shown in (15). Milsark claims that sentences such as those in (15b–e) are ungrammatical, but admits that "the nature of the principles involved here is at present beyond my ken" (Milsark 1979: 158).

(15) a. *There disappeared a man in front of us. (Breivik's example)
 b. *There ended a riot. (Milsark's example)
 c. *There died some people in that fire. (Milsark's example)
 d. *There vanished a book from this desk yesterday. (Milsark's example)
 e. *There left several people. (Milsark's example)

Breivik (1999) says: "If I am correct in claiming that *there* is a presentative signal, then this also provides a natural explanation for the restrictions it imposes on the verb", following which he gives the example in (15a) as well as all of Milsark's sentence in (15b–e). In his view, then, there is a *natural, logical* contradiction between the presentative nature of the construction and its use with predicates of non-existence. If this is true, though, why does grammatical negation with *not* survive?

Why is the logical fallacy of (14) felicitous? And finally, why do other languages, such as Hebrew, unproblematically accept such predicates in the EX S-pattern?

This behavior in English has become conventionalized for reasons I am not aware of, but first of all, these reasons are not logical, if we take logic seriously. Secondly, this behavior is not without exceptions. And the exceptions are well motivated pragmatically.

Erdmann's (1990: 67) work on EX sentences is corpus based, and his sample of lexically negative verbs is small. He has a sentence with the verb *want* in the sense of 'lack', which is highly literary and in an archaicizing style, and he also points out that *vanish* is acceptable, but no attested example is given to substantiate this claim.

Lumsden (1988: 237) goes one step in what seems to me the right direction. He provides a pragmatic criterion, not a lexical or logical one. In his view, (16a) is not acceptable in isolation; "however, providing the preceding discourse context contains material related to the verb in [(16a)], the strangeness can be mitigated", as is evident in (16b).

(16) a. There disappeared our own ship over the horizon.
 b. One by one during the day the vessels left until finally there disappeared our own ship over the horizon.

The pragmatic perspective is correct, but it has to be stated in explicit terms. Lakoff (1987: 570) suggests that the EX sentence is "specialized to narratives. It allows speakers to introduce a new narrative element, while simultaneously sketching a scene". One of his examples involves the verb *disappear*, as in (17a).

(17) a. From an asylum near Providence, R.I., there recently disappeared an exceedingly singular person.
 b. There recently ended the longest scoring streak in the history of professional hockey.

It is clear from the phrasing of sentence (17a) that it is an opening sentence of a narrative, even though Lakoff does not say so explicitly. The person in (17a) is introduced into the universe of discourse in highly mysterious terms ("exceedingly singular person"), which call for explanation, and there is a conventionalized expectation that this explanation will be provided in the subsequent text. In other words, the *disappearance* from the asylum is the way this person *makes an appearance* in the story. A very similar setup should be imagined for (17b), from Lakoff (1987: 574).

A similar attested example (18) from the LOB corpus performs exactly the same narrative function.

(18) *When the last leaf draps fae the auld aish tree*
The Boyds o' Penkill maun cease tae be
So runs an old rhyme which came sadly true when, in 1897, there died Miss Alice Boyd, 15th Laird of Penkill and the last of the Boyds.   (LOB F29 5)

Being placed at the opening passage of a narrative, the sentence *there died Miss Alice Boyd* combines the verb meaning with the discursive usage. The verb *die* is a verb of disappearance, and this is what is being reported of Miss Boyd. As such, it should be conventionally unacceptable in English. But if sentential non-existence is used for discursive appearance, special pragmatic conditions are established, which license this usage. Miss Boyd is introduced into the story by the EX sentence through her death. Her having existed before she died is key to understanding how her descendant Miss Evelyn May Courtney-Boyd eventually turned out to be the owner of the Boyd Estate.

We may summarize then that indeed English does not usually employ verbs of non-existence in the EX S-pattern, unless this use can be pragmatically justified by turning sentential non-existence into narrative introduction, usually at the very beginning of the narrative.

The issue of the lexical negation of existence will be revisited in the discussion of the Hebrew data in Section 3.3.2.

3.2.2   The evaluative S-pattern in English

The EV S-pattern is often called an *extraposition* sentence. In early transformational–generative theory (e.g Rosenbaum 1967), the sentences of (19) were viewed as having the InfP or the *that*-clause base-generated in the initial subject position, as they are in (20), and then moved (extraposed) to the final position.

(19) a. It is good to see you.
     b. It is good that they have a plan.
(20) a. To see you is good.
     b. That they have a plan is good.

Huddleston (1984: 16) sides with the original extraposition stance and views the sentences of (20) as the "unmarked kernel clauses" and those of (19) as "marked by extraposition". This view was later reversed in Chomskyan syntax, namely the InfP or *that*-clause came to be viewed as base-generated in the post-predicate position, and if they appear in the subject position, as in (20), they are there as a result of movement (Emonds 1976; Reinhart 2002). The term *extraposition* for the sentences of (19) has survived the reversal in the directionality of movement, and has been inherited also in post- and non-transformational literature (e.g Kaltenböck 2000; Van Linden & Davidse 2009).

Besides serving as the name for the EV construction, the term *extraposition* has been also used in syntactic literature for other movement operations, such as the shifting of heavy relative clauses to the end of the sentence, as in (21a), or left dislocation, as in (21b).

(21) a. And then a girl came, whose name I don't seem to remember now. (I)
 b. Mary, she is a good person. (I)

The term *extraposition* will be avoided here as the name of this construction, both because a movement operation is not premised here and because it is a broad term covering other phenomena as well.

Since the V S-pattern and the EV S-pattern have been viewed as two linearizations of the same proposition, linguists wondered about the difference in choice between the unmarked versus marked/extraposed sentence. When differences in linearization are addressed, two motivations are often brought up: weight and information structure. This was the case here as well. Huddleston (1984) mentions both factors. One motivation, in his view, has to do with weight: "a 'heavy' unit appears at the end of the clause, which makes for easier processing". The second motivation has to do with information structure: "a context where the content of an embedded finite clause or infinitival is given favors the unmarked construction". Aware of the incompleteness of this description, Huddleston admits that "there is of course no absolute correspondence between given and non-extraposed, new and extraposed, but there does appear to be some measure of correlation between them" (Huddleston 1984: 453–454).

In an attempt to motivate the choice between the two linearizations, Smith (2003: 221), basing her discussion on corpus data from Miller (2001), suggests that information structure considerations override weight, namely "familiarity status rather than heaviness is the determining factor in extraposition". This approach assumes that the two sentence forms of (19) and (20) are equal alternates. In Rosenbaum, Huddleston, and Smith's view, then, the EV sentence is nothing but a regular S1 sentence, which for various reasons got re-linearized. This view is, however, critically challenged by the examples of (22), which show that certain EV sentences do not have an S1 counterpart.

(22) a. (i) It seems that they are buddies.
 (ii) *That they are buddies seems.
 b. (i) It hit me that I will never see this team play again.
 (ii) *That I will never see this team play again hit me.

c. (i) (It is) fancy meeting you here.
   (ii) *Meeting you here is fancy.
d. (i) It remains to show that this formal limit really holds.
   (ii) *To show that this formal limit really holds remains.

Bolinger takes an important step in making a generalization about the evaluative function of this construction. Consider Bolinger's (1977: 72) examples 78–81, given in (23) with his own acceptability judgments.

(23) a. Try to realize this simple fact: to give in now would be fatal.
   b. ?Try to realize this simple fact: it would be fatal to give in now.
   c. I agree with you all the way: it would be fatal to give in now.
   d. ?I agree with you all the way: to give in now would be fatal..

Viewing the two linearizations as alternates, Bolinger suggests that factivity enhances the non-extraposed order. For the factive option Bolinger uses the expression "realize this simple fact" as context, which is indeed compatible with factivity. Note, however, that for the non-factive option, Bolinger uses the phrase "agree with you" (Bolinger 1977: 71–74) as context. In doing so, Bolinger in fact directs us to the *evaluative* context for his acceptability judgments. In Bolinger's presumed view, then, it is the situation type that motivates the choice between the two S-patterns. To this, Bolinger (1977: 74) also adds information structure considerations: "if the information value is increased, extraposition is not necessary".

In the constructional literature, Michaelis & Lambrecht (1996a) treat the EV S-pattern as a daughter construction of their *abstract exclamative construction*. The former inherits its semantics from the latter, and as such is said to be expressive of "an affective stance/expectation contravention" (1996a: 375). However, this semantic characterization is too narrow and only captures the most prototypical instances. Less prototypical examples, such as the sentences of (24), do not necessarily exhibit this property.

(24) a. It is time that the Republicans take a stance. (I)
   b. It has been suggested to have a campaign to raise awareness. (I)

Sentence (24a) may, but does not have to, express an affective stance, and (24b) does not do so at all, nor does it contravene any expectation. The way such sentences are associated with the EV S-pattern will become clear shortly.

In the rest of this section, the form and general function of the EV S-pattern as an independent S-pattern (not a variant of an S1 S-pattern) will be presented. The semantics of the EV predicates will be treated separately in Chapter 6.

The categorial affiliation of the evaluative predicate in the EV S-pattern is multivariate: the evaluative predicate may be a V (e.g. *turn out*), N (*riot*), A (*wonderful*), or P (*in*), as can be seen in (25).

(25) a. It turned out that the information was not credible. (I)
b. It's a riot to watch Fido chomp away at his favorite chew toy. (I)
c. But it is wonderful watching his blog and following his story. (I)
d. It is quite in order to ask for a dish which is out of reach. (I)

While it is quite ordinary, in the case of V, N, and A, to have bare predicates without complements, it is less common to find this behavior with P. Nevertheless, we might find an occasional use of *in* without a complement (representing the concept "in fashion", "in style", or "in vogue"). In most cases, writers encircle the P with scare quotes, see (26), as evidence of their awareness of the exceptional nature of this form.

(26) It is "in" to talk about minorities (I)

Since the predicate slot of this pattern may admit different parts of speech, without imposing any formal restrictions (such as agreement) on it, this position also "attracts freaks" (Kuzar 1996). In (27a), the predicate *OK* is used. This is a morphologically unique form, an interjection, which (at least initially) did not have categorial affiliation.

(27) a. Vatican: It's OK for Catholics to Believe in Aliens. (I)
b. It is "WOW" to be in this ornaments shop. (I)

One might object that in fact *okay* has undergone grammatical categorization and is already a regular word. It can be the head of an NP (*to give an okay*) or an AP (*this is more OK*). Sentence (27b) might be a rawer example of the use of a morphologically unique interjection in the predicate slot. The scare quotes surrounding "WOW" testify to the speaker's sense of the oddity of the expression (as do the capitals used). In Hebrew, as will be demonstrated in Section 3.3.3, there are more obvious and more central cases of morphologically unique predicates in the EV S-pattern.

The second major component of the EV S-pattern, the evaluee, is encoded in one of three nominalization constructions, i.e. constructions in which a proposition is packaged and embedded as a noun-like expression in the matrix clause. English has three such forms: the infinitive phrase (InfP), the gerund phrase (GrdP), and the *that*-clause. Among the two variants of GrdP, only the verbal type of GrdP (*It's good having deadlines*), not the nominal type (**it's good the having of deadlines*) (McCann 1979), may be used in the EV S-pattern. The term *nominal* will be used here as the superordinate label for the three nominalization constructions in terms of their categorial affiliation. The functional label of this component is *evaluee*.

Besides the predicate and the evaluee, there is an additional functional role, the *affectee*. Functionally stable, its form is rather elusive, in that it may be encoded in several syntactic slots. Sentence (28) will serve as a starting point for its elaboration.

(28)   It makes sense to me for Google to buy Twitter.   (I)

In this sentence we have several NP positions that require attention with regard to their role. The NP *sense* is the object of *make*. It complements its meaning. The evaluative stance cannot be derived in this sentence from the light verb *make* alone. It arises compositionally from the verb + object *make sense*.

The second NP is *me* in the PP *to me*. The role of this NP is affectee. It represents the person affected by the evaluative stance *makes sense*. Finally we have a *for*-phrase containing the NP *Google*, which is the subject of the InfP and is internal to it. This sentence, then, exhibits a discrete division of roles between *to me* as a modifier of the verbal expression *make sense* and *for Google* as the subject of the InfP *to buy Twitter*. If this sentence alone were taken as a model for the EV S-pattern, one might be tempted to assign a slot for an affectee (representing *to me*) in the formula, which would be VP-internal, hence InfP-external.

Interestingly, however, the person affected by the evaluative stance sometimes appears to be coded in seemingly similar sentences in other syntactic positions. Take, for instance, the two sentences of (29).

(29)   a.   It gives them pleasure to see all of these Aussie products.   (I)
       b.   It gives pleasure to God to give life to those who repent and trust Him.   (I)

In the dative alternation displayed in (29), the recipient of *pleasure* – be it direct (29a) or oblique (29b) – is the affectee of the evaluative stance. It follows, then, that the syntactic slot encoding the affectee may be variable.

The situation is even more complex, since there seem to be three additional positions in which the affectee may be encoded. In one case, the predicate itself is evaluative and does not need to establish evaluative meaning compositionally with an object. The object of the verb is then free to serve as affectee of the evaluative stance. The direct object of the verb *annoy* in (30a) and the PP complement of the predicative adjective *incumbent* in (30b) are used for the affectee role.

(30)   a.   It annoys him that you keep asking him what happened to your mom.   (I)
       b.   It is incumbent on them to exhibit this truth to the Church   (I)

Another case of affectee encoding is the use of an adjunct for this role, as shown in (31).

(31) a. Wow, it is unbelievable to me that we have already completed the first week of school. (I)
b. It is hard on me to let him pay for everything. (I)
c. It is important for us that the garment is easy to wear. (I)

Different prepositions (*to, on, for*) are used for the affectee adjuncts in (31). Yet, the preposition *for* seems to be the default choice for adjuncts, and indeed it may replace the others in the sentences above.

The use of a *for*-PP in front of the *that*-clause, as in (31c) raises the question whether the same position can be assumed to exist in front of an InfP as well. This question comes up, since in English, as we have seen in (28), the noun between *for* and *to* in this position is often considered the subject of the InfP, which is internal to the InfP. If both positions exist, then a sentence such as *it is important for me to go* should be ambiguous. In fact, Postal (1974: 152) quotes a suggestion made to him by McCawley (via personal communication) of a sentence in which the object position of the matrix clause and the subject position of the InfP are separately filled with two *for*-phrases, as in (32).

(32) It is important for me for you to visit my mother (Postal 1974: 152).

Actually, it is not so difficult to find attested examples of this kind, as shown in (33). These examples readily showed up by searching the Internet for "it is important for me for".

(33) a. It is important for me for my children to learn about Britain. (I)
b. It is important for me for the tone to be coming still from my amp. (I)
c. It is important for me for them to know that everybody has trouble along the way. (I)
d. It is important for me for you and your family to be safe anywhere in the country. (I)
e. Thus it is important for me for him to belong in these classes. (I)

The question, then, remains: should a single occurrence of *for* + NP preceding the infinitive be read as a complement of the matrix predicate or as the subject of the InfP? It is quite clear that in some cases the NP following *for* has to be interpreted as the subject of the InfP. This is the case in (34a–b), where *it* and *there* are expletive subjects that do not represent any referent, and therefore are grammatically prevented from serving as affectees, regardless of context. And since affectees are prototypically human, the NP following *for* in (34c) cannot be construed as affectee.

(34) a. Is it possible for it to rain oil? (I)
　　 b. It is essential for there to be no misunderstanding on this point
　　　　　　　　　　　　　　　　　　　　　　　(Huddleston & Pullum 2002: 1183).
　　 c. It is difficult for learning to take place in chaotic environments.
　　　　　　　　　　　　　　　　　　　　　　　　　　　　　　　　(COCA)

On the other hand, the evident equivalence in form between EV sentences having *that*-clauses and those having InfPs as evaluees – demonstrated in the almost-minimal pair of (35) – renders the separate appearance of the *for*-phrase *before* the InfP quite viable.

(35) a. It is important for me that I see things clearly and correctly. (I)
　　 b. It is important for me to see things in context. (I)

Such equivalence is even less questionable when there is no *for*, but rather an accusative NP, as in (36).

(36) a. It annoys me that I have to work at 7:00 tomorrow. (I)
　　 b. It annoys me to have to work on Sundays. (I)

Incidentally, some languages make a systematic distinction between these two positions. Barri (1977: 72) provides attested examples from Attic Greek for sentences with a dative affectee and an accusative subject of the embedded clause referring to different persons (see also Buyssens 1987 for a problematization of English corpus data).

　　Coming back to the question of the ambiguity of *it is important for me to go*, it should be kept in mind that the question rests on the premise of discrete constituency. This premise, maintained in several formal grammatical frameworks, may, however, be challenged by the concept of "event integration and clause union" (Givón 2001b), according to which a certain constituent may belong to both the matrix clause and the embedded clause. As such, the need to choose between two construals does not have to arise, and in fact in most cases it does not. *It is important for me to go* is usually not ambiguous.

　　At other times, the *for*-phrase in question may vacillate between two construals. In one construal, the *for*-phrase is related to *important*, hence the affectee is in the matrix clause, and the InfP implicitly shares its subject with it. In the alternate construal, the predicate is not directly followed by an affectee; it is phrased in general, impersonal terms, and what is generally taken to be *important* is the event encoded in the InfP, namely *for me to go*, which contains a subject *for*-phrase. Under this view, the option of splitting the shared slot "back" into its two discrete components is not ruled out. Nevertheless, the need to make such a distinction is in fact strikingly rare.

The last option for affectee encoding to be discussed here is a possessive expression incorporated in the object NP, as in (37).

(37) a. It suits my needs to control my settings and install my own plugins. (I)
 b. It blows her mind to even think about it. (I)
 c. It broke the little boy's heart that his father considered him a liar. (I)
 d. It stroked her ego that he got jealous over her. (I)

In these sentences, *my* of *my needs* and *her* of *her mind* (and so on) are the affectees. Given that both the subject of the InfP and the possessive element inside the NP are internal to their phrases, they will not appear as separate components of the EV S-pattern. (Another affectee encoding, which has the affectee incorporated in the *predicate* phrase, as in *it is my turn to be the designated driver*, will be separately discussed in Chapter 11).

There is a difference, then, between the question of affectee encoding, which involves different layers of sentence structure (sentential as well as phrasal), and the question of the possible affectee slots (sentential slots) in the formula of the EV S-pattern.

The formula of the EV S-pattern is shown in Figure 16. The EV S-pattern has a V and a COP variant, as does the EX S-pattern discussed in Section 3.2.1. In line with the practice suggested there, this variation is filtered out in the formula.

The fact that the evaluee might be InfP-internal cannot be explicitly spelled out in this formula, since the formula does not go into the details of the nominal evaluee (*that*-clause, InfP, or GrdP).

To keep things simple and consistent, and to maintain the functional analogies of the examples in (35) and (36), all *for*-phrases are treated here uniformly as objects of the matrix clause. This also makes sense from a functional perspective, since both object positions have the optional role *affectee*, a role that needs to be postulated at the level of the S-pattern itself.

As noted above, the object position is not always occupied by an affectee. In (38) there is an object that is not an affectee. This role is simply called *Obj* in the formula.

it	[$_{PredP}$	V/N/A/P	NP	NP/PP	]	Nominal
Expletive		Ev Pred	Obj/Affectee	Obj/Affectee		Evaluee

Figure 16. EV S-pattern in English

(38) It will open the gates of hell to let you out. (I)

The EV S-pattern, like the EX S-pattern, does not have a canonical subject. What counts as the canonical position of the subject in S1 S-patterns is filled in the EV S-pattern by the expletive *it*. This expletive is a constant of the formula of this S-pattern.

Finally, the copular variant of the EV S-pattern seems to be more liberal than its counterpart in the EX S-pattern in the range of copular verbs it admits, as is evident in (39).

(39) a. With technical matters it seems good to be relentless and focus on your needs. (I)
 b. It sounds good to be able to fine individuals so stringently for these violations. (I)
 c. It appears fair to allow the department to receive copies of those appraisals. (I)
 d. It became obvious that the five of us weren't going to be able to do this on our own. (I)
 e. It remains our view that a two-state solution, Israelis and Palestinians living side by side in peace and security, is in our interests and in the region's interests. (I)

I would nevertheless speculate, subject to future corpus based verification, that such sentences are less frequent than equivalent S1 COP sentences, thereby being also more highly marked.

The function of the EV sentence is stated in (40).

(40) Through the use of the evaluative predicate, the EV S-pattern evaluates the evaluee. The evaluation is made relevant to an affectee, if present.

A word on the choice of the terms *evaluative/evaluee/evaluation* is due here. Evaluation amounts to modal judgment on the part of the speaker. But since the term *modal* is occupied as a part of speech in English, this term is avoided here both in the naming of the S-pattern and in the description of its function. The full discussion of the various (modal) usages of the EV S-pattern will be conducted in Chapter 6, where the semantics of the EV predicates is discussed.

While the EX S-pattern in English does not have any linked sub-patterns, the EV S-pattern in English does. This is the Cost S-pattern, which will be discussed in the next section.

3.2.2.1 *The cost S-pattern in English*
The sentences of (41) display an extension of the EV S-pattern. Semantically, they characterize events in terms of the *cost incurred* by the event taking place. Two

prototypical cases of cost incurred are the time an event takes and the price it costs. The cost may be stated in general, or with respect to an affectee. Examples (41a–b) do not contain an affectee, while (41c–e) do. In (41e) the verb *save*, which also belongs here, conveys the lexical negation of *cost*.

(41) a. It takes an hour to make a five minute journey. (I)
b. It costs two dollars to take the subway downtown. (I)
c. It takes me an hour to get to work. (I)
d. It will cost a firm 13000 to do this. (I)
e. It may save you some trouble to read this first. (I)

The sentences of (41) may not be included in the EV S-pattern for several reasons. First of all, they are not evaluative in any of the four traditional senses of modality (deontic, attitudinal, evidential, and epistemic) to be elaborated in 6.2.1. In other words, a statement of cost is not an instance of an evaluative judgment.

Secondly, while the two post-predicate positions in the EV S-pattern are optional and, if filled, can be objects at large or affectees, in the Cost S-pattern the two post-predicate positions are well defined in terms of their role. The first object is optional and encodes the affectee, and the second object is obligatory and encodes the cost.

Finally, the nominal of the Cost S-pattern is usually an InfP, as in (41) above, sometimes a GrdP, as in (42a), but never a *that*-clause, as evident from the ungrammaticality of (42b).

(42) a. It costs a lot having to throw away a 6 months-old TV. (I)
b. *It costs a lot that I have to throw away a 6 months-old TV.

It may, therefore, be concluded that the sentences of (41) displays a genuine pairing of form and function, different from the EV S-pattern.

In addition to time and money, other kinds of cost may be expressed in this S-pattern, as exemplified in (43).

(43) a. It takes much courage to proceed when all others are fleeing. (I)
b. It takes a lot of energy to invest life with meaning. (I)
c. It uses up too much memory to slurp all of that data into Ruby objects. (I)
d. It takes me effort and concentration to track down and "process" [...] how I am "feeling" at any given time. (I)
e. If a house is empty all day, it wastes energy to keep it heated at 72 degrees. (I)

In all the examples of (43), the verb used is a cost verb (*take, cost, use up, waste, save*). It is possible, however, to express the cost compositionally as well, so that the predicate itself does not express cost, but its complement bears this meaning, as in (44).

(44) Sometimes it involves paying a fee to set up the DNS. (I)

The expression *involves paying a fee* amounts to *costs money*, but it is not the verb *involve* but rather its complement gerund phrase *paying a fee* that render this VP a cost predicate.

An affectee may be used in this construction as well. It may be viewed as the subject of the InfP, as in (45a), or as a direct object of the verb, as in (45b). On rare occasions, both slots may be filled, as in (45c).

(45) a. It will cost a fortune for greyhound to have any sort of metal detector. (I)
 b. It would probably cost me my job to give you remote access. (I)
 c. It costs me a fortune for myself and four kids to get our haircuts. (I)

While the Cost S-pattern is clearly a separate construction, its affinity to the EV S-patterns is evident. Much of the structure of the Cost S-pattern is inherited from the EV S-pattern. As for its function, although the Cost S-pattern does not convey evaluation in a straightforward modal way, the circumstances of stating the cost of an event often make it subjectively relevant to a (present or implied) affectee, namely the event is not just measured but also evaluated as cheap or expensive. If it costs only $5 per session to use the gym, this means it is cheap, so that (46a) amounts to (46b), which is a regular EV sentence.

(46) a. It costs $5 per session to use the gym at work.
 b. It is cheap to use the gym at work.

Many situations in which a cost is discussed are such that the cost is subjectively evaluated as low, just right, or too much. It is therefore the situation type of implied evaluation that functionally connects the Cost S-pattern to the EV S-pattern.

This evaluative overtone may be sensed when the difference between (47a) and (47b) is considered. Whereas the S1 sentence in (47a) is a more objective choice of encoding the proposition, probably as a background statement in a narrative sequence, the P1 wording of (47b) is more likely to be a statement of cost with an implied evaluative comment.

(47) a. The trip to Berlin takes six hours.
 b. It takes six hours to get to Berlin.

For all these reasons, it makes sense to view the Cost S-pattern as an independent construction, in opposition to the S1 rendering of the same argument structure of

it	[VP	V	NP	NP	]	Nominal
Expletive		Cost Pred	Affectee	Cost		Evaluee

Figure 17. The Cost S-pattern in English

the V S-pattern, and related to, but also different from, the EV S-pattern. The formula of the Cost S-pattern is shown in Figure 17.

In this formula the two Objects have been assigned separate slots, and they have been assigned the distinct functional names *Cost* and *Affectee*. The function of the Cost S-pattern is phrased in (48).

(48) Through the use of the cost predicate, the Cost S-pattern states the cost incurred (to the affectee, if present) by the event encoded in the evaluee.

The presentation of the P1 family of S-patterns in English will be concluded with the environmental (ENV) S-pattern, presented in the next section.

3.2.3 The environmental S-pattern in English

In many languages, environmental conditions are expressed through zero-place predicates, i.e. predicates with zero argument structure. In some languages, these predicates are accompanied by expletive subjects. For a comprehensive discussion of the status of these expletives in sentences expressing environmental conditions, see Ruwet (1991: 82–170) and Alba-Salas (2004). Since expletive subjects are merely a formal requirement of certain languages, the sentences of (49a–b) are viewed here as instantiating equivalent constructions in English and Hebrew, comparable in their form and function.

(49) a. It is drizzling.
     b. *metaftef.*
        drizzles
        'It drizzles'/'It is drizzling.'

The term Environmental (ENV) S-pattern is used, in keeping with the practice of giving meaningful names to constructions. The name *weather verbs*, which is current in the literature (Bolinger 1977: 66; Levin 1993: 276; Haegeman & Guéron 1999: 43; Radford 2004: 297), is inadequate for two reasons. First of all, the predicates in this S-pattern are not only verbs, and secondly, these predicates express environmental conditions that go beyond weather, such as the noun *Sunday* or the adjective *crowded*.

Environmental conditions do not *have* to be encoded in this construction. Other prevailing means of representing environmental conditions are existential constructions (50a), intrinsic (50b) and tautological (50c) predicate expressions, or reference to the world at large as subject (50d).

(50) a. There is wind.

b. *yored gešem.*
descends rain

c. *hivrik ha-barak.*
lightened the lightning

d. *id-dunya šoob* (dialects of Palestinian Arabic)
the world hot
'It is hot.'

The diversity of means for expressing environmental conditions necessarily results in different choices in different languages. Hence, for example, the condition of rain is expressed in English in the ENV S-pattern, whereas in Hebrew it is expressed in the EX S-pattern through the intrinsic predicate *yarad* 'descend', as in (51).

(51) a. It is raining.

b. *yored gešem.*
descends rain

What is similar between the English and Hebrew ENV S-patterns is, therefore, not the actual stock of predicates used in this construction, but rather their general formal and functional properties.

The formula of the ENV S-pattern in English is presented in Figure 18.

The ENV S-pattern has zero argument structure. One may, therefore, wonder whether it is not redundant to assign a special S-pattern to these predicates. Why not just fit them into their equivalent S1 S-patterns. For example, the verb *rain* may be inserted into the V S-pattern, in which case it will have no arguments; an expletive *it* will be inserted as a default syntactic operation, as is done in Chomskyan syntax, and the sentence will be a felicitous V sentence in terms of its form.

While formally this is a descriptive option, it does not make sense from a constructional point of view. The V S-pattern expresses a categorical judgment, i.e. it

| *it* | [$_{PredP}$ | V/N/A |] |
| Expletive | | Env Pred | |

Figure 18. The ENV S-pattern in English

has a built in bi-partition into a subject and a predicate phrase, and a default information structure of topic–comment/predicate focus. In discourse, it is used, by default, as a narrative sentence, contributing to the unfolding of the storyline. The ENV S-pattern is a thetic construction, i.e. it consists of comment alone; it has no semantic role assigned to a subject position and no topic, not because it idiosyncratically is missing a subject, but because it is by its very nature not about anything. In discourse, it typically interrupts the narrative, providing background information to the unfolding storyline. In other words, it fulfills a function similar to the other two P1 S-patterns.

Furthermore, if the different environmental predicates are inserted in their respective S1 S-patterns, the functional generalization over them is lost. As a designated P1 S-pattern, it exhibits diversity in the categorical affiliation of the predicate, similar to that observed in the other P1 S-patterns, and sharply in contrast to the S1 S-patterns, which are defined by the part of speech of their predicate. Finally, it will be demonstrated in Section 7.1 that the conceptual category of environmental predicates is organized according to the same principles as the conceptual categories of existence and evaluation.

The three parts of speech that may serve as predicates of the ENV S-pattern, V, N, and A, are instantiated in (52).

(52) a. It is raining.
     b. It is Sunday.
     c. It is cold.

The function of the ENV S-pattern is given in (53).

(53) Through the use of the environmental predicate, the ENV S-pattern provides the condition of the contextually relevant environment.

The "contextually relevant environment" could be the world at large as experienced by the speaker, or any part of the world, implicitly or explicitly pointed out. The statement of (54a), for example, might be pronounced in a bus, a train, or a stadium. Hence, these sentences are often accompanied by a locative expression, as in (54b). The term *environmental* should be understood in a broad sense, referring not only to the spatial but also to the temporal conditions, as in (54c–d).

(54) a. It is crowded.
     b. It is crowded in here.
     c. It is winter.
     d. It was winter when we first met.

A detailed discussion of the semantics of the ENV S-pattern will be taken up in Chapter 7.

3.3 Predicate-initial S-patterns in Hebrew

Hebrew, like English, expresses existential, evaluative, and environmental statements in the P1 word order. However, while English does so in three distinct constructions, Hebrew only has one form for the EX and the EV S-patterns. This is so for two reasons: First, Hebrew does not require expletives, so the difference between the two expletives of the two constructions in English (*there* vs. *it*) is annulled in Hebrew. Second, the existent and the evaluee, which are different in structure in English, are not so in Hebrew. In English, the existent is an NP and the evaluee is a nominal. In Hebrew, this is true for the unmarked case, but there are also existents that are nominals and evaluees that are NPs. So if both S-patterns lack expletives, and both may have in their last slot both an NP and a nominal, then in terms of form, there is no difference between them.

The fact that Hebrew does not require expletives has further consequences. In English, the use of an expletive subject *it* in the copular variety of the EV S-pattern triggers a dual sentence structure. First a pleonastic grammatical predication takes place between *it* and the predicate through the copula (*it is good*), and then the true predication takes place between the predicate and the evaluee (*good to see you*). In other words, the expletive does not just stand there, at the beginning; it enters a formal relation with the predicate. The same is true for the copular variety of the EX S-pattern (first there is a predication in *there is extant* then in *extant three manuscripts*). In Hebrew, there is no expletive, nor copula, so the P1 S-pattern is P1 simply by virtue of its word order. Consequently, there is no visible difference between the verbal and the copular P1 S-patterns. In both patterns, the predicate (be it V, N, A, or P) appears literally at the beginning of the sentence, followed by the object (if there is one) and the final component: existent or evaluee.

The question whether Hebrew has separate EX and EV S-patterns, or perhaps it is one common construction, will be addressed in Section 3.3.3. This delay is necessary, since the answer has to do not only with the forms, briefly presented above, but also with the functions of these forms, yet to be discussed. For the time being their accounts will be kept apart.

In addition, the ENV S-pattern is simpler than its English counterpart. In English the ENV sentence is bipartite, exhibiting a pleonastic predication relation between an expletive subject and the predicate. In Hebrew, the predication is expressed by the predicate alone. This difference has some consequences that will be discussed below. The EX S-pattern in Hebrew is discussed in Sections 3.3.1 and 3.3.2, the EV S-pattern in 3.3.3, and the ENV S-pattern in 3.3.4.

3.3.1 The existential S-pattern in Hebrew

Two theoretical diversions are needed before embarking on the presentation of the formula and the examples of the EX S-pattern. In the following two sub-sections, *morphologically unique* and *endemic* predicates and the use of a *possessor* object in the EX S-pattern will be discussed.

3.3.1.1 Morphologically unique and endemic predicates

The first diversion concerns morphologically unique and endemic predicates. Hebrew uses the existential predicate *yeš* 'there is', along with its lexical negation *en* 'there isn't'. Historically, both had some residual copular roles in Biblical Hebrew, but in Israeli Hebrew the use of *yeš* as a copula is obsolete, and the use of *en* as a negative copula is restricted to the literary and formal registers. In either case, these words do not have any categorial affiliation, i.e. they are *morphologically unique*. Furthermore, since *yeš* only appears in the EX S-pattern, and nowhere else outside the EX S-pattern, it will in addition be referred to as being *endemic* to the EX S-pattern. Its negation *en* is morphologically unique as well, but it is not endemic to the construction, since it is also used for negation in other constructions (e.g. the V S-pattern) in the literary style. In the upcoming examples and discussion, *yeš* and *en* will be glossed as EXIST and NOT.EXIST respectively.

The term *morphologically unique* and *endemic* will also be useful in the discussion of the EV S-pattern forthcoming in 3.3.3.

3.3.1.2 The possessor

The second diversion concerns the use of the EX S-pattern with an oblique object to express a possessive statement. In this context, not all objects that appear in the existential sentence are alike. The one that calls for attention is the PP with the preposition *le* 'to'/'for', namely *le*-NP. Example (55) instantiates an EX sentence with such a object.

(55) *yeš le-dani harbe sfarim*
    EXIST to Danny many books
    'Danny has many books.'

For the sake of simplicity, this object will be called here the *possessor*, since the translational equivalent in English would be the possessor in a possessive sentence with the verb *have*. But we should be cautious not to view this form as a separate possessive construction. Rather, the recruitment of the affectee role in a possessive situation type gives the affectee the appearance of possessor. In other words, unlike in English, a transitive EX sentence in Hebrew is a canonical instantiation of the EX S-pattern. The argument structure of the existential predicate *yeš* includes intransitive and (oblique) transitive behavior. The semantic integrity of intransitive and transitive *yeš* arises from the exchange in (56), uttered by a student of mine, telling me about a conversation she had with her sick grandfather (note: *l-* is an allomorph of *le-* 'to', before vocalic possessive suffixes).

(56) *hu amar l-i: "yeš be'ayot".*
he said to me: "EXIST problems".
'He said to me: "there are problems".'
az ša'alti oto: "le-mi yeš be'ayot, le-xa?"
so I.asked him: "to whom EXIST problems, to you?"
'So I asked him: "Who has problems, you?"'

The English translation in (56) cannot capture the continuity between the two Hebrew sentence forms, because of the unavoidable switch in English from the EX S-pattern in the statement of the grandfather to the possessive V S-pattern in the response of the speaker. In Hebrew, however, the sentential construction is the same, the only difference being that the predicate *yeš* behaves intransitively in the statement of the grandfather and transitively in the granddaughter's response. This kind of behavior is what would be expected of any predicate with an optional object. It is, however, not a typical case of null-instantiation (Fillmore, Johnson & Petruck 2003), because the absence of an object does not imply its existence. Nevertheless, if such an object is not uttered, it may be asked about, just as is generally the case with null-instantiation. Consider the difference between (57a) and (57b).

(57) a. He told me: "I ate", so I asked him: "What did you eat, soup?"
b. *He told me: "I am starving", so I asked him: "Who are you starving, your dog?"

While the exchange in (57a) constitutes a coherent piece of discourse, since *eat* may be used both intransitively and transitively with no change in the meaning of the predicate, and with no alternation of the semantic role of the subject, the exchange in (57b) is infelicitous, because intransitive and transitive *starve* have different meanings, and the subject in each has a different semantic role. Hebrew *yeš*, as we see from the exchange in (56), may be used both ways felicitously.

The sentences of (57a) were constructed for the purpose of clear exposition. An attested example, displaying similar behavior, comes from the Corpus of Hebrew Political Call-In Radio Programs (Dori-Hacohen 2007: Conversation 1016L Lines 236–241):

(58) 236 Caller: ... *z--e,*
this
'that is'

237		*..kše-ata adam katan,*
		when you person small
		'when you are an ordinary person'
238		*ve-ezrax eh ragil*
		and citizen eh regular
		'and a regular eh citizen'
239		*... en lexa im mi ledaber.*
		NOT.EXIST to.you with who to.talk
		'You have nobody to talk to.'
240	Interviewer:	*Mhm*
		Mhm
241	Caller:	*.. en im mi ledaber*
		NOT.EXIST with who to.talk
		'There is nobody to talk to.'

What in English requires two different constructions (possessive: *you have nobody to talk to*; existential: *there is nobody to talk to*) is done in Hebrew through the transitive and intransitive variants of the same predicate instantiating the same EX S-pattern: NOT.EXIST (*to.you*) *with who to.talk*.

The position advocated here, that existence and possession constitute one semantic and syntactic category in Hebrew, stands in sharp contrast to Heine's (1997: 42) view that possessive and existential constructions should be kept apart, since "they are simply different in meaning and speakers are usually aware of this difference".

What is flawed in Heine's position is the lack of distinction between pragmatic–communicative needs and the ways they are encoded in the grammar of each language. The expression of possession is a universal need, and therefore "any human language can be expected to have conventionalized expressions for it" (Heine 1997: 1). Similarly, the expression of existence is a basic human need. Despite the universality of these communicative needs, they may be grammaticalized in many ways.

> Possession is a relatively abstract domain of human conceptualization, and expressions for it are derived from more concrete domains. These domains have to do with basic experiences relating to what one does (Action), where one is (Location), who one is accompanied by (Accompaniment), or what exists (Existence) (Heine 1997: 45).

But Heine goes further to claim that at the end of the diachronic process that gives rise to the construction, it undergoes decategorialization. "With the new function that the source schema assumes, the items making up the source schema tend to lose their erstwhile properties" (Heine 1997: 77).

This must indeed have been the case when we look at the emergence of the EX S-pattern in Biblical Hebrew from some copular expression with *yeš*, which even in Biblical Hebrew is already archaic and residual. In Israeli Hebrew, however, *yeš* no longer serves as a copula, and the existent is no longer a canonical subject. The addition of a *le*-NP affectee is a synchronic option in Israeli Hebrew, which cuts across several constructions, and the existential construction is no exception in this respect. The diachronic process of decategorialization described by Heine has not happened in the case at hand. (A view that is closer to Heine's was expressed by Rosén 1977a: 108, who characterized the sequence *yeš le-* 'there-is to' as a verboid and the existent with the object features as a regular object.)

In Langacker's framework, the notion of existence is the *reference point* (Langacker 2000: 173–174) for the notion of possession. Differences in reference point may account for slight differences in the actual encoding and language-specific employment of the communicatively needed concept of possession. In this sense, the universality of possession is challenged, assuming nuances in the very conceptualization of possession in different languages.

In support of the claim made here that possession in Israeli Hebrew is merely a transitive variant of existence, we may recall that it is not at all unusual to find an important pragmatic function being expressed indirectly in the grammar of different languages. The expression of time distinctions, for example, is an important human need, yet Biblical Hebrew (among other Semitic languages) expresses the past indirectly, through the perfect form of an aspect system. Pragmatically, Biblical Hebrew is capable of expressing past time, but grammatically it lacks past tense. It expresses time *in terms of aspect*. Similarly, Israeli Hebrew is able to express possession, but it does not have a designated construction for it. Hebrew expresses possession *in terms of existence*. In the transitive EX S-pattern, then, we have an existent-turned-possessed and an affectee-turned-possessor,

Hebrew, Aramaic, Greek, and Latin all have a way of expressing possession in terms of existence. Because of the centrality of these languages in Judeo–Christian culture, some word-for-word translations of these constructions have penetrated English, and have become so familiar that their structural oddity is barely noticed. For instance, (59a) has the Greek text of 1 Corinthians 8:6. (The verb ἐστί 'is' is missing, but this ellipsis is allowed in Greek, and the sentence has the same existential–possessive meaning without and with it.)

(59) a. Ἀλλ' ἡμῖν εἷς θεός.
    but to.us – one God.

  b. Yet to us there is one God.

Chapter 3. Predicate initial sentence patterns 91

    c. i. Néanmoins pour nous il n'y a qu'un seul Dieu.
        ii Toutefois, nous n'avons qu'un seul Dieu.
    d. So haben wir doch nur einen Gott.

Ten English translations consulted in this matter unanimously have *to us there is*, as in (59b) (with minor irrelevant differences between them, such as *for us* instead of *to us*), four French translations are split evenly between (59ci) and (59cii), and two German translations have the form in (59d) (http://scripturetext.com/1_corinthians/8-6.htm). English, then, is most consistent in following Greek syntax, French goes both ways, and German does not use it at all.

A comparison of the English and German translations of the Hebrew verse from Ecclesiastes 3,1 in (60) yields similar results. (Here too the existential predicate *yeš* is absent: its ellipsis is allowed in Biblical Hebrew just as it is in Classical Greek.)

(60) a. *l-a-kol zman.*
        to the all – time

      b. To every thing there is a season.   (KJV)

      c. Ein jegliches hat seine Zeit.   (Revised Martin Luther Version)
         an everything has its time
         'Everything has its time.'

English, again, follows the Hebrew source construction verbatim, while German uses the possessive verb *haben* 'have'. These findings exhibit the hesitation in the translation of holy scriptures between a maximal preservation of the original text in a word-for-word translation as opposed to the preservation of its content in a thought-for-thought translation. However, the word-for-word translation can only be carried out, since the transitive variant is a dormant option in English, which is theoretically possible. It is not a total aberration from possible grammatical norm.

Indeed, Modern English makes some use of the option of the existential construction with a PP possessor, even if very rarely and only with peripheral meanings of possession. In (61) there are two EX sentences, the first with and the second without the *to*-NP possessor.

(61) There is no end to it, [...]; there is only more of the same.   (I)

Central meanings of possession, such as the expression of ownership of property, would never appear in English in the EX S-pattern (*there is to me a book*/*there is a book to me*), but rather with the verb *have* in the S1 V S-pattern. In Hebrew, there is no conceptual gap between "existence" and "existence-to". All possessive meanings, central and peripheral, can only be expressed in terms of "existence to" an entity.

The possessor may be used not only in association with *yeš*, but with many other existential predicates, such as the verbs *nosaf* 'be added' and *nigmar* 'be finished'/'run out', and the adjective *daruš* 'needed', yielding similar possessive statements. This mechanism is, however, constrained by individual argument structure restrictions. For example, the adjective *kayam* 'exist.adj.' does not tolerate a possessor, at least in the speech of some native speakers, including myself. (See example (159) of Chapter 5 for an exception.)

Some verbs, e.g. verbs of motion, take an object which is not a possessor (e.g. *azav et ha-xeder* left ACC the-room). However, these verbs do not take a possessor. Being in complementary distribution, the possessor and the object occupy the same slot (separated by a slash) in the formula of the EX S-pattern in the next section.

Having completed the two deviations, on the unique and endemic predicates and on the possessor, we may return now to the discussion of the EX S-pattern in Hebrew.

3.3.2 The existential S-pattern in Hebrew – continued

The morphologically unique existential predicate *yeš/en* is not a verb, hence it has no tense dimensions. In the past and future tense, it is suppleted by the past and future forms of the verb *haya* 'be'. In the examples, the expressions 'EXIST' and 'NOT.EXIST' in SMALL CAPS are used as glosses of *yeš* and *en*. The verb *be* is used as a gloss for *haya* 'be'. The adjective *kayam* 'exist' also has a similar meaning. It will be represented as 'exist.adj' in the glosses.

In addition to morphological variation, *yeš* also undergoes syntactic variation, which involves two domains: agreement and case. Regarding agreement, *yeš* and *en* are indeclinable forms, but when the verbal forms of *haya* are used in standard written language or in careful speech, agreement in number and gender is maintained between the verb and the existent, as can be seen in (62a) with agreement tags on the Hebrew text and the glosses. In casual spoken and written Hebrew, *haya* is used as an indeclinable form, as in (62b).

(62) a. *hayu*.C.PL *gam leylot*.M.PL *alizim*.M.PL. *yoter.*   (I)
        were.C.PL. also nights.M.PL. cheerful.M.PL. more
        'There were also more cheerful nights.'

   b. *buša ve-xerpa od me'at lo iye*.M.SG. *[iye=yihye] avoda*.F.SG.   (I)
        shame and disgrace another little not will.be.M.SG. work.F.SG
        'It's a disgrace! In a little while there won't be any work.'

As for case, Hebrew is a language that has no morphological case on nouns or NPs. The only exception is the marking of the definite object NP as accusative with the particle *et* placed in front of the NP. This particle is considered a case marker, rather than a preposition, because it alternates with zero when the object is indefinite, and because syntactically, verbs that take these objects behave like normal transitive verbs in other languages, i.e. they are subject to passivization.

When the EX sentence does not have a definite existent (which is its usual behavior), the question of case cannot arise. However, when the existent is definite, the case issue becomes relevant. This happens, for example, in possessive statements, where there is no "indefiniteness restriction" on the existent-turned-possessed. Lexical definite NPs are still used in careful prescriptively inspired speech (say, on the news) without the accusative marker *et*, sounding stranger and stranger to the native ear as the decades go by. Pronouns can no longer be used in the nominative form in this position (as observed by Rosén 1966: 34–35 as early as 1966). Such forms would be judged by any native speaker of Hebrew to be just as odd as an English speaker would judge a sentence such as *I have they*. An adherent of normative Hebrew would resort to circumlocution (e.g. *hem be-yaday* they in. my.hands 'they are in my hands') rather than use pronominal forms.

A constitutive act in the acceptability of the accusative forms in mainstream Hebrew was the publication of a novel by Yehudit Katzir, whose title – a quote attributed to Picasso – is given in (63).

(63) *le-matis yeš et ha-šemeš b-a-beten*
to Matisse EXIST ACC the-sun in-the-belly
'Matisse has the sun in his belly.'

One has to appreciate this act of liberation in the context of Hebrew normativism. For some militant normativists, this is tantamount to publishing a title containing a four-letter word in a respectable publishing house in the US or UK.

There is nowadays a growing acceptability of the accusative forms, less so with respect to the lack of agreement. Usually the two are related; i.e. when there is accusative case there is also an indeclinable form of *haya*, but the processes are not fully aligned and hybrid forms do exist. Example (64a) has a possessive sentence with the indeclinable *haya* aligned with the accusative case on the possessed. A hybrid form is instantiated in (64b), where the verb agrees with the possessed, as prescriptively required, but the possessed is in the accusative form, as practiced in spoken Hebrew.

(64) a. *lo haya*.M.SG. *l-a et kol ha-xomarim*.M.PL (I)
not was.m.sg to-her all the materials.m.pl

b. *hayu*.C.PL. *l-ahem et ha-emca'im*.M.PL. (I)
were.c.pl to-them ACC the means.m.pl

Rosén (1977a: 107–108) sees *yeš le-* jointly as a verboid, an explanation that accounts for the accusative case of the post-verbal NP. In spoken Hebrew, which Rosén calls "substandard", he suggests that the Left Dislocation construction with *yeš* has lost its LD power and appears to some extent to serve as an S1 variant of the P1 construction, as in (65). Presumably, *haya-lo* in this example is a verboid taking the possessed *ha-kesef* as a direct object with the *et* accusative marker (see discussion in Netz & Kuzar 2011).

(65) *yosef haya l-o et ha-kesef* (Rosén 1977a: 108).
    Joseph was to him [=had] ACC the money
    'Joseph had the money.'

The issues of agreement and accusative existent in actual usage in the EX S-pattern await corpus work. This issue will not be further pursued here.

The formula of the EX S-pattern in Hebrew is presented in Figure 19. It differs from its English counterpart precisely in having the possessor PP, in addition to the regular object, in the complement slot. The fact that *yeš/en* are morphologically unique is marked by the addition of Unq to the list of parts of speech licensed in the predicate slot. Another difference from the English formula is the absence of an expletive slot in the Hebrew formula.

[PredP	Unq/V/A/P	NP/PP	]	NP/Nominal
	Ex Pred	Obj/Possessor		Existent/Possessed

Figure 19. EX S-pattern in Hebrew

Some schematic examples of the EX sentences with an NP existent are listed in (66). They contain some of the major options of predicates and their argument structures, namely the use of intransitive and transitive *yeš* in (66a–b), intransitive and transitive *en* in (66c–d), the use of the verbs *nosaf* 'be added' and *azav* 'leave' in (66e–f), of the adjective *kayam* 'exist.adj (intransitive) and *daruš* 'needed' (transitive) in (66g–h), and finally of the PP *beyaday* 'in my hands' as predicate in (66i).

(66) a. *yeš bxirot.*
        EXIST elections
        'There are elections.'

    b. *yeš l-anu bxirot.*
        EXIST to us elections
        'we have elections.'

    c. *en hafsaka.*
        NOT.EXIST intermission
        'There is no intermission.'

d. *en l-ahem hafsaka.*
      NOT.EXIST to them intermission
      'They do not have an intermission.'
   e. *nosfu l-a studentim xadašim.*
      were.added to her students new
      'She has new students added (to her class).'
   f. *azvu et ha-ir 20,000 tošavim.*
      left ACC the town 20,000 residents
      '20,000 residents left the town.'
   g. *kayamot šaloš efšaruyot.*
      exist.ADJ. three possibilities
      'There exist three possibilities.'
   h. *daruš l-a-xevra menahel nimrac.*
      needed to the company a.director energetic
      'The company needs an energetic director.'
   i. *be-yaday salim kvedim.*
      in my.hands baskets heavy
      'In my hands there are heavy baskets.'/'I am holding heavy baskets.'

The use of *azav* 'leave' exhibits one major difference between the English and Hebrew equivalent constructions. Predicates of non-existence, which generally do not appear in the English EX S-pattern, prevail in this construction in Hebrew. The issue of negated existence is discussed further below in this section.

Hebrew is a language of relatively free word order. Since the existential S-pattern is constructed through word order only, without an expletive, the question of the distinction between the EX S-pattern and an inverted word-order alternation of the S1 sentences comes to mind, especially where the same predicate may be used in both. In (67a) we have an S1 sentence which happens to use the verb *azav* 'leave'. In (67b) the sentence could be both an unmarked P1 sentence and an S1 sentence marked by a word order alternation.

(67) a. *20,000 tošavim azvu et ha-ir*
        '20,000 residents left the city.'
     b. *azvu et ha-ir 20,000 tošavim*
        '20,000 residents left the city.'

The use of (67b) as a marked S1 sentence with a word order alternation may be seen in the constructed example of (68). This should be read as a continuous passage, presented here in three numbered sentences for ease of reference.

(68) a. *mispar holex ve-gadel šel tošavim noteš et ha-ir b-a-šanim ha-axronot.*
a.number going and growing of residents deserts ACC the city in the years the last.
'An ever-growing number of residents has been deserting the city in recent years.'

b. *lifney šnatayim azvu et ha-ir 5,000 tošavim. lifney šana – 10,000.*
before two.years left ACC the city 5,000 residents. before a.year – 10,000,
'Two years ago 5,000 residents left the city, a year ago – 10,000.'

c. *ve-hašana azvu et ha-ir 20,000 tošavim.*
and this.year left ACC the city 20,000 residents.
'And this year, 20,00 residents left the city.'

In the sentences (68b–c) of this passage, the VP *azvu et ha-ir* 'left the city' is in the presupposition. It echoes the VP *noteš et ha-ir* 'deserts the city' of (68a) and is placed in first position, so as to allow the specific numbers of deserters/leavers to be in final focus position. Lambrecht (1994: 111–112) is reluctant to call such a phrase topic, since it consists of a VP rather than the canonical NP referent. Chafe's (1994: 72) use of *idea* rather than *referent* more easily allows calling a VP *topic*. But even if not topic by name, the VP is clearly *in the presupposition*, and the subject of the sentence carries a narrow focus by being placed in accented sentence-final position. Since English cannot do this through word order, the subjects of the English translations would have to carry a (narrow) argument focus to reach the same effect.

In the passage of (69), an attested example, we have a similar sentence, but this time it is an unmarked P1 EX sentence. The sentences of the passage are sequentially numbered, but this is one continuous passage.

(69) a. *siman rišon le-txilat ha-haxanot l-a-ona ha-ba'a ecel ha-alufa ha-triya?*
sign first to the.beginning.of the preparations to the season the next by the champion the fresh?
'[do we see] the first sign of the beginning of preparations for the next season among the fresh champion [team]?'

b. *hayom axar-ha-cohorayim azvu et ha-arec nešotehem šel šne saxkane beytar ha-brazila'im José Ramalho ve-Tuto Ruschel.*
today after the noon left ACC the country their.wives of the.two.of the.players.of Beytar the-Brazilian José Ramalho and Tuto Ruschel
'This afternoon, the wives of the two Brazilian players of Beytar, José Ramalho and Tuto Ruschel, left the country.'

c. *be-beytar makxišim še-ha-šnayim šuxreru me-ha-kvuca.* (I)
in beytar they.deny that the two were released from the team
'Beytar sources deny that the two have been released from the team.'

Sentence (69b) of this passage provides a negative EX sentence, reporting the non-existence in the country, due to leaving, of the wives of the players. The VP *azvu et ha-arec* 'left the country' is not presupposed; it is part of a thetic sentence, a Sentence Focus construction, in which the VP is part of the focus domain, hence it is part of the asserted news which culminates in the presentation of (the wives of) the Brazilian players. This is the first sentence in a bi-clausal construction. The second sentence is a topic–comment construction, in which the NP *ha-šnayim* 'the two [Brazilian players]' is in topic position.

To summarize this discussion, Hebrew forms the EX S-pattern by means of word order only. Consequently, two sentences might have the same (neutralized) form: an S1 sentence with marked word order and an EX sentence with unmarked word order. An examination of the context of such sentences would reveal that they have two different information structures attached to them. Even if the accent falls on the same component, this accent has to be interpreted as representing a narrow NP focus in one case, a wide sentence focus in the other.

So far, the EX S-pattern discussed here had an NP existent, parallel to the behavior of the EX S-pattern in English. Let us now turn to a case not paralleled in English. Here, the existent is a nominal, not an NP. Hebrew does not have a form equivalent to the verbal GrdP (see 3.2.2 above), so the term *nominal* in the case of Hebrew covers only InfPs and *that*-clauses.

The InfP as the existent of an EX sentence is used primarily in the representation of a situation type of talking about a task waiting to be accomplished. Hebrew speakers may use intransitive and transitive (i.e. possessive) EX sentences for this purpose, as in (70).

(70) a. *le-maxar yeš lehavi et kol ha-sfarim be-xešbon.* (I).
for tomorrow EXIST to.bring ACC all the books in arithmetic
'Tomorrow one has to bring all the arithmetic books.'

b. *yeš l-i lixtov xibur be-anglit.* (I)
EXIST to me to.write an.essay in English
'I have an English essay to write.'

In (70a), the task is stated in general terms, without a prospective doer in mind, whereas in (70b), the prospective doer is encoded as the possessor. The English equivalent of the latter would be a possessive sentence with either an InfP, as in (71a) or with an NP that incorporates an InfP modifier, as in (71b). If, however, the task is formulated in general terms with no doer in mind, the proposition may be encoded in English in the EX S-pattern, but only with an NP incorporating an InfP, as in (71c). What cannot be done in English is using an InfP directly as the existent of an EX sentence, as is evident from the ungrammaticality of (71d), which is precisely what Hebrew does, as demonstrated in both sentences of (70).

(71) a. I have to write an essay.
b. I have an essay to write.
c. There is an essay to write.
d. *There is to write an essay.

Note, however, that (71a) would normally have a modal rather than a possessive reading in English, i.e. it usually means *I must* rather than just *I have the task*.

The license to use InfPs in Hebrew existential sentences is not limited to *yeš*. The same can be done with other existential verbs, such as *nišar* 'remain', as in (72).

(72) *nišar l-i livdok et ha-rištit.* (I)
remained to me to check ACC the retina
'I am left with a retina checkup.'

The EX S-pattern can accommodate also a *that*-clause in the existent slot. Such a sentence is typically uttered when a state of affairs comes and goes or exhibits distributive existence. Thus it is translatable into English by phrases such as *it happens that*, or by adjuncts such as *here and there* or *occasionally*. Example (73) instantiates a rare case of an entire passage consisting of three consecutive sentences of this kind, describing the distribution of landscape types in Tuscany.

(73) *yeš še-ha-adama mexusa bi-xramim u-vesadot,*
EXIST that the ground is.covered with vineyards and fields
"Here and there the ground is covered with vineyards and fields".
yeš še-hi menumeret be-xoršat acei zayit ksufim,
EXIST that it is.dotted in grove.of trees.of olive silvery
"Elsewhere it might be dotted with silvery olive trees".
ve-yeš še-hi atufa be-xelkot ya'ar yerukot. (I)
and EXIST that it is.wrapped in plots.of forest green
"And in other places you might find it wrapped in green plots of forest".

While this form is quite literary and rare, it is highly common when the existential predicate appears in the infinitive form (i.e. *lihyot*, the infinitive of *haya* 'be') and is preceded by the raising adjective *yaxol* 'able', i.e. *yaxol lihyot* 'could be', as in example (74).

(74) *yaxol lihyot še-ha-olam hifsid psantranit gdola.* (I)
able to.be that the world lost pianist great
'The world may have lost a great pianist.'

This is a borderline case between the evaluative (*could*) and existential (*be*) meaning, to be further discussed in Section 3.3.3 below.

The EX S-pattern may also be used with a *that*-clause when an event is said to have been reported in the mass media, as in (75). In this kind of statement, the media source in the adjunct PP is obligatory.

(75) a. *haya b-a-iton še-iša be-gil 60 yalda.* (I)
was in the paper that woman at age 60 gave.birth
'There was a report in the paper that a woman aged 60 gave birth.'

b. *haya baxadašot še yalda bat 11 macʼa et ha-šaršéret šelo.* (I)
was in the news that a.girl aged 11 found ACC the necklace of.his
'There was a report on the news that a girl aged 11 found his necklace.'

Clearly, then, The EX S-pattern in Hebrew is more liberal than its English counterpart in that it licenses both NPs and nominals in the existent slot.

Hebrew is also more liberal than English in the expression of non-existence, or the negation of existence. The primary predicate of existence *yeš* cannot be negated by sentential negation. It has its own lexical negative counterpart *en*. Other existential verbs (including the past and future forms of *haya* 'be') may freely be negated with the sentential negator *lo* 'not', as can be seen in (76). This is equally true for intransitive as well as transitive (possessive) forms of the EX sentence.

(76) a. *lo haya imut.* (I)
not was confrontation
'There was no confrontation.'

b. *lo hayta l-i xavera af paʼam.* (I)
not was to me a.girlfriend even once
'I have never had a girlfriend.'

c. *lo nišʼar kesef le-meʼacev mikcoʼi.* (I)
not remained money to a.designer a.professional
'There was no money left for a professional designer.'

So far, this is not very different from English. But Hebrew allows also lexically negated existential predicates, as can be seen in (77).

(77) a. *nigmeru ha-klementinot.* (Advertisement for citrus fruits)
ran.out the tangerines
'The tangerines ran out'/'We are out of tangerines.'

b. *metu šloša mi-pcuʼey erua ha-dkira be-tokiyo.* (I)
died three from the.wounded.of the-event.of the stabbing in Tokyo
'Three of the people wounded in the stabbing event in Tokyo died.'

c. *ne'elam l-i aykon ha-safa.* (I)
disappeared to me the.icon.of the language
'The language icon disappeared on me.'

The fact that Hebrew is more liberal than English in the details of the employment of the EX S-pattern has been demonstrated so far in two domains: the use of an affectee-turned-possessor in possessive statements, and the use of lexical negation to express non-existence or disappearance. These behaviors touch upon the long debated question of the "indefiniteness restriction" on the existent (Milsark 1979: 215). Milsark's claims have been problematized in Rando & Napoli (1978), Lakoff (1987: 561), Hannay (1985: 130), Birner & Ward (1998: 113–152) (with an exhaustive bibliography of both sides of the debate), and Melnik (2006) for Hebrew. A pragmatic, rather than grammatical criterion was suggested as early as 1952, by Fries (1952: 161).

The relatively narrow scope of situation types covered by the EX S-pattern in English may have led Milsark and others to view the indefiniteness restriction as a grammatical matter. The logic behind the restriction is quite clear: you do not assert the existence of an entity whose existence is already established in the general awareness of the hearer. However, verbs of non-existence often do not just assert non-existence, but rather disappearance. In this case, it is not illogical to assert the disappearance of an entity whose existence is known to the hearer. In fact, this is the ordinary case in statements of non-existence or disappearance in Hebrew. The entity might even be highly active, in which case the speaker still has the choice between producing an S1 or a P1 (negative existential) statement about it.

Given, for example, the context in (78a), both (78b) and (78c) are felicitous continuations by the same speaker, with the slight difference between a more storyline oriented categorical judgment in (78b) as opposed to the use of an S-pattern specifically designated for thetic existential statements, which often interrupt the storyline (78c). In this case, although the existent is active in the consciousness of the interlocutors, the thetic construction renders this piece of information holistically new. Put differently, the difference in meaning is that sentence (78b) is a continuation of the narrative, whereas (78c) interrupts the narration in order to make an existential statement.

(78) a. Yesterday I bought tangerines. About twenty of them. I thought they would last a whole week. But my kids love them. Now have a look at the fruit basket.

b. *kol ha-klementinot nigmeru.*
all the tangerines ran.out

c. *nigmeru kol ha-klementinot.*
ran.out all the tangerines.

A similar "violation" of the indefiniteness restriction may be observed with possessive statements. There might be felicitous discourse conditions for asserting the possession of entities either active or inactive in the hearer's awareness. Now, since the possessed entity in Hebrew is the existent-turned-possessed of an EX sentence with transitive *yeš*, the sentences of (79) are both perfectly felicitous, given the right contexts.

(79) a. *yeš l-i misxak xadaš b-a-maxšev.*
EXIST to me a.game new in the computer
'I have a new game on my computer.'

b. *yeš l-i et ha-misxak ha-ze b-a-maxšev.*
EXIST to me ACC the game the this in the computer
'I have this game on my computer.'

Another situation type where the EX S-pattern is used unproblematically with a definite NP is shown in (80). It involves the indication of confidence that a certain active or accessible entity is in a particular location (see Ziv 1982, who considers it as a separate construction).

(80) a. *be-ezor ha-horadot yeš et ha-safa ha-ivrit le-horada.* (I)
in the.zone.of the downloads EXIST ACC the Hebrew language for downloading
'In the download zone you/one may find the Hebrew support download.'

b. *ve-šam leyad ha-kur yeš et ha-knafe haxi tov be-teheran.* (I)
and there near the reactor EXIST ACC the knafe most good in Teheran. (I)
'And there, right by the reactor, you may find the best knafe [kind of dessert] in Teheran.'

c. *im atem medabrim al ma še-ani medaberet xa-xa, yeš et ze be-kol xanut diskim.* (I)
if you are.talking on what that I am.talking ha-ha EXIST ACC this in every shop.of disks
'If you are talking about what I am talking about, ha-ha, you may find it at any disk store.'

Due to the stronger applicability of the indefiniteness restriction on existents in English, this situation type is not encoded in the English EX S-pattern. Usually it is conveyed through the phrase "you/one may find the X at Y" or "the X may be found at Y", as has been done in the English translation of the sentences in (80). In Hebrew, "the X" is instantiated as the existent of the EX S-pattern.

While the EX S-pattern in English has no sub-patterns, the Hebrew one has. In the following subsection such a case is discussed. It is the Deteriorating-entity S-pattern in Hebrew.

3.3.2.1 *The deteriorating-entity S-pattern in Hebrew*

Sometimes negative existentials do not mark the non-existence or the disappearance of an entity, but merely its deterioration. This is so in a situation type where the entity is no longer what it used to be, or what it is supposed to be. The entities are prototypically inalienable possessions within the immediate vicinity of the affectee, or if there is no affectee, the relevant person in the context. Examples are given in (81).

(81) a. *nikre'u l-i ha-mixnasayim.* (I)
tore to me the pants
'My pants tore on me.'

b. *nifram l-i ha-srox b-a-na'al ha-yemanit.* (I)
got.undone to me the shoe.lace in the shoe the right
'The shoelace of my right shoe got untied.'

c. *nitka l-i ha-oto.* (I)
got.stuck to me the car
'My car broke down on me'

d. *nistam ha-kiyor b-a-ambatya.* (I)
got.clogged the sink in the bathroom
'The bathroom sink clogged up (on us/me/them...).'

While in English the expression *on me* is often used to personalize such expressions, as has been done in the translation of (81a and c–d), in Hebrew this effect is achieved by the use of the Deteriorating-entity S-pattern. The presence of an affectee may enhance the deteriorating-entity construal of such a sentence, but it is not solely responsible for it, as is evident in (81d), where no affectee is expressed.

It is a common human experience that inalienable entities disintegrate and fall apart spontaneously, but much less do we experience spontaneous recovery of such entities. There are, of course, also spontaneous processes of improvement, such as ripening. Yet the unacceptability of (82a) with the verb *hivšil* 'ripen' shows that Hebrew only encodes the more central human experience of deterioration of entities in this construction, as we have seen in (81) above, not their much less frequent amelioration, as attempted in (82a). The ripening of fruits will be encoded in Hebrew via an S1 V sentence, as in (82b).

[VP	V	PP	]	NP
	Deterioration Pred	Affectee		Affectee's deteriorating entity

Figure 20. The Deteriorating Entity S-pattern in Hebrew

(82) a. *hivšilu ha-perot b-a-salsila.
     ripened the fruits in the basket.
     'The fruits in the basket have ripened.'

  b. ha-perot b-a-salsila hivšilu.
     the fruits in the basket ripened
     'The fruits in the basket have ripened.'

Incidentally, if *hivšil* 'ripen' is used metaphorically, for abstract entities such as *tna'im* 'conditions', then its meaning is not 'improve' but rather 'come into being (after ripening)'. In this case, *hivšil* acts as an existential verb in the regular EX S-pattern, as in (83).

(83) hivšilu ha-tna'im le-hafsakat eš.   (I)
     ripened the conditions for a.cessation.of fire.
     'The conditions for a cease fire have been created.'

The conceptual connection between deterioration and lack of existence is quite clear. When something stops being what it is supposed to be, in some sense it ceases to exist as such. Hence one might think that all these cases may be handled simply under the EX S-pattern. Yet the difference in meaning and the restriction against amelioration events suffice to view it as a separate sub-pattern with its own unpredictable meaning. What has been the *existent* in the EX S-pattern is now the *deteriorating entity* in the Deteriorating-entity S-pattern. The formula of the Deteriorating Entity S-pattern is given in Figure 20.

This ends our discussion of the Hebrew EX S-patterns and its extended Deteriorating-entity sub-pattern. In the next section, the Hebrew EV S-pattern will be presented.

3.3.3 The evaluative S-pattern in Hebrew

The presentation of the EV S-pattern starts with a discussion of the case that is familiar from English, namely where the evaluee is a nominal. Then the less familiar case, where the evaluee is an NP, will be addressed.

104   Sentence Patterns in English and Hebrew

[PredP	Unq/V/N/A/P	NP/PP	]	Nominal
	Ev Pred	Obj/Affectee		Evaluee

Figure 21. EV S-pattern in Hebrew with a nominal as evaluee

An interim formula of the EV S-pattern (at this point with a nominal as evaluee) is presented in Figure 21.

While in the EX S-pattern only one predicate, *yeš/en*, has been found to be morphologically unique, in the EV S-pattern, Hebrew parades some ten morphologically unique predicates, which are endemic to the EV S-pattern. Historically, they have come from various sources, and their way into this position has been differently grammaticalized in each case. Among these forms one finds a preposition + interjection compound (*keday* 'worthwhile', from *ke-day* 'like enough'), a passive participle (*mutav* 'had better', literally 'made better'), an adverb of obscure origin, possibly a Persian borrowing (*efšar* 'possible'), a verb in the future (*yitaxen* 'may be possible'), an interjection (*xaval* 'too bad', *day* 'enough'), and a feminine passive participial form *suma* 'obligatory' of the verb *sam* 'put', namely "being put [on someone]".

The forms that originate from verbs are conceived as being in the present tense, irrespective of their morphological tense of origin, and when turned into the past or future tenses, they are accompanied by past and future forms of the verb *haya* 'be', as if they were adjectives. Three of the morphologically unique predicates are demonstrated in (84)

(84) a. *efšar še-ha-macav yištaper.* (I)
possible that the situation will.improve
'It is possible that the situation will improve'/'The situation may improve.'

b. *mutav še-tiškeli hit'abdut.* (I)
better that you.will.consider suicide
'You'd better consider suicide.'

c. *keday l-a-memšala lilmod historya.* (I)
worthwhile to the government to.learn history
'It would be worth the government's while to learn history.'

In addition, the interjection *oy va-avoy* 'woe and alas', a hendiadys form, may be inserted in this pattern, see (85a). This kind of usage dates back to Biblical Hebrew, see (85b), and is sometimes wittily echoed in present-day English as shown in (85c). It is clear however, that the expression in (85c) has not finished becoming an

English EV sentence, or else it would have had the standard form with the expletive *it* and a copula, as attempted in the ungrammatical sentence of (85d).

(85) a. *oy va-avoy l-anu še-ze dor ha-atid šelanu.* (I)
 woe and alas to us that this generation.of the future of.us
 'It is too bad for us that this is our future generation.'

 b. *oy l-i imi ki yelidtini.* (Jeremiah 15, 10)
 woe to me, my.mother, that you.gave birth.to.me
 Woe is me (Standard Version)/Woe to me (New American Standard Bible), my mother, that you bore me.

 c. Woe to me that I set forth on this task. (I)
 d. *It is woe to me that I set forth on this task. (I)

We see, then, that even in English, the predicate slot of the EV S-pattern may be filled by an interjection, i.e. a morphologically unique predicate. But this is an under-grammaticalized variant of this S-pattern (under-grammaticalization in English is discussed in Chapter 9). The interjection *OK* is more grammaticalized, since it is acceptable to say *it is OK to do so and so*.

This intriguing group of morphologically unique endemic predicates of the EV S-pattern in Hebrew was first discovered by Haiim B. Rosén in the 1960s (see Rosén 1977b: 113 for the English exposition). Rosén assigned them a special part of speech, and called them by the Hebrew acronym *X.G.M.* (pronounced *xagam*), which stands for "lacking person, gender, and number", i.e. indeclinable. In English, Rosén called them *Impersonals*, which amounts to more or less the same notion.

In Rosén's writings, however, the morphologically unique evaluative predicates are not set apart from the adjectives appearing in this S-pattern, In Rosén's view, some adjectives have two categorial affiliations, either as declinable adjectives in the predicative position of the S1 A COP S-pattern (*ha-seret tov* the movie.m.sg good.m.sg 'the movie is good'; *ha-hacaga tova* the play.f.sg good.f.sg 'the play is good'), or as impersonal predicates of the P1 EV S-pattern, appearing in the default zero-affix indeclinable masculine singular form (*tov še-bata* 'good.m.sg that you.came).

A more restrictive view is offered here. Adjectives are adjectives, even if they are declined in one construction and indeclinable in another, since they do not show any structural peculiarities in either case. The morphologically unique predicates of the EV S-pattern do not, at first sight, strike one as a part of speech, since we are used to seeing parts of speech display some morphological uniformity. But if distribution is the sole criterion for membership in a part of speech, then the morphologically unique endemic predicates of the EV S-pattern indeed form a class unto themselves.

Clearly, not *all* members of the other parts of speech (V, N, A, and P, may serve as predicates in the EV S-pattern. Which members of each part of speech qualify to participate in the EV sentence is not a lexical but a semantic question. This issue will be addressed in Chapter 6.

Some examples of the use of other parts of speech in the EV S-pattern are given in (86). The nouns *xoxma* 'wisdom' and *xova* 'duty' are used in (86a–b), the adjective *bari* 'healthy' in (86c), and the PP *kamuvan* 'as understood' in (86d).

(86) a. *lo xoxma lihyot yašar kše-lo osim klum.* (I)
not wisdom to.be honest when not doing anything
'It doesn't take brains to stay honest when doing nothing.'

     b. *xova al kol mištameš likro et ha-xukim.* (I)
duty on every user to.read ACC the rules
'It is incumbent on all users to read the rules.'

     c. *yoter bari le'exol et ha-pri bi-šlemuto.* (I)
more healthy to.eat ACC the fruit in its.entirety
'It is healthier to eat the whole fruit.'

     d. *k-a-muvan še-ha-nasi lo yevater kol-kax maher.* (I)
like the understood that the president not will.give.in so.much fast
'It is obvious that the president will not give in so fast.'

So far, we have looked at instances of the EV S-pattern with the evaluee being a nominal, the way it is in English. Let us now turn to the less familiar case, in which the Hebrew EV S-pattern also admits NPs as evaluees. This option exists both in the literary (87a) and the colloquial (87b) registers.

(87) a. *mutav cipor axat b-a-yad mi-štayim al ha-ec.* (a proverb)
better bird one in the hand than two on the tree
'A bird in the hand is worth two in the bush.'

     b. *haxi tov telefon dor rišon.* (I)
most good telephone generation first
'The best would be a first-generation phone.'

When the predicate is an adjective, as is the case in (87b), it often remains in the unmarked masculine singular form, regardless of the gender and number of the evaluee NP. In (87b) above, *telefon* is masculine, so the issue of gender and number is invisible. But *tov* 'good' remains in the masculine singular form even if the evaluee NP is *maclema* 'camera', a feminine singular noun form, as in (88).

(88) *haxi tov maclema digitalit.* (I)
most good.m.sg a.camera.f.sg digital.f.sg
'The best would be a digital camera.'

However, Hebrew fluctuates between agreeing and non-agreeing forms. In (89) we have an agreeing form.

(89) *nexucot l-i hanxayot yoter specifiyot.* (I)
needed to me instructions more specific
'I need more specific instructions.'

The noun *hanxayot* 'instructions' is in the feminine plural form (with the suffix *-ot*), as is the predicate *nexucot* 'needed'. The motivation for the distribution of agreeing or non-agreeing forms still awaits research (see some initial discussion in Kuzar 2002). Clearly, though, the spoken language exhibits a stronger tendency to forgo agreement, while the formal style maintains it.

The EV S-pattern with the NP as evaluee may admit also an affectee, as can be seen in (90a–b).

(90) a. *keday le-xa maxšev xadaš.* (I)
worthwhile to you computer new
'It is worth your while to have/get/own/buy a new computer.'

b. *keday le-xa šamayim behirim.*
worthwhile to you sky clear
'You'd better have a clear sky (e.g. on your day trip).'

Often the evaluee NP does not stand for an entity but metonymically represents an event in which this entity is imagined to plays a central role. Note the felicity of (90a–b) versus the infelicity of (91).

(91) **keday le-xa amud akum.*
worthwhile to you pillar crooked
'*It is worth your while to ___??? a crooked pillar.'

The felicity of (90a–b) stems from the fact that in these sentences an event may be metonymically reconstructed around the NP, based on conventional assumptions regarding new computers or a clear sky, as is evident from the translations of these sentences to English. This is not so in (91), where no event is conventionalized involving a crooked pillar.

Some conventionalized situation types are associated with the predicate *efšar* 'possible'. Sentences (92a–b) are felicitous, since they evoke the *frames* (Fillmore 1985) of a restaurant and a (jewelry) store respectively, but (92c) remains frameless, at least as long as we have not come up with some unusual situation that would render it acceptable.

(92) a. (a) *efšar tafrit/xešbon?*
Possible menu/bill?
'May I have the menu?'/'The bill, please.'

(b) *efšar šaršeret zahav?*
possible chain-of gold?
'May I look at a gold necklace?'/'May I offer you a gold necklace?'

(c) **efšar šaršeret harim?*
possible chain-of mountains?
'Is it possible to ___??? a mountain range?'

In these sentences, the difference between English and Hebrew, then, is not in the intended meaning, which is in either case an event, but in the encoding of that event. In the EV S-pattern in English, the event has to be encoded by a nominal, whereas in Hebrew it may additionally be metonymically inferred from an NP representing one of the participants of the event, provided that the event can be reconstructed from a conventionalized frame or pragmatically derived from a given situation.

A similar metonymic process has been identified in the nominal extraposition construction in English, as in *it's amazing the people you SEE here* (Michaelis & Lambrecht 1996b). *The people you see here* is described there as representing "a state of affairs involving the people in question", or put differently, "a proposition which bears the thematic role content" (Michaelis & Lambrecht 1996b: 220). The Hebrew sentences discussed above cannot be considered equivalent to nominal extraposition in English, though they do belong to the same family of constructions.

There are, however, some other EV sentences with an NP evaluee, as in (93), in which the evaluee cannot be viewed as metonymically representing an event, but merely as a plain entity alone.

(93) a. *le-motorola drušim studentim le-handasat xašmal.* (I)
to Motorola needed students for engineering.of electricity
'Wanted: Motorola seeks electrical engineering students.'

b. *nexuca l-i sifrut hadraxa al mexkar narativi.* (I)
required to me literature.of guidance on research narrative
'I am in need of reference literature on narrative research.'

Note, though, that the concept *needed* is on the borderline between existence and evaluation, since *needed* means *isn't there*, but *should be*. "Being there" is existential, whereas "should" is evaluative. This proximity to the existential meaning may explain the naturalness of the NP as an evaluee–existent in Hebrew. After all, the EX and the EV S-patterns in Hebrew share the same form.

Another variant of this S-pattern with an NP as evaluee is given in (94).

(94) a. *meyaseret oti ha-maxšava še-lo hevanta.* (I)
 turtures me the thought that not you.understood
 'I am tortured by the thought that you haven't understood.'

 b. *lo šixne'a otam ha-uvda še-l-a-aguda en yexolet axifa mišpatit.* (I)
 not convinced them the fact that to the association NOT.EXIST an.ability
 of enforcement legal
 'They were not convinced by the fact that the association had no power of legal enforcement.'

 c. *maca xen be-eynay ha-ra'ayon šel paskol eytiz be-rubo.* (I)
 found favor in my.eyes the idea of a.sound.track.of eighties in its.
 most
 'I was pleased by the idea of a mostly-eighties soundtrack.'

In (94a–b) the evaluee NP consists of a shell noun (Schmid 2000) (*maxšava* 'thought', *uvda* 'fact'), modified by an appositional content clause, which brings this form quite close to the EV sentence with a nominal as evaluee. In (94c), however, the shell noun *idea* does not have a modifying clause following it. The complement of this noun, however, metonymically represents such a proposition, namely *the idea of a mostly-eighties soundtrack* is equivalent to *the idea that we should produce a mostly-eighties soundtrack*, which is what was intended in the context.

The sentences of (93) and (94) display agreement between the verb and the evaluee, as would be expected from a carefully thought out written text. In the prescriptive view (and as commonly practiced in written texts), the evaluee is considered to be a subject, agreeing with the verb. The same contents may, however, also be uttered without agreement. A full-page ad, promoting a morning radio talk show, uses the colloquial style of this construction, without the agreement, as shown in (95). (The graphical display here imitates that of the ad from 12.5.06 in the daily *Haaretz*.)

(95) a. *meša'amem oti*
 bores me
 'I am bored by'

 itoney xag, mesibot itona'im, koktelim, ptixot ve-sgirot šel mis'adot
 newspapers.of holidays, parties of journalists, cocktails, openings and closings of restaurants.
 Holiday supplements, press conferences, cocktails, openings and closings of restaurants.'

b. *meša'amem oti*
   bores me
   'I am bored by'
   > *ma'amarim be-itonim še-orkam me'al amud exad*
   > articles in newspapers that their.length over page one
   > 'Newspaper articles longer than one page.'

c. *radyo.*
   radio.
   > *me'anyen oti radyo.*
   > interests me radio.
   > 'What interests me is radio.'

The total number of sentences describing what bores the speaker in the original ad is six. Four of them following (95b) have been omitted here. They all display the same lack of agreement between the singular verb *meša'amem* 'bores' and the plural entities that are enumerated after it. In (95c), the agreement with the masculine noun *radyo* is inadvertent.

All these examples with an NP evaluee bring us back to the question whether it is justified to talk about a unified P1 constructions of EX and EV sentences in Hebrew. As a reminder of the formal affinities, recall that Hebrew has no expletives and both constructions allow NPs as well as nominals as the final component (existent or evaluee). There are other similarities between them. For example, in both, there is a tendency to forgo agreement under certain (yet unstudied) circumstances in the spoken language.

The formula of the unified P1 S-pattern, common to both existence and evaluation, is shown in Figure 22.

As far as function is concerned, however, there are two quite distinct predicate types – existential and evaluative – operating in this unified construction, and two functionally distinct final components – existent and evaluee – with some borderline cases between them. This unity of form along with a division into two domains of meaning is reminiscent of what Kay & McDaniel (1978) called *composite categories*, with regard to color terms that cover two adjacent color foci. The conceptual categories of existence and evaluation are indeed "adjacent" in a very real

[$_{PredP}$	Unq/V/N/A/P	NP/PP	]	NP/Nominal
	Ex Pred	Obj/Existent/Possessor		Existent
	Ev Pred	Obj/Affectee		Evaluee

Figure 22. Unified P1 S-pattern in Hebrew

sense, namely in that they share borderline cases between them. The fact that they are adjacent is true for Hebrew as well as for English. In (96), we have three predicates *necessary*, *needed*, and *required*, that have been shown in the discussion of their Hebrew equivalents to combine both existential and evaluative meaning. Ignoring irrelevant nuances, they all have the basic meaning *something does not exist but should exist*.

(96) a. There would then have not been necessary the thousands of years which the ages span. (LOB D12)
b. There are needed policy changes in trade regulations and debt relief. (I)
c. In each county to which this article applies, there is required a valid certificate of emission inspection. (I)

Interestingly, these hybrid predicates get encoded in English in the S-pattern which is able to contain them in terms of their form. When the "something" that does not exist but should exist is an NP entity, the proposition is encoded in the EX S-pattern, as in (96) above. On the other hand, when the same predicate refers to a situation represented by a nominal, the proposition is encoded in the EV S-pattern, as shown in (97).

(97) a. In doing so it will be necessary to improve the quality of teachers. (I)
b. In order to attain it, it is needed that the Commissioner shall be both willing and able to enforce this responsibility. (I)
c. It is required that children get a chickenpox booster shot at age 4 to 6 years. (I)

Hence, the association of a predicate with a construction in borderline cases is not determined in English by the semantic nature of the predicate, but merely by the formal dimensions of the hosting construction. This suggests that not only in Hebrew, but also in English, are the EX and EV S-patterns one construction with two form variants, existing side by side in complementary distribution. The choice of *there* or *it* as expletive is indeed in complementary distribution, depending on the nature of the final component.

In Hebrew, such sentences are straightforward, since in terms of form there is indeed only one construction. But in Hebrew, interesting borderline behavior may also be observed. This behavior may involve polysemy in predicates that may appear in the P1 construction in distinct existential and evaluative meanings.

The predicate *yeš* 'EXIST', for example, is used with InfPs in two distinct senses. In the colloquial style, it has existential meaning, but in the written formal style, *yeš* has a deontic meaning of obligation similar to *carix* 'necessary'. Since the EV S-pattern is impersonal, it is often employed for gender-neutral written instructions, using *yeš* as its predicate, as in (98).

(98) *yeš lehasir et ha-atifa lifne ha-šimuš.*
      EXIST to.remove ACC the cover before the use
      'It is necessary to remove the cover before use'/'Remove cover before use.'

Hence, sentence (70a), discussed above and repeated here as (99), has in fact two distinct meanings.

(99) *yeš lixtov xibur.*
      EXIST to-write composition

If a child is asked by a friend about homework, the answer in (90) will be interpreted in the existential meaning as being informative about the content of the assigned homework. In this case an affectee–possessor may be present, preceded by the preposition *le-* 'to' (*yeš l-anu lixtov xibur* EXIST to us to.write an.essay). However, if the sentence appears in a text of instructions written by the teacher of these children, it will be read as a gender-neutral deontic predicate, instructing them to do it. In this case, the addition of an affectee is ungrammatical.

Similar behavior is exhibited by the adjective *xaser* 'missing'. With a noun as existent it means literally 'missing', as in (100a), but with a *that*-clause it has a modal meaning of stern warning against non-compliance, as in (100b).

(100) a. *xaser le-xa tik avodot.*   (I)
          missing to you a.portfolio.of works
          'You are still short of a portfolio of your work.'

      b. *xaser le-xa še-lo tagia maxar.*   (I)
          missing to you that not you.will.arrive tomorrow
          'If you don't show up tomorrow, you are dead meat.'

The verb *higia* 'arrive' is even more interesting: it is polysemous between an existential and an evaluative reading, but this time, both appear with an NP entity, as is evident in the almost-minimal pair of (101).

(101) a. *lo higia l-i ha-iton haxodeš, ve-ani lo mocet et ha-mispar šelahem.*   (I)
          not arrived to me the-paper this.month, and-I not find ACC the number of.them
          'I haven't received the paper this month, and I can't find their number.'

      b. [Talking about the exaggerated fringe benefits of elected public officers]
          lo magia l-ahem iton xinam.   (I)
          not arrive to them a.paper free.of.charge
          'They don't deserve/are not entitled to a paper free of charge.'

The evaluative meaning of *arrive* (or *come*) was apparently a borrowing into Hebrew from Yiddish (see 102). This is clearly Yiddish (not German) influence, since German does not have a similar expression.

(102) *hob ikh shoyn farzindigt on keyn takone az s'kumt mir shoyn shtarben?* (I)
       have I already sinned without no repair that it comes to.me already to.die
       'Have I sinned so badly beyond repair that I deserve to die?'

The employment of a Polysemous word in a context that allows both meanings to emerge may have a comic effect, and is fertile ground for puns, such as (103), which was a slogan of the messianic followers of the Lubavitcher Rabbi:

(103) *magia lanu mašiyax.*
       'Messiah is arriving to us'/'We deserve a Messiah.'

All these borderline cases in English and Hebrew demonstrate that the two conceptual categories of existence and evaluation are indeed adjacent. In Hebrew, they form two foci in one formal category, i.e. a composite category. In English, the composite construction has two distributionally conditioned form variants, which respectively host the two conceptual categories of existence and evaluation.

In borderline cases in Hebrew, the distribution of *meanings* is determined by the prototypical behavior of each variant. If the same predicate co-occurs with both NPs and nominals (*xaser* 'missing' vs. 'had better not'), its meaning will be existential with NPs and evaluative with nominals. This state of affairs proves that even though Hebrew is liberal in accepting both NPs and nominals in both constructions, nevertheless, the prototypical (and therefore unmarked) case is that existential statements go with NPs and evaluative ones with nominals. The contrary options are marked. However, this distinction is not always available, as was the case with *yeš* 'EXIST' in (99) and *magia* 'arrives' in (103), which are both existential and evaluative with an NP existent/evaluee.

In borderline cases in English, the distribution of *forms* has been shown above to be determined by the form of the existent/evaluee; namely, if the predicate co-occurs with an NP, it will appear in the existential variant, but if the predicate co-occurs with a nominal, it will appear in the evaluative variant.

Although it has been shown that in both languages the two sentential constructions may be viewed as one construction with two variants, for practical reasons, they will keep on being referred to here by the two distinct terms EX and EV S-patterns.

The Cost S-pattern, which has been presented as a sub-pattern of the EV S-pattern in English (in Section 3.2.2.1), also exists in Hebrew and will be discussed in the following subsection.

[PredP	V	PP	NP	]	Nominal
	Cost Pred	Affectee	Cost		Evaluee

Figure 23. The Cost S-pattern in Hebrew

3.3.3.1 *The cost S-pattern in Hebrew*

Hebrew has the Cost sub-pattern just like English, except that in the Hebrew construction, there is no expletive. Another minor difference involves the form of the affectee. While the affectee in English is a direct object NP, in Hebrew it is an oblique object PP with the preposition *le* 'to'. The formula of the Cost S-pattern appears in Figure 23.

The function of the Cost S-pattern is repeated in (104).

(104) Through the use of the Cost predicate along with the Cost object, the Cost S-pattern states the cost incurred by the event encoded in the evaluee.

The examples are practically identical to those in English; see (105). While the sentences of (105a–b) specifically talk about money and time costs, the one in (105c) presents the human cost, in this case courage, that is incurred by the evaluee.

(105) a. *lo ole matayim šekel lezayef matbea šel asara škalim.* (I)
 not costs two.hundred shekel to.counterfeit a.coin of ten shekels
 'It doesn't cost two hundred shekels to counterfeit a coin of ten shekels.'

 b. *lokeax l-a-rikma ha-tomexet zman lehagiv l-a-tipul.* (I)
 takes to the tissue the supporting time to.respond to the treatment.
 'It takes the supporting tissue time to respond to treatment.'

 c. *lokeax harbe omec la'asot et ma še-asita.* (I)
 takes much courage to.do what that you.did
 'It takes much courage to do what you have done.'

Whereas in English, the Cost S-pattern is the only sub-pattern of the EV S-pattern, Hebrew has a few more. These will be described in the following subsections.

3.3.3.2 *The body-part-condition S-pattern in Hebrew*

In English, statements about the condition of a body part do not have a designated construction. This situation type is mostly encoded in the S1 S-patterns. The unmarked V S-pattern may be used in English, either with the person as subject and the possessive verb *have* taking the condition as object, as in (106a), or with the body part as subject and the verb describing the condition, as in (106b). Otherwise, the A COP S-pattern may be used, as part of its general use for expressing states, with the subject representing the person and the adjective expressing the condition, as is shown in (106c). Finally, the person may be the subject of a V sentence, and the body part a post-verbal PP, as in (106d).

(106) a. (i) I have a neck ache.
 (ii) I have a nose bleed.
 b. (i) My head is spinning.
 (ii) My neck hurts.
 (iii) My nose is bleeding.
 c. (i) I am dizzy.
 (ii) I feel nauseous.
 d. I am bleeding from my nose.

Though Hebrew may use these S1 options as well, it has *in addition* a P1 S-pattern that is specifically designated for expressing Body-part-conditions, as in (107).

(107) a. *ko'ev l-i ha-cavar.*
 hurts to me the neck

 b. *mistovev l-i ha-roš.*
 rotates to me the head.

 c. *yored l-i dam me-ha-af.*
 descends to me blood from the nose.

 d. *barax l-i pipi* (I)
 escaped to me pee
 'I had an accident.'

The affinity of these sentences to the other P1 constructions is complex. On the one hand, they are similar to evaluative statements. The affected person is encoded as an affectee, the bodily state, just like the attitude in modal expression, is a predicate that represents a state with spontaneous, non-agentive onset. This is not necessarily obvious from the predicates themselves, since *yarad* 'descend' or *barax* 'escape' are typically used in the V S-pattern as agentive verbs. On the other hand, the affected body part is an NP, and as such more similar to an existent of a negative existential sentence. If the well being of humans is taken as the norm, then negatively affected body parts are not what they should be. In some sense, then, they are absent, not there for their owner. Note the gradual move from pain to non-existence in (108a–c).

(108) a. *ko'evet l-i ha-regel.*
 hurts to me the leg
 'My leg is hurting.'

b. *nirdema l-i ha-regel.*
fell.asleep to me the leg
'My leg fell asleep/went numb.'

c. *halxa l-i ha-regel.*
went to me the leg
'My leg is gone.'/'I lost my leg.'

In (108a) the leg just hurts. In (108b) it becomes numb, which is a way of not being there for you. Finally, in (108c) it has become mutilated or amputated. Sentence (108c) is, in fact, very similar to the deteriorating entity S-pattern (Section 3.3.2.1) of the kind repeated in (109).

(109) a. *nikre'u l-i ha-mixnasayim.*
got.torn to me the pants
'My pants tore.'

b. *nitka l-i ha-oto.*
got.stuck to me the car
'My car broke down on me.'

There is a difference, though, between the deteriorating entity S-pattern and the Body-part-condition S-pattern. Body parts may act negatively, but also positively, on a person. They can get sick, for example, and then spontaneously get better. Entities tend to naturally deteriorate with time, but not to spontaneously get better. Examples of positive bodily states are given in (110).

(110) a. *nirpa l-i ha-šever b-a-af.* (I)
got.healed to me the fracture in the nose
'My broken nose is all better now.'

b. *rak lifne yomayim nisgar l-i ha-peca.* (I)
just before two.days closed to me the wound
'Just two days ago my wound closed up.'

c. *kol pa'am še-ani ro'e ota, omed l-i ha-zayin.* (I)
every time that I see her stands to me the penis
'Every time I see her I get a hard on.'

All these situations have their negative or positive construal only in the prototypical cases. These situations may, however, be also accompanied by the opposite attitude. One may be very glad that somebody else has a neck ache, as one may be very troubled to have an erection in the wrong situation. Either way, these situations types are conducive to emotions affecting the person that is undergoing them.

[PredP	V	PP	]	NP
	Bodily Process Pred	Affectee		Body Part

Figure 24. The Body-part-condition S-pattern in Hebrew

Nevertheless, all these statements may also be uttered with no particular attitude, just as an objective description. As was the case with the Cost S-pattern, the expression of these situation types in the P1 pattern has become conventionalized and is no longer necessarily read off as an intention to express emotive states, even if this is still so in the majority of cases.

Statements about certain body parts have been conventionalized as metaphorical expressions of emotive states. The meaning is thereby shifted from the physical to the emotional, as in (111). This shows again how close these meaning domains are.

(111) a. *nišbar l-i ha-lev me-ha-sipur šelxa.* (I)
    got.broken to me the heart from your story
    'My heart was broken by your story.'

  b. *nišbar l-i ha-zayin me-ha-avoda ha-masrixa ha-zot.* (I)
    got.broken to me the penis from the work the stinking the this
    'I am sick and tired of this crappy job.'

The formula of the Body-part-condition S-pattern appears in Figure 24. This sentence pattern employs only verbs (no other parts of speech) in the predicate slot, which is another reason for keeping it separate.

The function of the Body-part-condition is presented in (112).

(112) Through the use of the bodily process predicate, the Body-part-condition S-pattern expresses the Body-part-condition affecting the affectee (often viewed evaluatively, as unfortunate or beneficial to the affectee).

3.3.3.3 *The animal-induced-condition S-pattern in Hebrew*

Sentence (113) was introduced into the discussion of P1 S-patterns by Melnik (2006: 7).

(113) *akca oti dvora.*
    stung me a.bee
    'I was stung by a bee.'

Melnik wonders to what extent this sentence may be characterized as presentational, since it is quite clear that the bee does not usually actively persist as a topic in the subsequent discourse. This question intrigues Melnik, since the object of her inquiry is primarily verb initial constructions with an NP at the end, namely existential sentences. This is why she also expects this sentence to have some presentational sense. I will return to this puzzle below. But first, some more examples of animal-induced human conditions are given in (114). The sentence in (114c) is the punchline of an Israeli joke.

(114) a. *hikiš oti nexaš cefa.* (I)
 bit me a.snake.of viper
 'I was bitten by a viper snake.'

 b. *kol šniya metapeset al-ay nemala al ha-regel.* (I)
 every second crawls on me an.ant on the leg
 'Every second another ant crawls on my leg.'

 c. *50,000 iš hayu b-a-ictadyon ve-rak al-ay xirbena cipor.* (I)
 50,000 people were in the stadium and only on me shat a.bird
 'There were 50,000 people in the stadium, and I was the only one the bird shat on.'

Actions of animals that do not involve people being affected are not candidates for being encoded in this construction, as is evident from the unacceptability of (115a). Such propositions will be encoded in the regular S1 V S-pattern, as in (115b).

(115) a. **histabxa be-kurei ha-akaviš b-a-maxsan dvora.*
 got.tangled in the.webs.of the spider in the shed a.bee
 *'There got tangled in the spider web in the shed a bee.'

 b. *dvora histabxa be-kurei ha-akaviš b-a-maxsan.*
 a.bee got.tangled in the.webs.of the spider in the shed
 'A bee got tangled in the spider web in the shed.'

The formula of the Animal-induced-condition S-pattern is shown in Figure 25.
The function of the Animal-induced-condition S-pattern is given in (116).

(116) Through the Animal's action predicate, the Animal-induced-condition S-pattern expresses the condition inflicted on the affectee by the animal.

Note that the Animal-induced-condition and the Body-part-condition are similar in form, though the parts of the constructions have different functions and different names. The similarity is brought out in (117).

[$_{PredP}$	V	PP	]	NP
	Animal's Action Pred	Affectee		Animal

Figure 25. The Animal-induced-condition S-pattern

(117) a. *nirdema l-i ha-regel.*
fell.asleep to me the leg

   b. *akca oti dvora.*
stung me a.bee

Although the last part of the construction is in both cases an NP, in (117a) the verb is a predicate of *spontaneous* action ("unaccusative"), hence this body part NP *undergoes* the experience on behalf of the affectee, whereas in (117b) the predicate is an agentive verb, and the NP animal *inflicts* the condition on the affectee. It should be kept in mind, however, that all these actions carried out by animals are not really volitional. Bees sting, snakes bite, and birds relieve themselves in an instinctual way, sometimes as an automatic reaction to a person's action. Similarly, ants climb on people's legs with no intention of doing so and no awareness of consequences, just using people as a climbing surface. In other words, there is not much agentivity in these acts when performed by these animals, and their appearance in a P1 construction supports this construal. Their appearance in out-of-the-blue sentences is perceived as natural and fully acceptable. A very similar situation type, with people as attackers, does not get encoded in this construction in out-of-the-blue sentences, as can be seen in (118).

(118) a. **hitkif oti šoter.*
attacked me a.policeman

   b. **ca'ak al-ay pakid.*
yelled on me a.clerk

This concludes the discussion of the sub-patterns associated with the EV S-pattern. In the next section the ENV S-pattern in Hebrew is discussed.

3.3.4 The environmental S-pattern in Hebrew

The ENV S-pattern in Hebrew has been treated very briefly in the literature (Rosén 1966: 209, 222; Rubinstein 1968: 162; Berman 1980: 766; Glinert 1989: 183–184; Coffin & Bolozky 2005: 331). This S-pattern is similar to its English counterpart, but it lacks an expletive. It also differs from its English counterpart in that it has a sub-pattern, which will be discussed in the next section.

The three parts of speech that may serve as predicates of the ENV S-pattern, namely V, N, and A, are exemplified in (119).

(119) a. *Maxšix.*
is.darkening
'It is getting dark.'

b. *stav.*
Autumn
'It is autumn.'

c. *kar.*
cold
'It is cold.'

The level of visibility of sentence structure in Hebrew is lower than in English. The presence of an expletive and a copula in English produce a bipartite sentence form, even though the sentence contains only one lexical word, namely the predicate. In English, therefore, there is a clear difference between ENV sentences and monopartite interjections (consisting of one-word or one endocentric phrase). There is no semantic constraint on what may serve as a monopartite interjection. In English, then, the interjections of (120a–b) are equally grammatical, but the ENV sentences associated with the same nouns are subject to semantic constraints. This is why (120c) is acceptable, whereas (120d), (to be read with an expletive *it*), is not.

(120) a. Winter!
 b. a new computer!
 c. It is winter.
 d. *It is a new computer.

In Hebrew, only the verbal ENV sentence is clearly identifiable as a full sentence, since it has a finite (third-person singular) form. In fact, it is precisely the lack of any subject that identifies it as an environmental statement, since in the V S-pattern, a third-person singular verb form cannot appear without an overt subject (lexical or pronominal). This is part of the mixed nature of Hebrew with regard to null-subject behavior. A third-person singular verb is one of the cases where a null subject is not permitted, unless it appears in a sequence of verbs sharing the same subject. This is why (121a–c) are acceptable, while (121d) is not, if the reading of the verb *tiftef* in the sense of *drip* is attempted. The lack of an overt subject in (121d) forces the listener to interpret the verb *tiftef* as an environmental predicate, meaning *drizzle*.

(121) a. *ha-berez tiftef.*
the tap dripped
'The tap was dripping.'

b. *ha-berez asa kolot muzarim ve-tiftef.*
the tap made noises funny and dripped
'The tap made funny noises and was dripping.'

c. *hu tiftef*
he [=it, the tap] dripped
'It [the tap] dripped.'

d. *tiftef.*
drizzled/*dripped
'It drizzled.'

If noun-based and adjective-based monopartite expressions are in the past or future tense, they are easily interpreted in Hebrew as sentences, since they are, in that case, accompanied by the verb *haya* 'be', or *nihya* 'become' as shown in (122).

(122) a. *yihye nora xam.*
will.be awfully hot

b. *nihya erev.*
became night.

Only if a noun or an adjective expression stands alone, may it be interpreted as an interjection. This is why environmental nouns and adjectives tend to appear with time or place adjuncts, meaning *now, already, not yet, in Australia*, etc., as in (123). Such expressions make it clear that these are sentences, not interjections.

(123) a. *axšav me'unan.* (Title of a popular song by the pop singer Aviv Gefen)
now cloudy
'It is cloudy now.'

b. *kvar boker, ve-ha-forum radum.* (I)
already morning, and the forum is asleep.
'It's already morning, but the forum is still asleep.'

c. *od lo šamati havdala, az adayin šabat.* (I)
yet not I.heard Havdala [=Close of the Sabbath ceremony] so still Sabbath
'I haven't heard Havdala yet, so it must still be the Sabbath.'

d. *be-ostralya kayic.* (I)
in-Australia summer
'In Australia it is summer.'

The opaque structure of non-verbal ENV sentences in Hebrew has brought about various proposals regarding their syntactic analysis. Ornan (1979: 39) suggests that in the sentence *haya xam* 'was hot' the adjective *xam* 'hot' is subject. Aware of the oddity of an adjective as subject, Ornan notes that the adjective might be perceived here as an abstract noun. In Ornan's analysis, *haya* 'was' is the predicate. As a transformational-generative linguist, Ornan holds that when *xam* occurs alone instantiating a grammatical sentence form, the predicate in it has undergone ellipsis. Rubinstein (1968: 65) correctly observes that these single sentence-words are predicates, and that in the sentence *ata layla* 'now night', *ata* is an adjunct.

Sentences with adjuncts should not be conflated with an inverted P COP sentences. Hence, sentence (123c), should not be confused with the sentences of (124).

(124) a. *mi-yamin ha-bama, mi-smol ha-kahal.*
from right the stage, from left the audience
'On the right is the stage, on the left – the audience.'

b. *be-od šavua ha-bxirot.*
in another week the elections
'In another week there are the elections.'

The sentences of (124) are inverted P COP sentences with a marked word order variant involving a fronted predicate. The PP is a component of the S-pattern, not an adjunct. The NP expressions *ha-bama* 'the stage' and *ha-bxirot* 'the elections' cannot stand on their own as sentences under any circumstances, since they do not express environmental conditions. On the other hand, expressions such as *šabat* 'Sabbath' and *kayic* 'summer' may stand on their own. As full sentences, they may be embedded, as in *ani yodea še-šabat* 'I know that [it is] the Sabbath'.

Indeed, embedding is a clear test for the sentencehood of such expressions, since interjections do not get embedded. The nouns *kayic* 'summer' in (125a), and *layla* 'night' in (125b), are embedded clauses. The noun *šulxan* 'table' cannot be similarly embedded, as is evident from the ungrammaticality of (125c).

(125) a. *im xašavtem še-tipatru mi-meni biglal še-kayic, az mamaš lo.* (I)
if you.thought that you.will.get.rid from me because that summer, then decidedly not
'If you thought you'd get rid of me because it's summer, forget it.'

b. *boker tov le-kulam (ken, ani yodaat še-layla...).*
morning good to all (yes, I know that night...)
'Good morning to you all (yes, I know it is night).'

c. a. *hey, tir'e. šulxan.*
hey, look. a.table.

b. **ani yodea še-šulxan.*
I know that a.table

The formula of the ENV S-pattern in Hebrew is presented in Figure 126.

```
[_PredP   V/N/A      ]
         Env Pred
```

Figure 26. The ENV S-pattern in Hebrew

The function of the ENV S-pattern in Hebrew is given in (126).

(126) Through the use of the environmental predicate, the ENV S-pattern provides the condition of the contextually relevant environment.

The ENV S-pattern has a sub-pattern linked with it: the PredP-alone S-pattern. This is the topic of the next subsection.

3.2.4.1 *The PredP-alone S-pattern in Hebrew*

The PredP-alone S-pattern is a sub-pattern of the ENV S-pattern. It is similar to it in form, except that the predicate has an affectee in the form of a PP with the preposition *le-*. Like the ENV S-pattern, the PredP-alone S-pattern does not have a final component, such as evaluee or existent. This is why the PredP-alone S-pattern is linked to the ENV S-pattern as a sub-pattern. In terms of its function, the PredP-alone shares only a small number of predicates with the ENV S-pattern. In fact, its stock of predicates has more in common with the EV and the Body-part-condition S-patterns. This might be, then, a case of double inheritance (see "multiple inheritance" Goldberg 1995: 73, 97–98,), where the form comes from the ENV S-pattern, but the function from the EV and Body-part-condition S-patterns. Due to this double inheritance, the PredP-alone S-pattern may not be viewed simply as a transitive option of the ENV S-pattern.

As a first example of this S-pattern consider the sentence in (127).

(127) *mešaʿamem l-i.*
  boring.Adj to me.
  'I am bored.'

The adjective *mešaʿamem* 'boring' appears also in the EV S-pattern, where it may have an evaluee InfP, as can be seen in (128).

(128) *mešaʿamem l-i laševet b-a-bayit kol ha-yom.* (I)
  boring to me to.sit in the house all the day
  'I am bored sitting at home all day.'

As an EV sentence, its modality is attitudinal, and boredom is pronounced vis-à-vis the state of "sitting at home all day". However, boredom is also a general state of being, one that does not have to be associated with a particular event or state; hence the acceptability of (127) in the PredP-alone S-pattern.

Not all evaluative predicates, however, have the capacity of indicating a general state of being, when their evaluee is removed. Given the right context, any evaluative predicate may of course be used elliptically, without its evaluee, but in such cases, the ellipsis is felt. Example (129) represents an elliptical use of the EV predicate *keday* 'worthwhile'.

(129) A: [Do you want to buy a new car?]
B: *lo keday l-i.*
B: not worthwhile to me
B: 'It is not worth my while.'

The elliptical nature of the Hebrew sentence in (129) does not come through in the English translation, because the moment the evaluee is absent in English, the word *it* is construed as a pronoun rather than as an expletive. But this is not what is intended here. In Hebrew, as well, the demonstrative pronoun *ze* 'this' may be used as a pronoun (*ze lo keday li* 'it is not worth my while'), in which case, the sentence would be perceived as complete. Yet without the pronoun *ze* in Hebrew, the sentence necessarily feels elliptical.

The evaluative predicate *keday* 'worthwhile' is purely attitudinal, hence it cannot be uttered without the evaluated event that serves as the target of that attitude. The predicate *keday* cannot be construed as conveying a general state of being that is newsworthy on its own.

Adjectives that may be used in the PredP-alone S-pattern are given in (130). The adjectives *kar* 'cold' and *xam* 'hot' may be used in the ENV S-pattern to convey environmental conditions. Once an object is added, the sentence is transferred from the ENV to the PredP-alone S-pattern, thus the environmental effect is lost, and the condition is personalized as the state of being of the affectee, as in (130a). The predicates *tov* 'good' and *ra* 'bad' may also be peripherally used in the ENV S-pattern (see Section 7.5), provided that an appropriate environment is supplied by a place adjunct, such as *po* 'here' (*tov po* 'it is good in here'). In (130b), this form is transitive, and the adjunct is no longer obligatory, since the predicate does not refer to environmental conditions but to a personal state of being.

The sentence *tov l-ax* 'it shall be well with thee' (KJV) happens to have been used in Biblical Hebrew as well (Psalms 128,2). Sentence (130c) is a routinely used apology formula in Israeli Hebrew. In Biblical Hebrew it was used with an adjunct PP *al-exa* 'on you' indicating the object of sorrow. The Biblical sentence is given in (130d).

(130) a. *kar/xam l-i po.*
cold/hot to me here
'I am cold/hot here.'

b. *tov/ra l-i (b-a-avoda).*
good/bad to me (in the work)
'I feel good/bad (at work).'

c. *car l-i.*
distressful to me
'I am sorry.'

d. *car l-i al-exa, axi yonatan.*   (2 Samuel, 1,26)
distressed to me on you, my.brother Yonatan
'I am distressed for thee, my brother Jonathan.' (KJV)

In addition to adjectives, the predicate slot of the PredP-alone S-pattern admits also verbs. Some of the verbs come from the Body-part-condition S-pattern, with the argument being implicitly incorporated into the verb. In two cases the motivation for incorporation is clean language, as is the case in (131a–b). In these sentences the implied body part is *ha-zayin* 'the penis'. (For expressions that do include this NP, see Section 3.3.3.2). While every Hebrew speaker is aware of the fuller version in these sentences, this is not the case with (131c), where the shorter form *holex l-o* goes to him 'he's doing well' has been fully conventionalized. Only a fraction of Hebrew speakers can still associate it with the original expression *holex l-o klaf mešuga* goes to him a.card crazy 'he has a wild card going for him', i.e. 'he is doing very well'. The negative sentence in (131c) would not make sense with the implied argument restored.

(131) a. *b-a-pa'am ha-rišona še-nisinu bixlal lo amad l-i.*
in the time the first that we.tried at.all not stood to me.
'The first time we tried I couldn't get it up.'

b. *day! nišbar l-i. ani lo yexola yoter.*   (I)
enough! got.broken to me. I not able.F any.more
'That's it! I am at my limit. I can't stand it any more.'

c. *makabi tel aviv lo mesaxakim tov ve-lo holex l-ahem.*   (I)
Maccabi Tel-Aviv not are.playing well and not goes to them
'Maccabi Tel-Aviv are not playing well, and they are not doing so well.'

By the way, the speaker in (131b) happens to be a woman (*yexola* 'able' is in the feminine form). Women may use the full phrase as well (to the extent that they are inclined to use profane language). The sense is, in any case, metaphorical, so if your penis does not *really* break, it does not matter if you do not actually have one.

There is also an idiom which appears exclusively in the PredP-alone S-pattern, i.e. it does not show up in other P1 S-patterns. It involves the passive verb *busam* 'be perfumed' followed by the preposition *le* 'to'. It may be preceded by *še* 'that' which acts as an optative particle (a grammaticalized abbreviation of *I wish that*). A translational equivalent may be *so be it* or *see if I care* or *who am I to judge*.

(132) *im hi roca lehitxaten be-gil 16, še-yevusam l-a.* (I)
if she wants to.get.married in age 16, that will.be.perfumed to her
'*If she wants to get married at the age of sixteen,* who am I to judge her?'

The formula of the PredP-alone S-pattern appears in Figure 27.
The function of the PredP-alone S-pattern is given in (133).

(133) Through the use of an affecting predicate, a state of being is rendered relevant to the affectee.

The PredP-alone S-pattern is semi-productive. Occasionally one hears people playfully use (134a) instead of (134b), the latter being the standard way of speaking in the given situation types.

(134) a. *raev/ayef l-i.*
hungry/tired to me
'I am hungry/tired

b. *ani raev/ayef.*
I hungry/tired.

In the same playful manner, the radio reporter Yoav Limor uttered sentence (135). This is a more complex construction, since the affectee is left-dislocated, but otherwise it exemplifies the same phenomenon.. What the reporter did here is constructional rhyming. Normally, one would say *xam l-o* hot to him 'he is hot', and *hu mazia* 'he sweats'. Instead, the reporter forced the second sentence into a non-canonical one-time usage in the PredP-alone S-pattern, resulting in *mazia l-o* sweats to him 'he sweats'.

(135) *ha-israeli be-xodeš ogust be-ikar xam l-o, mazia l-o.* (10.7.2011, Network B)
the Israeli in month August in main hot to him, sweats to him
'The Israeli during the month of August is mainly hot, he sweats.'

[$_{PredP}$	V/A	PP	]
	Affecting Pred	Affectee	

Figure 27. The PredP-alone S-pattern in Hebrew

Similarly, in the promo to a docu-drama on Israeli rich women who are not embarrassed to spend a lot of money on expensive fun things to do, one of these women says (using the English word *fun*):

(136)   elohim, barata kol-kax harbe fanim še-fan l-i.   (3.12.2011 TV promo)
        God, you.created so many "funs" that "fun" to me
        'God, you have created so many fun things that I am having fun.'

As our discussion of the various P1 S-patterns is drawing to its conclusion, it is worth noting that the differences between the various P1 S-patterns on the one hand, and the partial similarities between them on the other hand, are fertile ground for puns. A playful exchange, playfully acted out by children in Israel, may demonstrate this interaction between S-patterns. It is based on the kindred constructions the PredP-alone S-pattern and the Animal-induced-condition S-pattern. The only difference between them in terms of form is the presence or absence of a final NP. The humorous effect emerges from the different meanings of the same predicate in the two constructions. The exchange is demonstrated in (137).

(137)   a. A: *holex le-xa!*
                goes to you
                'You are doing great!'
            B: *ma holex li?*
                what goes to me?
                'what do you mean I am doing well?' Lit.: 'what is going to me?'
            A: *ǧuk al ha-katef.* (slapping B's shoulder to kill an imaginary bug)
                a.bug on the shoulder.
                'A bug [is going] on your shoulder.'

Speaker A starts the exchange by complimenting speaker B for doing very well. Caught by surprise by this out-of-the-blue compliment, B echoes A's statement with a preceding *ma* 'what', which is intended to ask for a clarification: "what [do you mean by] I am doing well?". However, this question may also be construed as asking for a missing argument, namely: "what is walking to me?" ("to me" in this construal is the affectee, even though no affect has been pronounced yet), to which A replies "a bug on you shoulder". As a favor to his friend, A takes the opportunity to slap B's shoulder to kill the imaginary bug.

This concludes the discussion of the ENV S-pattern and its sub-pattern the PredP-alone S-pattern, as well as the discussion of the P1 S-patterns in Hebrew in particular and of P1 S-patterns in general. The following section will provide a summary and conclusion of this chapter.

3.4 Summary and conclusion of Chapter 3

The chapter starts (Section 3.1) with a justification of the concept of P1 S-patterns. Goldberg's suggestion of plugging P1 argument structures into the network of S1 patterns, with a word-order override instruction, is rejected on two grounds. First, since the procedure for stating linearization facts has not been explicitly stated with regard to the S1 S-patterns, the same problem persists with the P1 S-patterns. It is also not clear at what part of the S1 network the P1 proto-pattern would be attached, nor is it obvious whether there would be one or several P1 S-patterns hanging in different locations on the network.

Secondly, argument structure patterns have been developed for sentences with a V predicate, but the P1 S-patterns accommodate multiple parts of speech in their predicate slots. It is not clear how the unity of constructions with multiple class membership and the generalizations over them would be handled in an argument structure framework, which is atomizing by nature.

It should be added here as a further conclusion that polysemy differentiates meanings of predicates according to the S-pattern they appear in. The same predicates when used in S1 or P1 S-patterns sometimes have different meanings. Typically, the predicates used in the P1 sentences have an existential, evaluative, or environmental twist to them. Thus, the adjective *car* 'narrow' as predicate in the COP S-pattern becomes 'distressful'/'sorry' in the EV S-pattern. The adjective *xaser* 'missing' in the COP S-pattern is a borderline case between the EX and EV S-patterns when the existent/evaluee is NP, and it means in that case 'is missing or absent and should be replaced or replenished'. The adjective *xaser* undergoes a further shift when the evaluee is a *that*-clause, meaning "you are in trouble if" (as if to say "all you are missing for me to chop your head off is that you..."). Similarly, in English, the adjective *clear* has several meanings in the COP S-pattern, such as 'free of obstruction' 'translucent', 'unblemished', 'cloudless', and 'easy to perceive', but in the ENV S-pattern *clear* only has the meaning 'cloudless' and in the EV S-pattern only 'easy to perceive' (see also the discussion of *develop* as an existential verb in Section 5.3.1). These processes of unpredictable, yet well motivated, metaphorical extensions of meaning across S-patterns have not been discussed in the literature on argument structure, since the V S-pattern has been the focus of attention in it.

The chapter is then divided into two parts: P1 S-patterns in English (Section 3.2) and P1 S-patterns in Hebrew (3.3). In each of them, the three major P1 S-patterns – EX, EV, and ENV – have been presented, including their sub-patterns.

The English P1 S-patterns are more constrained in their range of applicability than the Hebrew ones. English prefers to use the S1 word order for many situation types that are expressed in Hebrew in the P1 word order. One of the domains where this is visible is the use of objects. While in the EV S-pattern both languages have an object position that is part of the construction and has a role assigned to it, namely the *affectee* (or some role extended from it), in the English EX S-pattern there might be an occasional object, selected by some predicate (*there entered the room a girl*), but there is no object slot at the constructional level, with the affectee role assigned to it.

This is not the case in Hebrew, where the EX S-pattern has a functional object slot, namely the affectee-turned-possessor, whereby existential statements are made relevant *le* 'to' an affectee, thereby expressing possession. The ENV S-pattern in English does not have an affectee either, whereas the Hebrew one does, in the PredP-alone sub-pattern (*car li* distressful to me 'I am sorry' and *nišbar li* broke to me 'I'm at my limit').

We see, then, that the Hebrew P1 S-patterns are symmetrical, allowing an affectee slot in all three of them, whereas in the English P1 S-patterns, only the EV S-pattern has an affectee slot, while the EX and ENV S-patterns do not.

The meager use that English makes of the P1 S-patterns can also be seen in the strict division of labor between EX and EV S-patterns. The former admits only NPs in sentence-final position, the latter – only nominals. In Hebrew, both the EX and the EV S-patterns permit both NPs and nominals as final components.

Another place where English is more austere than Hebrew is the extension of patterns to sub-patterns. English only has one sub-pattern, the Cost S-pattern, which shoots out of the EV S-pattern. The English Cost S-pattern has a Hebrew counterpart, but in addition Hebrew has many more sub-patterns, extending from all three P1 S-patterns, used for situation types that English encodes via the S1 S-patterns.

Finally, we have seen that English uses lexically negative existential predicates very rarely. When this happens, the negative predicate is used to positively introduce the existent into the discourse. Hebrew, on the other hand, uses lexically negative existential predicates across the board in order to express non-existence or disappearance, fully parallel to the expression of existence.

The situation types for which Hebrew has conventionalized P1 S-patterns (sometimes alongside alternate S1 forms), while English uses only the S1 S-patterns, are as follows: negative existence, possession, negative possession, deteriorating entity, body-part condition, animal-induced condition, and affective and bodily states expressed by the PredP-alone. All these are summarized and exemplified in Table (1).

Looking at these data from a typological perspective, English and Hebrew appear on two poles of a scale in their use of P1 S-patterns. Other languages to be included in the same typology, namely languages that use S1 S-patterns for major narrative functions and P1 S-patterns for existential, evaluative, and environmental

Table 1. Situation types with Hebrew P1 versus English S1 S-patterns

Sit. Type	Hebrew	English
Negative existence	nigmeru ha-klementinot ran.out the tangerines	The tangerines ran out
Possession	yeš l-i sefer EXIST to me a.book	I have a book
Negative possession	ne'elam l-i ha-darkon disappeared to me the passport	My passport disappeared.
Deteriorating entity	nikre'a l-i ha-xulca tore to me the shirt	I tore my shirt/My shirt tore
Body-part condition	nišbar l-i ha-af broke to me the nose	I broke my nose/My nose broke
Animal-induced condition	akca oti dvora stung me a.bee	I was stung by a bee/a bee stung me
Affective & bodily states (via PredP)	meša'amem l-i boring to me omed l-i stands to me	I am bored I have a hard-on

statements (including their sub-patterns), will presumably get located on this scale somewhere along the continuum formed by these two languages, or perhaps mark new poles beyond them, depending on the particular situation types that get encoded by these S-patterns or by ones that are extended from them.

What remains to be checked is whether there is any rationale, any systematic pattern, in the choice that speakers make when they decide on a particular S-pattern for a particular situation type. In the upcoming Chapters 5, 6, and 7, it will be suggested that this kind of choice is guided by semantic motivation. The three P1 S-patterns will be shown to be organized semantically in three conceptual categories (CCs) of existence, evaluation, and environmental conditions. These CCs will be shown to be prototype-based radial structures. With these CCs established, it will be claimed that the sentences with predicates at or near the core will tend to appear in P1 sentences as their unmarked form, based mostly on their very situation type, whereas at the periphery, predicates will get encoded in S1 or P1 constructions, based on narrative needs and information structure considerations.

The question whether the EX and EV S-patterns are really two constructions has been brought up on several occasions. In Hebrew the situation is clear: the two constructions have the same formula and the same distribution of parts of speech in it. The domains of existence and evaluation are adjacent, as is evident from borderline cases. Hence it has been suggested that they form one composite category with two meaning foci in it.

In English the EX and EV S-patterns may be considered two variants of the same construction as well, since they operate in complementary distribution; namely, if the final component is an NP, it is construed as an existent in the EX S-pattern; if the final component is a nominal, it is construed as an evaluee in the EV S-pattern. The choice of expletive *there* or *it* follows this choice. Borderline cases are therefore technically distributed between the two S-patterns in line with their form. The borderline predicate *needed* thus forms both the EX sentence *there are needed policy changes in trade regulations and debt relief* and the EV sentence *it is needed that the Commissioner shall be both willing and able to enforce this responsibility*, with no difference in the meaning of the predicate *needed* itself.

In Chapter 3, the three P1 S-patterns have been presented, with their English and Hebrew sub-patterns. What has not been discussed yet is the architecture of the whole domain of S-patterns. This will be done in the next chapter. Some of this architecture has been already described: certain S-patterns have been viewed as sub-patterns of parent S-patterns. Furthermore, all S-patterns have been classified into the two groups of S1 and P1 S-patterns. In the next chapter, S-patterns will be viewed as being in a *field*, either as networks or as stand-alone entities.

CHAPTER 4

A field of sentence patterns

4.1 Fields

The *constructicon* (see Section 1.2) is the storehouse of all constructions (Fillmore 2006). In light of the view in cognitive linguistics that lexical and grammatical structures in language are all expressible as constructions, the constructicon does in fact include the lexicon. This brings up the question of the structure of the constructicon. The constructicon cannot just be a random list. This early view about the random nature of the lexicon as a list of idiosyncrasies – in Bloomfield's (1933: 274) terms "a list of basic irregularities" – cannot be extended to the constructicon, given all we know today about the many regularities prevailing both among lexical entries and among constructions.

Without making any global commitment with regard to the architecture of the constructicon at large, the group of all S-patterns is viewed here as a section within the constructicon: the *field* of all S-patterns. This field is different in architecture from Goldberg's network of argument structure constructions. While in Goldberg's (1995) view, all argument structure constructions fit into a single network, it is suggested here that the field of S-patterns contains both unordered and ordered materials. It contains both stand-alone constructions and networks of constructions.

In the next section, the field of S-patterns in English and Hebrew will be presented with emphasis on the organization of the networks of the major S-patterns.

4.2 The field of S-pattern networks in English and Hebrew

In English and Hebrew, there are major and minor S-patterns (see Section 1.9). Minor S-patterns have not been focal in the present study. It stands to reason that at least some of the minor S-patterns are stand-alone constructions, not linked to any network. These are not represented in the diagrams of Figures 28 and 33, which contain a partial representation of the field of S-patterns in English and Hebrew respectively. Only the major S-patterns discussed in earlier chapters show up in these diagrams.

The networks in the diagrams sketch out a hierarchy of nodes from left to right. A node that contains the phrase "S-pattern" in its label is a *instantiated node*: it represents a construction that has actual linguistic instantiations. The root node and other intermediary nodes leading to the instantiated nodes are *generalizing nodes*. They represent generalizations over instantiated nodes. Their form and function may be represented in formulas similar to those used in the S-pattern, but they have no actual linguistic instantiations.

Instantiated nodes that are daughters of instantiated nodes are sub-constructions, in our case sub-patterns. In the diagrams below, they also carry the phrase "S-pattern" in their label, just like any first-generation S-pattern. Branches represent *inheritance links* in the direction of the hierarchy (from left to right). The daughter node may contain additional or contradictory (overriding) properties, relative to its mother node. These diagrams are partial representations of the descriptive mechanism discussed earlier. A full formalization of the mechanism offered here remains a desideratum at this point.

The diagram of the field of the networks of major S-patterns in English is given in Figure 28.

The details of the structure of the field of S-patterns in English will be elaborated in the following paragraphs, but since the general structure in English and Hebrew is the same, most of this description will apply to Hebrew as well. The diagram of Hebrew networks will be presented following this elaboration.

The major S-patterns of English and Hebrew fall into two networks, headed by the root nodes S1 and P1. The S1 group of S-patterns is a coherent group, sharing a bipartite syntactic structure [NP PredP], which also translates into a functional bipartite structure of a categorical judgment (Brentano 1874; Kuroda 1972;

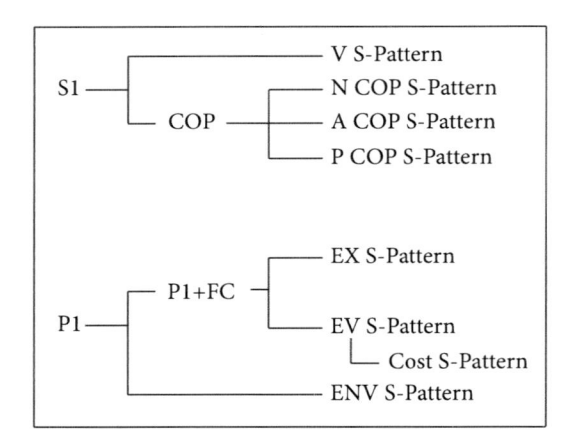

```
S1 ─┬──────────── V S-Pattern
    │         ┌── N COP S-Pattern
    └── COP ──┼── A COP S-Pattern
              └── P COP S-Pattern


             ┌── EX S-Pattern
    ┌─ P1+FC ┤
P1──┤        └── EV S-Pattern
    │            └── Cost S-Pattern
    └──────────── ENV S-Pattern
```

Figure 28. The field of S-patterns in English

NP	PredP
Logical Subject	Logical Predicate

Figure 29. The S1 root node for English and Hebrew

Sasse 1987), represented in the formula as "logical subject" and "logical predicate". Categorical judgments have the unmarked bipartite information structure of topic–comment (Lambrecht 1994). The formula of the root node of the S1 network is given in Figure 29. It applies equally to English and Hebrew.

On one of the S1 branches, the V S-pattern directly inherits the S1 root node's generalizations. On the other branch, the COP node mediates between the S1 root node and the three COP S-patterns. This configuration assumes the more conservative view of three separate COP S-patterns. Naturally, if only one COP S-pattern is assumed (Section 2.4.6), the latter would not be an intermediate generalizing node, but a terminal instantiated node. The formula of the (intermediate) COP node is presented in Figure 30. It applies equally to English and Hebrew. The PredP component with the function "assigned predicate function" is further elaborated in the three instantiated COP S-patterns, featuring N, A, and P as predicates, with the more specific functions of equivalence, attribution, and relation respectively.

The P1 group of S-patterns is headed by the P1 root node, which has a monopartite syntactic structure [PredP], with the functional role of a thetic predicate. The formula of the P1 root node is presented in Figure 31.

On one of the P1 branches, the instantiated node of the ENV S-pattern directly inherits the P1 root node's generalizations. On the other branch, the P1 + FC generalizing node mediates between the P1 root node and the instantiated nodes of the EX and EV S-patterns. FC stands for the final component (NP or Nominal) that is added to the [PredP] of the P1 root node. Functionally, it is the "considered referent", namely the referent whose nature is considered in the PredP as being in existence (the "existent") or as being evaluated (the "evaluee"). The formula of the P1 + FC root node is given in Figure 32.

NP	COP	PredP$_{\text{non-verbal predicate}}$
Basis Subject	Assigner of Pred Function	Assigned Pred Function

Figure 30. The COP node for English and Hebrew

PredP
Thetic Predicate

Figure 31. The P1 root node for English and Hebrew

PredP	FC
Thetic Predicate	Considered Referent

Figure 32. The P1 + FC node for English and Hebrew

Figure 33 has the diagram of the Hebrew S1 and P1 networks. What arises quite clearly from Figures 28 and 33 is the typological similarity between the two languages on the one hand along with the difference in detail on the other. The fact that English and Hebrew share the same number of sentential networks, the same node structure of generalizing nodes, and the same first-generation instantiated nodes, shows how close the two languages are in their basic design. English and Hebrew differ mainly in second-generation instantiated nodes. While English only has one, namely the Cost S-pattern, Hebrew has five, as listed in Figure 33.

Obviously, the diagrams only show the details relevant to the structure and the function of the constructions. Many other differences that have been discussed throughout this book are not represented in these diagrams. For example, avoiding the use of the EX S-pattern for lexically-negative existential statements cannot be shown on this diagram. The use of the transitive existential sentence for possession only appears in the formulas associated with the diagrams, but cannot be seen in the general design of the network.

What comes through very clearly from the diagrams is the choice of situation types that get expressed in different S-patterns. For example, the situation of an animal performing an injurious act on a person is encoded in English (1a) in the

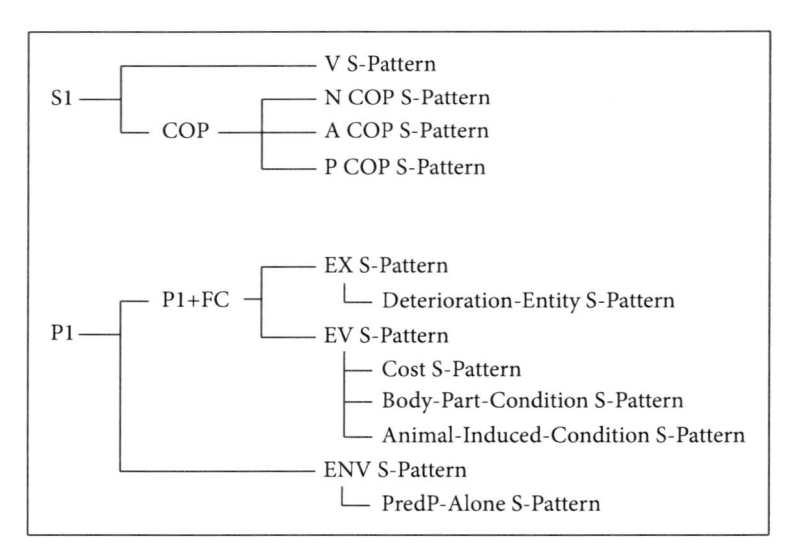

```
S1 ─┬─────────── V S-Pattern
    │       ┌─── N COP S-Pattern
    └─ COP ─┼─── A COP S-Pattern
            └─── P COP S-Pattern

          ┌──────── EX S-Pattern
          │         └─ Deterioration-Entity S-Pattern
    ┌ P1+FC ─────── EV S-Pattern
P1 ─┤           ├─── Cost S-Pattern
    │           ├─── Body-Part-Condition S-Pattern
    │           └─── Animal-Induced-Condition S-Pattern
    └──────────── ENV S-Pattern
                  └─ PredP-Alone S-Pattern
```

Figure 33. The field of S-patterns in Hebrew

passive form of an unmarked V sentence. In Hebrew (1b), a designated construction, the Animal-induced S-pattern, is used.

(1) a. I was stung by a bee.
    b. *akca oti dvora.*
       stung me a.bee

In English, then, this situation is reported as a categorical judgment, with the information structure topic–comment, encoding the human being in the topical subject position, in keeping with the general tendency of English to encode the human participant as subject. In Hebrew, this situation type is expressed in a thetic statement, encoding the human being as a secondary topic affectee.

Interestingly, in both languages the inflicting animal, here the bee, is the final accented component of the sentence, even though it is quite clear that in a typical surrounding narrative, in most cases it is not the bee that will persist as the topic of subsequent discourse. Putting the animal participant in that position in English does not give it narrow argument focus. On the contrary, given the constraint of having the human participant as subject in English, the only position left for the animal is the final position. The final accent on the NP representing the bee is the unmarked focus structure of subject–predicate sentences. The focus signaled by the accented last component has a broad VP focus which covers *stung by a bee* as a whole, not just *bee* alone.

In Hebrew too, the final NP representing the bee is accented. This is the default accent of this kind of thetic sentence, interpreted – as in English – as broad sentence focus, not as narrow argument focus. As a result, in English the human participant is a *primary topic* (subject) and in Hebrew it is a *secondary topic* (affectee) (Lambrecht's 1994 terms, slightly modified here), a difference that is discussed in more detail in Section 8.2.

Based on the diagrams of Figures 28 and 33, the V S-patterns seem to be similar in both languages. This is so, due to the difference in *granularity* between the V S-pattern and all other S-patterns. Granularity is discussed in the next section.

4.3 Granularity

Formal taxonomy does not always correspond to the basic level (Rosch 1978) functional categories that humans perceive. This is an effect of language being a species-specific embodied (Lakoff & Johnson 1999) mechanism.

The domestic dog *Canis lupus familiaris*, for example, is usually classified in zoological taxonomy as a variety (sub-species) within the species of the wolf, but the human eye is blind to its narrowly defined scientific designation. The dog is a basic level category, since it is such an important animal in human experience. Even its different breeds (sub-varieties) are visible to the average human beholder. Animals that have lesser relevance to human life, such as butterflies, rarely get classificatory attention, unless you happen to be a collector. Lizards are a sub-order, yet human beings rarely care to know their families, genera, and species. People might be puzzled by the difference between crocodiles and alligators, but nobody would mistake a Poodle for a German Shepherd. In such cases, we may talk about *granularity*, *grain size*, or *resolution*, terms that originate in the world of photography.

In a similar manner, it is suggested here that S-patterns operate at different resolutions in our experience as speakers. In some sense, the level of argument structure is the most salient level of categorization in the V S-pattern, since it captures situation types. Situation types are the basic level categories we are looking for in an explanatory taxonomy of sentential constructions. This is probably why the level of argument structure constructions *within* the V S-pattern has been identified first, and has consequently drawn much scholarly attention. The S-pattern level of the V S-pattern is a superordinate taxonomic level, which is functionally more abstract and less salient in human experience.

In the P1 S-patterns, on the other hand, the argument structure level – if such a level of analysis may at all be discerned – is too subliminal to serve as a relevant theoretical category. It does not capture situation types, but rather predicate-specific idiosyncracies (until proven otherwise). In the P1 S-patterns, it is the S-pattern that captures situation types, thus it is the basic level category in a taxonomy of sentential constructions. Furthermore, in the P1 S-patterns, the expression of situation types cuts across the categorial affiliation (parts of speech) of predicates, while in the V S-pattern, only verbs are involved.

What arises from the networks in the field of S-patterns is, therefore, taxonomically correct, but functionally deceptive. The V S-patterns of English and Hebrew look similar at the taxonomic level of S-patterns, but they differ greatly at the level of argument structure constructions (not discussed in this book).

The formulation of S-patterns in the present project offers, therefore, different moves in the various branches of the S1 and P1 networks. In the V S-pattern branch of the S1 network, the formulation of the S-pattern is a corrective addition to the theory of argument structure constructions, proposed due to the fact that argument structure constructions cannot encode linearized sentence forms. A comprehensive comparison of English and Hebrew argument structures (not pursued here) still awaits scholarship, and would be a welcome addition to our knowledge.

In the COP branch of the S1 network and in the P1 network, the S-patterns are what we as human beings conceptualize as basic level categories. Indeed, EX-sentences, EV-sentences, and ENV-sentences have traditionally been understood as constructions in linguistic literature, but they have not been systematically classified. The classification offered here gives this understanding a systematized theoretical home.

4.4 Summary and conclusion of Chapter 4

In this chapter, it has been suggested that S-patterns are organized in a field within the constructicon (Section 4.1). A partial representation of the field of major S-patterns is offered (Section 4.2). Major S-patterns fall into two networks: S1 and P1. The general design of the networks in the two languages is identical. At the level of S-patterns, there is no difference between the S1 networks of the two languages.

The P1 networks are different, though. English has only one sub-pattern in the whole system, whereas Hebrew has several. This is explained by the fact that many marginal situation types are encoded in Hebrew in the P1 S-patterns, while in English they are encoded in the unmarked V S-pattern. It stands to reason that other languages of the same typology will have yet other variants of pairing situation types with S-patterns.

Finally (Section 4.3), it has been suggested that what is conceptually most relevant to sentential encoding is situation types. Although the V S-patterns seem to be similar in English and Hebrew at the level of S-patterns, the relevant level at which situation types are visible is the argument structure level, not the S-pattern level. On the other hand, in the COP and P1 S-patterns, the salient level of analysis where situation types are visible is the S-pattern. This is, then, a difference in granularity.

The following three chapters will be devoted to the semantics of the predicates licensed in the three P1 S-patterns: the EX, EV, and ENV S-patterns.

CHAPTER 5

The conceptual category of existence

5.1 Preliminary discussion

Existential meaning is not one uniform category. It may be classified into groups of meaning, such as existence, presentation, introduction into the scene, movement, aspect, intrinsic property, etc. Such a classification, however, does not display any organizing principle. Rather, it is proposed here that the semantics of existence as expressed in the EX S-pattern is organized within a *conceptual category* (CC). The CC of predicates used in the EX S-pattern has an organizing principle: a prototype based categorization pattern.

Before embarking on the actual discussion of the semantics of the EX S-pattern, some preliminary issues need to be addressed. First to be discussed is the choice of level at which generalizations are made. Then, the status of *be* as an existential predicate will be revisited. Finally, the question of the distinction between existential and locative statements will be addressed.

As has been said in the Introduction (Section 1.11, and see also 4.3), choosing the level of generalization at which one wishes to elegantly capture commonalities of form and meaning has to be a conscious and well-informed decision. Now, if one takes certain formal features of the P1 constructions as distinctive, as does Melnik (2002: 95–96), for example, one ends up with five different sub-constructions of what I have been calling the EX S-pattern, namely (in Melnik's terms) VS_{agr}, VS_{nonagr}, VDS_{agr}, VDS_{nonagr}, and VOS (D stands for dative; those with D have possessive meaning; subscripted *agr* and *nonagr* stand for agreement and non-agreement between the predicate and the existent). While such a distinction between these technically separate syntactic sub-constructions is justified in Melnik's framework and for the purposes that she uses them, they share some important common properties of both form and meaning that justify keeping them all under the heading of the EX S-pattern. Hence, it is useful to treat the semantics of all these forms jointly. Internal divisions in the EX S-pattern (including also Milsark's 1979 division discussed previously in Section 3.2.1) atomize the wholeness of what is believed here to be usefully kept together for the semantic analysis of its predicates.

There are many ways to express existence. In the current study, however, it is not existence in general that is of concern, but existence as encoded in constructions specifically designated for it. This excludes other ways of expressing existence, especially those encoded in the V S-pattern, such as *God exists* or in the COP S-pattern, such as *Two books are on the table* (considered to be EX sentences by Kuno 1971: 333 and Breivik 1981). Here our object of analysis is the semantics of the CC of existence as manifest in the EX S-pattern. The fact that the range of predicates of this CC is coextensive with the range of predicates used in the Locative Inversion construction is plausible ("the same general type" Givón 1993: 208), but its verification has not been pursued in the current study.

Another issue that needs to be attended to, prior to the discussion of the semantics of the predicates, is the status of the verb *be* in EX sentences. Radford (1988: 434) calls the verb *be* in the sentence *there is a strike* "the existential predicate *be*". Viewing *be* as a lexical verb, however, has its problems. As a lexical verb, it should be capable of being a predicate, with independent meaning and with its own argument structure. Yet elsewhere in English grammar, the verb *be* functions as an auxiliary or as a copula, i.e. as a grammatical verb. This has resulted in McNally's (1998) suggestion that *there* and *be* jointly form a single predicate *there-be*. Through this supposed chunking, the verb *be* is semantically bolstered beyond its usual grammatical role, so as to appear lexical. Another candidate for the predicate role is the word *there* alone, as suggested by Moro (1997). The cycle of candidates is completed by Hazout (2004), who suggests viewing the existent as predicate, demoting the verb *be* back to a grammatical role as copula. This short survey shows that every slot of the EX S-pattern has been suggested by some linguist as its predicate position.

Despite the difficulty of viewing the verb *be* as predicate, this is the position that is adopted here. It is, in fact, not so unusual to find a word in both its grammatical and lexical functions. English itself does so with the verb *have* (on lexical versus grammatical *be* see also Benveniste [1960] 1971). In FrameNet, a similar view has been adopted: "some uses of *be* with a target noun do not bear the label COPULA. For example, when *be* occurs as part of the existential construction, it is tagged with the EXIST label" (Ruppenhofer, Ellsworth, Petruck, Johnson & Scheffczyk 2006: 32); in other words, it is the predicate of the EX S-pattern. While it is maintained in this chapter that *be* is a lexical existential verb, a modification of this view in terms of patterning rather than predication will be presented in Section 10.2.

For now, then, *be* is taken to be equivalent to other verbs that occupy a parallel role in this construction, and to the Hebrew predicate *yeš* that has always been unproblematically viewed in the literature on Hebrew syntax as a predicate, despite its morphologically unique form. As a predicate, then, the verb *be* has argument structure: its sole argument in English is the existent.

A second area of interest and a bone of contention has been the relation between existence and location. Some linguists draw a clear line between *bare* and *extended* EX sentences. A bare EX sentence "simply postulates the existence of some entity or entities" (Quirk, Greenbaum, Leech & Svartvik 1985: 1406), while Extended EX sentences "contain, in addition to *there*, *be*, and the displaced subject, an extension. [...] These elements are of relevance to the existential construction, being either complements or adjuncts" (Huddleston & Pullum 2002: 1393). These extensions can be divided into several groups: locative and temporal, predicative, infinitival, participial, and relative clause extensions (Huddleston & Pullum 2002: 1394–1396; see also Givón 1993: 207–208).

Among these, locatives have received the most attention. According to Lyons (1969: 389), "the 'existential' use of 'the verb *to be*' in English is not common except with a locative or temporal complement". Therefore, he argues, the existential construction is strongly related to the locative construction (Lyons 1969: 390). More strongly stated: "For prototypical existential sentences, namely, those that function as presuppositions of existence, the world as a whole is the Location" (Paducheva 2007: 2).

The opposite position is taken here: existence is viewed as the quintessence of existential meaning, location being added to it as "existence someplace". This is done selectively and discretely, i.e. while *be* draws the addressee's attention to the existence of an entity, a locative expression – when present – relates this existence to a location. Such a location, however, may also be available outside the sentence. This is the case of (1a), whose locational reading is supported in the preceding context by the expressions *on the island* and *there*. Conversely, the existence of a locative expression may be vacuous, used for other purposes than indicating location, as is the case in (1b), where the locative expression *in the world* does not add any locational information to the sentence, but rather is used to magnify the salience of the existent's *ontological* existence.

(1) a. There are few animals on the island. Not even rats live there [...] There are mice, but these did not arrive until [...] (I)
 b. I doubt if there is in the world a single problem, whether social, political, or economic, which would not find ready solution. (I)

Purely ontological statements are indeed relatively rare. Even when such sentences are pronounced, the concept in question is usually already there as an entity, as in (2a–c). Entirely new entities, though, may be proposed to exist by modifying the concept of an existing entity with a new or atypical attribute, as in (2d–e).

(2) a. There is a God.
 b. There is a Santa Claus.
 c. There are no boogeymen.
 d. There are yellow frogs.
 e. There are no spiders with seven legs.

Typically, though, the existent is an entity whose ontological status is not in question, in which case the EX sentence functions to "bring something into awareness" of the hearer (Bolinger 1977: 92–93), or to designate "a mental space in which a conceptual entity is to be located" (Lakoff 1987: 542). The spatial or temporal container of this speech act may be irrelevant, may be relevant but not stated, or may be salient and therefore stated.

The difference between the basic meaning of asserting existence and the pragmatic uses to which such a statement may be put have already been discussed in Section 3.2.1. One of these uses is the introduction of a referent into the discourse in order to use it as a topic in subsequent statements. This is, then, one of the *pragmatic* applications of the existential meaning, not an additional meaning.

It is appropriate to mention at this point Hatcher's (1956) taxonomy of P1 sentences in Spanish. It is the earliest, and probably the most detailed corpus-based account of the different meanings of verbs in the EX S-pattern in Spanish, a language that belongs to the type of languages discussed here. What Hatcher's study lacks is an organizing principle, which is hopefully supplied in the current study in the form of a CC.

In the following sections, a discussion will be offered of the semantic and pragmatic characterization of the predicates and predicate phrases (PredPs) licensed in the EX S-pattern.

5.2 Conceptual category

The term *conceptual category* as used in cognitive psychology originates in the research conducted by Rosch and her associates, e.g. Rosch & Mervis (1975). Its adoption into cognitive linguistics harks back to Lakoff (1987) and Brugman & Lakoff (1988). The concept is not problem-free. It raises the question of the division of labor between semantics and pragmatics, either as two distinct domains or as a continuum, as well as methodological questions of how to define multiply-related meanings (see discussions in Sandra 1998 and Tyler & Evans 2003).

Meaning variation within a CC is taken here to be expressible in a prototype-based radial category (Lakoff 1987: 91–117). In this view, the core of the CC is unmarked, while the periphery becomes progressively marked. The core might have a single member in it, e.g. the verb *be* in the EX S-pattern, or it may have a number of members, as will be the case with the predicates expressing modal evaluation in the EV S-pattern (discussed in the next chapter).

The relation between the core and the periphery is such that the specific and marked meanings of a predicate in the periphery are always at least partly expressible in terms of the meaning of a core predicate. Put differently, the unmarked meaning of a core predicate is always implied by the more specific, marked meaning of a peripheral predicate. Thus, the sentence *there came three people to my house* implies the meaning *there are three people in my house*, but provides also information on how the people got there. The verb *arrive* is, therefore, a peripheral predicate in the CC of existence.

The CC is organized not only semantically, but also pragmatically, displaying the continuity between the two domains. In the core and the closer periphery of the CC of existence, there are predicates that inherently belong to this CC, since they have a component of existence built into their own meaning. In the more distant periphery, there are predicates that are not inherently existential, but they acquire existential meaning pragmatically. This effect is sometimes achieved compositionally, i.e. by associating the predicate with elements that possess or imply existential meaning, e.g. the verb *burst* in the VP *burst into view*, culminating in existential meaning. The most radical pragmatic procedure of attaining existential meaning takes place when a non-existential predicate (or a non-existential PredP) is inserted in the EX S-pattern. In this case, the construction itself "imposes" (Goldberg 1995: 53) or "coerces" (Jackendoff 1997: 52) the existential meaning on the PredP, as is the case with the verb *wait*, in *there waited for me a bottle of wine*. Even in this distant periphery, the core meaning, namely *there was a bottle of wine*, is implied by the more specific meaning.

The CC of existence has a core and three rings of periphery. The core contains the verb *be* in English and *yeš* (with all its allomorphs) in Hebrew. The core meaning is unmarked (Lakoff 1987: 60–61), namely (a) it is non-specific, (b) it has a wide range of possible meanings, and (c) it has much freedom to combine with various entities whose existence is asserted. (These are Moravcsik & Wirth's 1986 three criteria of unmarkedness.) The first ring around the core contains predicates that are existential. Existence is one of the components of the semantics of these predicates. Since they contain additional semantic material in them, they are more specific in their meaning. For example, a predicate may contain a component of instantaneousness, as in the verb *occur*, or of duration, as in *prevail*, etc.

In the second ring, there are predicates that do not have a component of existence in them, yet they express the intrinsic state or prototypical behavior of the existent (Levin's 1993: 250 "verbs of entity-specific modes of being"), such as *hang* for a picture, *glimmer* for a light, or *ring* for a bell. In such cases, existential meaning is arrived at compositionally, as the predicate and the existent are positioned next to each other in the EX S-pattern. Naturally, the existential sense is also secured by the very use of the EX S-pattern itself.

In the third ring, there are predicates or PredPs that have no component of existence in them. Here the force of the S-pattern is crucial in effecting the existential meaning. A verb such as *wait*, for example, is not existential in its lexical semantic makeup, yet there is nothing wrong with *in the hotel room, there waited for them a bottle of wine*. This is so, only thanks to the power of the S-pattern – as a construction – to impose its meaning on the PredP *waited for them*.

The core and the three peripheral rings of the CC of existence will now be presented in a detailed and data-rich account. English will be discussed in Section 5.3, and Hebrew in 5.4.

5.3 Core and periphery of the conceptual category of existence in English

5.3.1 The core of the conceptual category of existence in English

The core of the CC of existence consists of one predicate only: the existential verb *be*. The meaning of *be* is unmarked in the sense that it is broad and relatively unrestricted. It may be used for concrete as well as abstract existents, as in (3a–b), for durational processes or instantaneous events, as in (3c–d), for entities with steady or fleeting existence, as in (3e–f), and so on.

(3) a. On my property there is a little house outback. (I)
    b. All of a sudden, there was silence in the room. (I)
    c. There was a storm outside. (I)
    d. There was an accident reported that night. (I)
    e. There is a tendency to move into cash. (I)
    f. There were ripples on the lake. (I)

Because of its broad polysemous nature, the core verb *be* may be implied, each time in a slightly different sense, by the more specific peripheral existential verbs. Hence, the occurrences of *be* in the sentences of (3) may be substituted by various more specific predicates, discussed in the next section.

5.3.2 The first ring of the conceptual category of existence in English

The first ring around the core is populated by predicates that are inherently existential in meaning, i.e. one of their meaning components indicates existence. There are, however, additional meaning components in them, which make them more specific in various ways.

The verb *exist*, for instance, indicates existence, but this existence is further characterized as being steady, hence the verb *exist* is compatible with NPs representing steady existents, whether concrete, such as *an island* in (4a) or abstract such as *a trend* in (4b).

(4) a. How I wish that somewhere there existed an island for those who are wise and of good will. (I)

Chapter 5. The conceptual category of existence 147

  b. In these days of ever-increasing technology, there exists a new trend that could cause serious problems for local businesses. (I)

Note the use of *exist* with *silence* in the attested example of (5a), where silence is a persistent attitude, compared to the unacceptable attempt to combine the two in a momentary situation in (5b).

(5) a. Where there existed silence about, or avoidance of, race and racial issues, African-American students expressed frustration and discomfort. (I)
  b. *For a moment, there existed silence in the room.

Existence may also be accompanied by some emphasis on the wide distribution of an existent phenomenon through the verb *prevail* (6a), on the existent being an event (as opposed to an entity) through the verb *occur* (6b), or on the holistically perceived nature of the event through the verb *happen* (6c).

(6) a. There prevails a fanciful opinion among a certain class of people, that [...]. (I)
  b. On 15th, at Wellington, there occurred a severe hail, rain, and thunder storm. (I)
  c. There happened a funny incident that day itself. (I)

The long duration of a state or a process may be expressed through verbs such as *continue, go on, remain,* and many others. The differences between them do not concern us here. What they share is a component of duration added to their existence. See the examples in (7).

(7) a. Yet there continue efforts to nail down a measurable deviant personality. (I)
  b. For a good while, there has been going on in this nation a process that I have termed the secularization of America. (I)
  c. However, there remained a critical shortage of trained lawyers in most parts of the country. (I)

Predicates of appearance, such as *appear, come, emerge, arise,* and many others, highlight the inchoative perspective of existence, as in (8a–b). The gradual nature of appearance may be expressed via the verb *develop*, as in (8c).

(8) a. Suddenly in the sky there appeared birds in large numbers. (I)
  b. In the 1990s, there emerged a scary new version called multi-drug resistant TB. (I)
  c. Through these early years there developed much unrest in the colonies. (I)

The verb *develop* belongs to a group of predicates that are polysemous, having an existential meaning among other non-existential meanings. In the non-existential sense, *develop* may be used to express the transition of an entity from one phase to another. In the S1 V sentence this may assume the form of (9a). This kind of meaning, however, may not be encoded in the EX S-pattern, as witnessed in (9b). Examples (9c–d) come to show that the definiteness of the existent is not the issue here. Rather, the unacceptability of both (9b) with the definite existent and (9d) with the indefinite one – vs. its felicitous counterpart, the S1 V sentence in (9c) – ensues from the fact that a child cannot "develop" in the sense of "coming gradually into being", yet this is the only sense that is sanctioned when the verb *develop* enters the EX S-pattern.

(9) a. During this time, the child develops very rapidly. (I)
 b. *During this time, there develops the child very rapidly.
 c. During this time, a child develops very rapidly.
 d. *During this time, there develops a child very rapidly.

As long as a polysemous verb contains some kind of existential meaning, the verb belongs to the first ring. In many cases, this can be tested in the S1 order, where the predicate should be open to an existential reading *in addition* to other readings. For example the verb *grow* is polysemous in a similar way to *develop*, hence the S1 V sentence may represent two meanings as in (10a–b). Because of the existential meaning of *grow* in (10b), it may be paraphrased in the EX S-pattern (10d), which is not the case for (10a), as evident in (10c).

(10) a. A pine tree will grow 0.5 meters each year. (I)
 b. A few years ago some petunias grew in my garden where none had grown before. (I)
 c. (i) *There will grow 0.5 meters each year a pine tree.
  (ii) *There will grow a pine tree 0.5 meters each year.
 d. A few years ago there grew some petunias in my garden where none had grown before.

The locative sense of arrival or appearance on the scene also belongs in the first ring. The verbs *come*, *arrive*, and *enter*, among many others, are exemplified in (11).

(11) a. Then there came two men well skilled in the handling of ships. (I)
 b. In the meanwhile at JB Hut, there arrived a kind Ozzie man, called Collin. (I)
 c. At this point there enters an element which occurs repeatedly in the history of cybernetics – the influence of mathematical logic. (I)

Chapter 5. The conceptual category of existence   149

The EX S-pattern is also open to phrasal verbs, which act as a single lexical unit. Such verbs may have different semantic compositions, and they are licensed in the first ring as long as they include existential meaning. See the use of *pop up, show up*, and *drive by* in (12).

(12) a. I continued to use my laptop and there popped up the warning from AVG. (I)
b. After developing the JVX system to this point, there showed up some interesting research topics. (I)
c. Hardly had he emerged when there drove by a motor in which, of all people, Lord Peebles was sitting. (I)

The predicate phrase may also contain direct and oblique objects, as in (13).

(13) a. For whatever reason there entered my head the image of a man in an upstairs room. (I)
b. And as I was sitting one day, there entered my apartment an old woman, (I)
c. And as this young woman weaved her way between deserted seats and TV commentary positions, there followed her a procession of journalists. (I)
d. There is constantly passing through the human brain a stream of impulses we call thoughts. (LOB F40 20)

What matters in the first ring is the fact that the *head* of the predicate phrase, namely the verb, contains existential meaning.

5.3.3 The second ring of the conceptual category of existence in English

In the second ring of the CC of existence, the predicate – whether alone or as the head of an entire predicate phrase – is not existential at all. What licenses the employment of such a predicate in this construction is the fact that existential meaning is arrived at compositionally. This may happen in two ways: either (a) the existential meaning is somehow supplied by the complement, or (b) it is supplied by the existent.

Let us look first at case (a). Verbs such as *burst, dance, limp*, or *drop* have no existential meaning, but when used in association with a path PP, in which the NP represents the target or the origin of motion, the added dimension of motion into or out of a real or metaphorical place gives it the meaning of appearance, i.e. existential meaning. These verbs with their path PPs are exemplified in (14).

(14) a. But suddenly, from around the point, there burst into view a steam yacht. (I)
b. There danced into my class one day a red-haired angel named Janie. (I)
c. Six months later there limped out of Chihuahua hospital a discharged patient. (I)
d. She drooped her flush face, lifting her handkerchief as a shield, when lo! there dropped from out its folds the little silken token he had left behind. (I)

The ability of the listener to construe these combinations as existential VPs arises not only from the compositional outcome of V + PP but crucially also from the meaning of the construction itself. The weaker the match between the meaning of the predicate and the meaning of the construction, the more pivotal the role of the construction in imposing its meaning on the predicate or predicate phrase.

Similarly, polysemous verbs that form existential collocations with certain NPs, such as the verb *hit* with the NPs *the news* or *the stands*, as in (15), belong here as well.

(15) There hit the stands a new journal. (Chomsky 1995: 343)

In Chomskyan literature, such sentences require special treatment: "It might be plausible that sentences such as [(15)] do not bear the 'subject of predication' feature in v in spite of their status as transitive sentences, which might in turn account for their marginality" (Tanaka 2002: 628). In the framework developed here, this sentence is only marginal in the sense that the collocation is not conventionalized in the P1 order. In the S1 order, however, it is highly conventional. A Google search of *there hit the news/the top ten list/the stands* yielded zero results, except for references to Chomsky's constructed (is it?) example, while its equivalent S1 forms (the same string without *there*) yields hundreds of thousands of results.

The verb *hit* alone does not have existential meaning, but within the above collocations it has the meaning of *arrive at/reach* which has an existential component in it, implying *there is a new journal*, namely the core meaning.

Case (b) involves the existent itself as motivating existential meaning. In such a case, the predicate expresses the intrinsic property of the existent (or one out of a small number of such properties). Pictures hang, statues stand, bells ring, lights glimmer, fires burn, rivers flow, cars drive or park, and so on. By expressing the *way* an entity exists, its *existence* is asserted (or in Erich Kästner's words "Was tut der Wind, wenn er nicht weht?" 'What does the wind do, when it doesn't blow?'). Some of these combinations are exemplified in (16).

(16) a. Out of the black shadows there glimmered little red circles of light. (I)
 b. Outside the gates of a house, there parked a silver BMW sports car. (I)
 c. On the wall there hung a poster of Charles Manson.
 d. Between two big cities, Buda and Pest, there flows a river, called the Donau. (I)
 e. And off in the distance there rang a bell. (I)

There is an interesting difference between the two cases of the second ring. Whereas group (a) involves transitive verbs, Group (b) does not allow transitive verbs, even if the whole action is intrinsic. So *spreading the wings* for a bird or *spinning the web* for a spider (attempted in 17a–b) would not pass as acceptable.

(17) a. *On the highest branch there spread its wings a huge vulture.
 b. *In the upper corner of the room, there spun its web a large black spider.

It seems, therefore, that objects are licensed in this construction only to the extent that they are necessary for the construal of existential meaning. The commonly held rule that in EX sentences "the verb must be intransitive (exceptions are idiomatic or dubious)" (Quirk, Greenbaum, Leech & Svartvik 1985: 1408) is not accurate. In fact, exceptions are well motivated when they enhance existential meaning.

5.3.4 The third ring of the conceptual category of existence in English

In the third ring of the conceptual category of existence, neither the predicate itself nor any other component of the sentence, such as the complement or the existent, bear any degree of existential meaning. In this case, it is the power of the construction alone that imposes existential reading on the sentence, provided that the context is supportive of such a reading. To the extent that the predicates have objects, it is not the verb alone but the whole PredP that is rendered existential.

Two types of predicate phrases typically appear in the third ring. In the first case, we find transitive verbs with direct or oblique objects, in which the event is interpreted, due to the existential meaning of the construction, as an entity-presentation event, as in (18a–b).

(18) a. As I logged in there was a knock on our front door. There greeted me a young man wanting to know if we would be interested in getting our parking area black topped... (I)
 b. Inside those unfeeling and uncaring walls I assumed that there waited for me the same type of medical treatment and psychiatric misinterpretations that I had consistently received for the past several years. (I)

c. Through an open doorway, well to one side so that he could not see into the room beyond, there struggled a curiously faint, dim glimmer of light. (I)
   d. There might be floating some cheap secondhand D2x around. (I)

The difference between encoding a proposition in the V S-pattern vs. the EX S-pattern is significant. If one says *a young man greeted me*, this V sentence is unmarked in terms of the function of the S-pattern. But if one says, as is the case in (18a), *there greeted me a young man*, the phrase *a young man* is presented as the existent of an existential proposition, hence its referent is markedly introduced into the narrative. The act of greeting is thus perceived ad hoc as an act of appearance on the scene. This is a pragmatic matter: the *front door*, mentioned in the preceding sentence, is a typical location of appearance, a pragmatic fact that enhances the existential understanding. In a similar way, the act of waiting in (18b) constitutes an ad hoc act of appearance. If you are about to enter a certain place, the things that exist inside are metaphorically "waiting" for you. Again, it is the pragmatics of the scene that helps the construction to coerce its meaning felicitously on the semantically non-existential PredP. In (18c–d) a similar process turns *struggle* and *float around* into ad hoc expressions of existence.

The second type of PredP typical in the third ring has a verb in the passive form, exemplified in (19).

(19) a. In addition there were caught for local consumption and shipment 8 tons of herrings, 5 tons of flounders, 2 tons of perch [...] (I)
   b. There were sold more tickets than the actual capacity and many managed to come in with false tickets or even without tickets. (I)
   c. Out of it all there has been extracted, not unnaturally, enough of fact and inference to sustain the suspicion among Germans that Great Britain seeks to balk the ambition of Germany. (I)
   d. Drink a cup of water in which there has been boiled a piece of white paper of Chinese origin. (I)
   e. He has the potential to sound pretentious and he's nervous about it – but there is wrapped up in this self-awareness the Catch-22, as they say, that if he knows he sounds a certain way, he probably isn't that way. (I)

In these sentences, we witness a "reversed transitivity", whereby the verb–object relation of the active sense of the verb becomes a verb–subject relation of the passive form, expressing an intrinsic property. Typically, fish make their appearance by *being caught* (19a) and tickets – by *being sold* (19b) in the same way that pictures *hang* and bells *ring* (see Section 5.3.2). But even less typical events, that in the V sentence would just be reports about the topical subject of the sentence, become encoded as statements of existence, when encoded as passives in the EX S-pattern. Thus, when it is said in the V S-pattern that certain facts and inferences were extracted out of a given database of knowledge, that is a regular report of an event, but when the verb appears in passive morphology in the EX S-pattern and the verb's complement is placed in the existent position, the action of *being extracted* constitutes the ad hoc way of existence of facts and inferences, as is the case in (19c). The last two sentences of (19) are less typical, since paper is not typically boiled (19d), and the existence of the complex notion expressed in the *that*-clause modifying *Catch-22* in (19e) shows up as being *wrapped up* in the self-awareness of *the potential to sound pretentious*. In these examples, the capability of the construction to impose ad hoc existential–presentational meaning is brought to light in its most forceful manner.

To sum up this point, under passive morphology, the reversal of the lexical transitivity between an action and the object entity affected (or effected) by it is similar to the nexus between a subject entity and its intrinsic mode of existence, as expressed by active intransitive verbs. The EX S-pattern facilitates such a construal. At other times, the relation between the verb and the passivized existent is lexically more opaque, in which case it crucially requires the constructional support of the EX S-pattern to produce the existential or presentational effect.

Despite the lack of reliable statistical data, it may be safely suggested that some of the expressions in the third ring are more conventionalized than others, hence they are more entrenched and collocational than others. *Fish* being *caught* must be more entrenched than *catch-22s* being *wrapped*. The same goes for the first group in this ring, namely, the co-occurrence of *man* with *greeting* at the door is probably much more conventionalized than *glimmers of light struggling* through a doorway. If this is so, perhaps some of these expressions should be promoted closer to the core, since the chunk as a whole is not understood compositionally. However, this suggestion would require rigorous quantitative corpus verification.

As an anticipatory remark to the discussion of the Hebrew data, it should be noted that English has less presentational options available than Hebrew. English may place the subject of an S1 V sentence in the final focus position through passivization. The transitive S1 V sentence in (20a) has an S1 passive alternation in (20b). In this case, the focal *by*-phrase is used as a presentational device. This practice is much more common than our attested example of the EX sentence in (20c), which has a more dramatic presentational effect. What English does *not* have is a pure word order alternation that post-poses the subject, such as is ungrammatically attempted in (20d).

(20) a. A young man greeted me, wanting to know...
 b. I was greeted by a young man wanting to know...

    c.   There greeted me a young man wanting to know...   (I)
    d.   *greeted me a young man wanting to know...

As will shortly become evident, the Hebrew counterpart of (20d) is not prohibited. In the next section, the Hebrew EX S-pattern will be presented.

5.4 Core and periphery of the conceptual category of existence in Hebrew

While the general design of the English CC of existence is well suited to account for the Hebrew data as well, some details nevertheless are different. These differences will come up as the discussion unfolds. One difference that has already been discussed in Section 3.3.1.2 is the fact that Hebrew expresses possession via existence. This is the primary way of expressing possession in Hebrew. This is radically different from the very few cases of such expressions in English, where the *to-* or *for-*phrase is merely an ad hoc affectee, interpretable as a possessor in marginal meanings of possession (Section 3.3.1.2).

The fact that in Hebrew possession is expressed via transitive existence (with an affectee-turned-possessor) does not mean that *every* predicate of existence has a transitive counterpart. Transitivity is primarily a lexical fact listed in the argument structure of the predicate. There is, however, a certain amount of variation in usage. For example, in my own speech as a native speaker of Hebrew, the adjective *kayam* 'exist.adj' does not allow a possessor. I was therefore quite surprised to hear on television the sentence in (21).

(21) *le-mišteret israel kayamot be'ayot kašot be-zihuy kley ha-nešek še-yaru.*
(Mabat – the news magazine on Channel One)
to the.police.of Israel exist problems difficult in the.identification.of the.tools.of the weapon that shot
'The Israeli police has serious problems identifying the weapons that have fired.'

A Google search of the string "*kayam l-i*" 'exist.adj to-me' yielded some 16,000 results. Judging by the first few dozens at the beginning of the Google list, many were indeed true hits of the target string. There obviously is variation among speakers in this respect. The range of usage of possessors across the core and periphery of the CC of existence in Hebrew is another topic that awaits future rigorous scholarship.

The core and the different peripheral rings of the CC of existence in Hebrew will now be presented in the following sub-sections.

5.4.1 The core of the conceptual category of existence in Hebrew

Yeš is the predicate of existence par excellence in Hebrew, and it is the only predicate at the core of the Hebrew CC of existence. Like *be* in English, it is the most unmarked form. By and large, whatever can be said in an EX sentence with *be* in English can be said in an EX sentence with *yeš* in Hebrew. As a reminder of the morphological variability of *yeš*, here are some examples (22) with its negative allomorph *en* and its future and past allomorphs using the verb *haya*.

(22) a. *yeš kvar tapuzim! toxli harbe ve-tavri'i maher.* (I)
 EXIST already oranges! eat many and get.well fast
 'Oranges have already hit the markets! Eat many of them and get well fast.'

 b. *im en te'avon, efšar latet manot ktanot le-itim krovot.* (I)
 if NOT.EXIST appetite, possible to.give portions small for times near
 'If loss of appetite is experienced, consider giving small portions at short interval.'

 c. *hayu ve-od yihyu harbe še'arim yafim yoter mi-šel ronaldinyo etmol.* (I)
 were and still will.be many goals nice more than of Ronaldinho yesterday
 'There were, and still will be, many nicer goals than the one by Ronaldinho yesterday.'

Before the rings around the core of the CC of existence are discussed, the issue of *stylistic inversion* of S1 sentences has to be addressed. This elaboration is needed at this point, since there is some overlap between genuine P1 sentences and S1 sentences exhibiting stylistic inversion. The topic of stylistic inversion will be discussed in the next section.

5.4.2 Stylistic inversion of S1 versus genuine P1 order

In the V S-pattern in Hebrew, which is an S1 S-pattern, there is a tendency in the higher registers of Hebrew to carry out inversion of the subject and the predicate following the initial placement of a non-subject component (object, adjunct, *wh*-elements, and certain particles) (see Kuzar's 1989: 77, 164, "register–style inversion" and Shlonsky's 1997: 144–148, "triggered inversion"). A similar kind of subject–predicate inversion also existed in Biblical and in Mishnaic (Post-Biblical) Hebrew (Bendavid 1958; 1971: 807–810), but the two differed from one another in detail, and they differ from their counterpart in Israeli Hebrew as well. Subject–predicate inversion in Hebrew resembles German Zweitstellung, except that in Israeli Hebrew, inversion is a stylistic option, not an obligatory rule. As such, sentences exhibiting subject–predicate inversion mark their text as belonging to the higher register, as opposed to spontaneous speech, in which such inversion is not common.

The problem is that under certain circumstances, a P1 sentence with an initial adjunct looks just like an S1 sentence with the same initial adjunct triggering stylistic inversion. The sentences of (23) instantiate this problem.

(23) a. *ha-talmidim lomdim et teoryat ha-cva'im šel gete b-a-šana ha-rišona.*
the students learn ACC the.theory.of the colors of Goethe in the year the first
'The students learn Goethe's color theory in the first year.'

b. *b-a-šana ha-rišona lomdim ha-talmidim et teoryat ha-cva'im šel gete.* (I)
in the year the first learn the students ACC the.theory.of the colors of Goethe
'Im ersten Jahr lernen die Schüler Goethes Farbentheorie.'
'In the first year, the students learn Goethe's color theory.'

In (23a), the sentence is a regular V sentence in its unmarked word order. In (23b), we have a variant of this sentence with the adjunct *b-a-šana ha-rišona* 'in the first year' occupying initial position. This adjunct triggers Subject–predicate inversion, as a result of which the adjunct is followed by the verb *lomdim* 'study', which in turn is followed by the subject *ha-talmidim* 'the students'.

Note that only the finite verb is fronted. In the event that the sentence contains a habitual verb complex, which consists of a finite auxiliary *haya* 'was' followed by a participle such as *lomed* 'studying' (24a), or if the verb complex has an infinitive-taking verb such as *hitxil* 'started' followed by the infinitive *lilmod* 'to study' (24b), only the finite verb takes part in the inversion, leaving the participial (24c) or infinitival (24d) forms in situ.

(24) a. *ha-talmidim hayu lomdim et teoryat ha-cva'im šel gete b-a-šana ha-rišona.*
the students were learning ACC the.theory.of the.colors of Goethe in the year the first

b. *ha-talmidim hitxilu lilmod et teoryat ha-cva'im šel gete b-a-šana ha-rišona.*
the students started to.learn ACC the.theory.of the.colors of Goethe in the year the first

c. *b-a-šana ha-rišona hayu ha-talmidim lomdim et teoryat ha-cva'im šel gete.*
in the year the first were the students learning ACC the.theory.of the.colors of Goethe

d. *b-a-šana ha-rišona hitxilu ha-talmidim lilmod et teoryat ha-cva'im šel gete.*
in the year the first started the students to.learn ACC the.theory.of the.colors of Goethe

In such cases, stylistic inversion differs from P1 order, since in the P1 order, usually the whole VP appears in initial position.

Stylistic inversion raises a problem of syntactic syncretism. If a one-word verb is used (rather than a composite verb complex), and if that verb could be interpreted as existential, and finally if the NP is indefinite (the latter is not a strict requirement), as in (25a), then it can be construed either as a P1 EX sentence that happens to have an initial adjunct, or as an S1 V sentence with the same initial adjunct triggering stylistic inversion. Due to this duality, the unmarked linearization of (25a) might be either the V sentence of (25b) or the EX sentence of (25c).

(25) a. *l-a-migraš higi'u šloša otobusim.*
to the yard arrived buses three
'At the parking lot three buses arrived.'

b. *šloša otobusim higi'u l-a-migraš.*
c. *higi'u l-a-migraš šloša otobusim.*

The question whether a sentence such as (25a) should be read as part of the storyline or as an existential interruption can only be solved in context. A possible test would be to try and speculate how the passage would be in colloquial Hebrew (where there is no stylistic inversion) and to see whether the verb in the sentence at hand still precedes the NP. If it does, then the sentence is a genuine P1 EX sentence. If it does not, it is an S1 V sentence with stylistic inversion. Many contexts, though, would tolerate both readings.

To avoid the need for such equivocal tests, the examples used in this section either lack an initial adjunct, or if they do have one, they will not be subject to this syncretism. In other words, they will have either an auxiliary verb immediately followed by the main verb, as in (26a), or an indefinite existent, as in (26b), or there will be an object (or adjunct) following the verb and preceding the existent, as in (26c). An equivalent stylistically inverted S1 sentence would have the object *follow* the subject.

(26) a. *mi-šne ha-cdadim šel ha-kviš hitxil lehistarex tur lo katan šel mexoniyot.* (I)
from two.of the sides of the road started to queue. a.line not small of cars.
'On both sides of the road a sizable line of cars started to queue up.'

b. *axre xaci ša'a higia eze texnay rusi.* (I)
after half.of an.hour arrived some technician Russian
'After half an hour some Russian technician arrived.'

c. *pit'om kafca al ha-masax šeli hoda'a.* (I)
suddenly jumped on the screen of.mine a.message
'Suddenly a message popped up on my screen.'

The syntactic syncretism presented above requires more research. It will, however, be briefly revisited in Section 5.4.5. Recall that the core of the CC of existence hosts the predicate *yeš* 'EXIST' alone. Since this predicate is endemic to the EX S-pattern, the syncretism discussed above does not apply to it (there is no S1 V sentence with the predicate *yeš*). We are now ready to move on to the discussion of the periphery of the CC of existence. In the next section, the first ring of the CC of existence in Hebrew is discussed.

5.4.3 The first ring of the conceptual category of existence in Hebrew

In Hebrew, as in English, the first ring around the core is populated by predicates which contain besides the existential meaning additional components of meaning, which make them more specific in various ways. Since the data in Hebrew are very similar to those in English, the discussion in Section 5.3.2 will not be repeated here. The predicates *kayam* 'exist.adj.', *kara* 'happen', *himšix* 'continue', *nišar* 'remain', *hofia* 'appear', *ba* 'come', *nocar* 'emerge', *ala* 'arise', *hitpateax* 'develop', and *camax* 'grow' are used as first-ring existential predicates, as shown in the sentences of (27).

(27) a. *kayamim tkanim le-ma'akot betixut.* (I)
exist.adj. standards for rails.of safety
'There are standards for safety rails.'

b. *kara ason. orli šuv zarka oti.* (I)
happened disaster. Orly again dumped me.
'A disaster happened. Orly dumped me again.'

c. *mamšixot aliyot ha-še'arim be-wol strit.* (I)
continue the.risings.of the rates in Wall Street
Wall Street rates continue to rise.'

d. *nišara še'ela axat xašuva.* (I)
remained question one important
'There remains one important question.'

e. *hofia ha-sefer "tarmila'im ve-samim".* (I)
appeared the book "Backpackers and Drugs"
'The book "Backpackers and Drugs" has appeared.'

f. *etmol ba le-israel šliax ha-kvartet toni bler.* (I)
yesterday came to Israel the.representative.of the Quartet Tony Blair
'Yesterday, the representative of the Quartet, Tony Blair, came to Israel.'

g. *lo nocra beyn-ehen šum situacia minit.* (I)
not was.created between them any situation sexual
'There has not arisen between them any sexual situation.'

h. *b-a-sixot alta ha-efšarut šel ha'avarat yicur le-hodu.* (I)
in the talks arose the possibility of transfer.of production to India
'In the talks, the possible relocation of production to India has come up.'

i. *hitpateax macav šel milxemet ezraxim.* (I)
developed a.situation of a.war.of citizens
'There developed a situation of civil war.'

j. *camxu šam hamon praxim yafim.* (I)
grew there a.lot.of flowers pretty
'A lot of pretty flowers have been growing there.'

As noted in Section 5.4 above, the adjective *kayam* 'exist' has also been found to appear transitively, in a possessive statement with a *le*-phrase as possessor. Some other predicates of (27) may also be used transitively, as shown in (28). The expression *kara l-i* 'happened to me' is frequent and conventionalized. The others are less entrenched.

(28) a. *kara l-i ason nora'i etmol.* (I)
happened to me a.disaster terrible yesterday
'A terrible disaster happened to me yesterday.'
or: 'I had a terrible disaster happen to me yesterday.'

b. *ad etmol nimšax l-i dimum še-halax ve-nexlaš.* (I)
till yesterday continued to me a.bleed that went and weakened
'Till yesterday I had bleeding that got progressively weaker.'

c. *nišara l-a-cibur rak brera axat. lehaxrim et bet hamišpat ha-elyon.* (I)
was.left to the public just choice one. to.boycott ACC the.house.of the-trial the.supreme
'The public has just one choice left. To boycott the supreme court.'

d. *hofia l-i eize hoda'a muzara be-daf ha-eksplorer.* (I)
appeared to me some message strange in the.page.of the Explorer
'I had a strange message appear on my Explorer page.'

e. *im banu mi-kofim, me-eifo ba lanu koax ha-dibur?* (I)
   if we.came from apes, from where came to us the.power.of the speech
   'If we have come from apes, where did we get our ability to speak from?'

The translations of these forms into possessive sentences in English ("have a choice left", "have a message appear") show to what extent transitive EX sentences with *le* 'to' are indeed possessive statements, akin to those with *yeš le-* 'EXIST to'. Yet from a conceptual perspective, they are all on one continuum within the category of existence.

5.4.4 The second ring of the conceptual category of existence in Hebrew

In Section 5.3.4, it has been said of the second ring of the CC of existence in English that the predicates in it are not existential; rather, existential meaning is arrived at compositionally, in conjunction with either a complement/adjunct (*danced into my classroom*) or in an intrinsic relation with the existent (*parked a silver BMW*). This is exactly the situation in Hebrew.

In (29), we have examples of the first group of non-existential verbs. The verbs *azav* 'leave' in (29a), *nafal* 'fall' in the first sentence of (29b), and *hegiax* 'surface' in the second sentence of (29b) are all verbs of motion which along with their complements, and aided by the constructional force of the EX S-pattern, acquire existential–presentational meaning.

(29) a. *be-1992 azvu et ha-ir ve-avru le-yišuvim axerim b-a-arec karov le-16,000 nefašot.* (I)
   in 1992 left ACC the city and moved to settlements other in the country close to 16,000 souls
   'In 1992 some 16,000 people left the city and settled in other places in the country.'

   b. *lefeta nafal mi-kis ha-mixnas šeli ha-mafteax šel ha-bayit šeli.*
   suddenly fell from the.pocket.of the.pants of.mine the key of the house of.mine
   'Suddenly, my house key fell out of my pocket.'
   be'od ani mošit et yadi mata litpos oto,
   as I am.reaching ACC my.hand down to.catch it
   'As I reach my hand out to catch it'
   hegiax me-ha-mayim ha-baxur še-kafac lefanay im ha-mafteax.
   surfaced from the water the guy that jumped before.me with the key
   'the guy who had jumped before me with the key popped out of the water.'

The second group of this ring consists of verbs that express the intrinsic behavior or the mode of being of an entity. Hebrew is very liberal in this use of the existential construction, allowing various typical behaviors and states of being to count as the intrinsic property. The semantic range covered by these verbs is much broader than in English. Furthermore, the use of verbs expressing intrinsic behavior is also common in Hebrew in the colloquial register, which is not the case in English. See examples in (30). They are parallel to the English examples of (16).

(30) a. *doleket kan nurat azhara.* (I)
         is.glowing here a.bulb.of warning
         'A warning light is on here.'

     b. *midey kayic ve-b-a-xagim xonot kan kirkarot ec yefeyfiyot.* (I)
         every summer and in the holidays park here carriages.of wood magnificent
         'Every summer and also on holidays, magnificent wooden carriages are parked here.'

     c. *yom exad camax b-a-gina perax.* (I)
         day one grew in the garden a.flower
         'One day there grew a flower in my garden.'

Additional examples are given in (31). They differ from the ones in (30) as they do not translate into the EX S-pattern in English, either because the action is not perceived as intrinsic enough in English, or because the VP contains objects or adjuncts, which are not tolerated in English. In (31a), for instance, the verb *xaraf* 'winter' represents one of the typical behaviors of migratory birds. Similarly, in (31c), "swimming in the gravy" is a metaphorical description of a typical environment in which patties and potatoes may be found. These properties are intrinsic enough for Hebrew, but not so for English.

(31) a. *be-ona zo xorfim b-a-ezor me'ot kormoranim gdolim.* (I)
         in season this winter.V in the area hundreds.of cormorants big
         'In this season, hundreds of large cormorants winter in this area.'

     b. *leaxar miken alta le-diyun haca'a le'afšer hacba'a be'emca'ut yipuy koax.* (I)
         after that came.up for discussion a.proposal to.enable voting through validation.of power
         'Afterwards a motion was filed to enable voting by power of attorney.'

     c. *ha-hacaga ha-gdola kan hi šel ha-rotev ha-madhim, xum, samix ve-ta'im be-teruf,*
         the show the big here is of the gravy the amazing, brown, thick and tasty in craze
         'The big show here is the amazing gravy – brown, thick and insanely tasty,'

> *še-be-toxo soxim le-hana'atam kcicot asisiyot ve-tapuxe adama šxumim*
> *ve-nimoxim.* (I)
> that in.it swim to their.enjoyment patties juicy and apples.of ground tan and mushy
> 'in which juicy patties and tan and mushy potatoes were swimming to their heart's content.'

Intrinsic predicates may be used also with a possessor affectee, as in (32).

> (32) *le-saba ve-savta šeli camxu b-a-gina amnon ve-tamar.* (I)
> to-grandpa and grandma of.mine grew in the garden Amnon and Tamar
> 'My granma and gradndpa had pansy violets growing in their garden.'

Sometimes the verb and the noun are based on the same root. Unlike the European languages, which find such usage esthetically defective (**to dig a digging, *to run a quick run*), Hebrew, along with some other Semitic languages, finds this kind of tautological alliteration pleasing to the ear. The EX S-pattern provides an opportunity to do this with passive verbs whose existent is an effected entity. The three examples in (33) are *niftax petax* 'there opened an opening', *nif'ar pa'ar* 'there gapped-up a gap', and *nisdak sedek* 'there cracked a crack'. The expression *niftax petax* 'there opened an opening' can be used both literally and in a metaphorical sense meaning "the ground was set", as is the case in (33a).

> (33) a. *im hitpatxut ha-sipur, niftax ha-petax le-sibux nosaf.* (I)
> with the-development.of the story, opened up the opening for a.complication additional
> 'As the story unfolded, the ground was set for an additional complication.'
>
> b. *me'az ha-bxirot nif'ar pa'ar mesuyam beyn de'otay le-de'ot ha-miflaga.* (I)
> since the-elections opened.up a.gap certain between my.opinions to the.opinions.of the party
> 'Since the elections, some gap opened up between my opinions and the party's.'
>
> c. *kax nisdak ha-sedek ha-rišon beyn tnu'at šas ve-ha-mitnaxalim.* (I)
> thus cracked the crack the first between the.movement.of Shas and the settlers
> 'This is how the first crack appeared between the Shas movement and the settlers.'

In a number of cases, Hebrew has stretched this practice to an interesting extreme. There are a few idioms in which a verb has been extracted out of the root of a noun for use in this construction only. This tautological expression conveys the intrinsic existence of that entity. The verb is uniquely endemic to the construction. This happens with the nouns *mazal* 'luck', for which the expression *hitmazel ha-mazal* 'lucked itself the luck' has been formed, and the noun *kec* 'end', for which the expression *hekic ha-kec* 'ended the end' serves the same purpose. See examples in (34). These verbs have no life outside these expressions.

(34) a. *lo, ze lo kal, ax hitmazel ha-mazal ve-pagašnu otxa.* (I)
no, this not easy, but lucked the luck and we.met you
'No, this isn't easy, but luck had it that we met you.'

b. *kax hekic hakec al ha-fašízem ha-italki.* (I)
Thus ended the end on the Fascism the Italian
'This is how there came an end to Italian Fascism.'

5.4.5 The third ring of the conceptual category of existence in Hebrew

In the third ring, as was the case in English, neither the predicate itself nor another entity, such as the complement or the existent, bear any of the forms of existential meaning. In this case, it is the power of the construction alone that imposes an existential reading on the sentence, given that the context is supportive of such a reading.

The same two types of predicate phrases that have been identified in English appear here as well. In the first case, there are transitive verbs with direct or oblique objects, in which the event is interpreted, due to the existential meaning of the construction, as an entity-presenting event. Sentences of this kind are much more common in Hebrew than in English. Given the right context, practically any agentive action may be encoded in the EX S-pattern, turning the action into a constitutive act of the existence of the entity. Examples are given in (35). To grasp the effect, imagine you could say in English **there made the movie Steven Spielberg*, with *the movie* already active in the context. The sentence introduces Spielberg into the discourse as the maker of that movie. To achieve the same presentational effect, English resorts to the passive variant of the V S-pattern, as is shown in the English translation of (35a).

(35) a. *lefi meitav zixroni asa et ha-seret stiven spilberg.* (I)
according.to the.best.of my.memory made ACC the movie Steven Spielberg
'If memory serves, the movie was made by Steven Spielberg.'

b. *ba-aceret zo hidliku masu'ot yeladim še-niclu bi-draxim šonot.* (I)
in rally this lighted beacons children who survived in ways different
'In this rally, beacons were lit by children who survived in various ways.'

c. *be-exad ha-xiyugim halalu ana li kol seksi.* (I)
in one.of the dialings those answered to.me a.voice sexy
'In one of those dialing attempts I was answered by a sexy voice.'

Since the EX S-pattern differs from the equivalent V S-pattern in Hebrew only in word order (no expletives being involved), there is, in fact, no visible difference between the marked VOS arrangement of the V sentence and the unmarked order of the equivalent EX sentence with verbs of the third ring (which are absolutely non-existential). Since in this ring the sentence only gets its existential meaning from the construction, we see, in fact, a kind of constructional syncretism between the marked VOS arrangement of the V S-pattern, as motivated by considerations of information structure, and the inherent function of the EX S-pattern.

In (35c) above, for example, the text relates the story of a bored soldier on an uneventful duty shift, making random phone calls. The NP *kol seksi* 'sexy voice' is the anchor for the rest of the story about the ensuing blind date with the owner of that sexy voice. This is clearly the pragmatic function of introducing an entity into the discourse, associated with the EX S-pattern.

Finally, the third ring of the EX S-pattern in Hebrew also hosts passive forms in reversed transitivity (Section 5.3.4), used in order to turn the spotlight onto the existence, occurrence, or appearance of an entity, as in (36).

(36) a. *ha-layla ne'ecra la-xakira be-veyta toševet netanya ke-vat 43.* (I)
the night was.arrested for interrogation in her.house a.resident.of Netanya like-aged 43
'Last night, a woman around the age of 43 from Netanya was taken from her home into custody for interrogation.'

b. *yugash ktav išum neged ha-mora me-rexovot.* (I)
will.be.submitted a.document.of indictment against the teacher from Rehovot
'Charges will be filed against the teacher from Rehovot.'

c. *niftera be'ayat ha-reyxot b-a-šxuna ha-ma'aravit be-dalya.* (I)
was.solved the.problem.of the smells in the neighborhood the western in Dalya
'The problem of bad air in the western neighborhood of Dalya has been solved.'

d. *be-misgeret zo šudregu ha-rexovot laxalutin ve-nislelu me-xadaš,*
in framework this were.upgraded the streets completely and were.paved from new
"In this framework, the streets were entirely upgraded and were newly paved.'

huxlefu kol ha-taštiyot, hucvu rihut rexov xadaš u-te'urat rexov,
were.changed all the infrastructures, were placed furniture.of street new and lighting.of street
'The whole infrastructure was replaced, new street furniture and street lights were put up,'
ništelu ecim, nislelu midraxot, ve-xuley.
were.planted trees, were.paved sidewalks, et cetera
'Trees were planted, sidewalks were paved, etc.'

The list of achievements bragged about in (36d) is formulated in the EX S-pattern, a practice which emphasizes the novelty of the appearance of all these innovations. This is not a narrative that tells a story about these entities as familiar topics, but rather one that constitutes them as novel or improved entities. English cannot do this in a designated construction, and has to resort to the S1 V S-pattern in the passive form.

These meanings can also be used in sentences that contain a *le* 'to' PP as an affectee-turned-possessor, as in (37).

(37) a. *ulay kaxa yibanu l-anu kan od kama proyektim.* (I)
perhaps thus will.be.built to us here more a.few projects
'This way perhaps we will have a few more projects built.'

b. *yipasel l-o harišayon.* (I)
will.be.canceled to him the license
'He will have his license revoked.'

c. *nifteru l-anu 80% me-ha-be'ayot.* (I)
were.solved for us 80% from the problems
'We've had 80% of our problems solved.'

Here, the English translations use the V S-pattern with the verb *be* accompanied by a passive participle, which is the way English combines possessive and passive forms to express a spontaneous (non-agentive) event having happened to a person, while keeping the person as subject.

Despite the differences discussed above, both the active and the passive predicates in the outer periphery of the CC of existence share similar semantic and pragmatic behavior: they are not existential in their semantic makeup, but they are given ad hoc existential meaning by the existential construction.

5.5 Summary and conclusion of Chapter 5

It has been shown in this chapter that the meanings that may be encoded in the EX S-pattern are organized in a prototype-based radial CC of existence. This CC has a core and three rings of periphery. The periphery is related to the core by implying it. Every predicate or PredP in the periphery implies an equivalent statement with the existential predicate *be* or *yeš*. The CC of existence has only one predicate at its core. This will not be the case with the CC of evaluation and the CC of environmental condition, to be discussed in the next two chapters.

The first ring hosts existential predicates more specific in meaning than the core predicate, but they all contain a major existential component in their semantics. The second ring contains predicates that are not existential, but the VP acquires existential meaning compositionally, either from the object inside the VP or by expressing the intrinsic way of being of the existent. The third ring contains predicate phrases that have no lexical existential meaning at all, but the existential meaning of the construction itself renders them existential or presentational in a context that is conducive to such a reading.

Since the criterion for inclusion in the CC is implicational, it is justified to include the Hebrew possessive sentence forms in the CC of existence and in the EX S-pattern. This is so, since there is a meaning continuity (and syntactic behavior that supports it) between the intransitive and transitive occurrences of *yeš* EXIST. The affectee-turned-possessor may always be omitted, thus producing the equivalent EX sentence that is implied by it. The sentence *yeš l-i be'ayot* EXIST to me problems 'I have problems' implies "there are problems", which is the meaning of the same sentence with the possessor phrase *li* 'to me' omitted.

Because of the gradual shift from lexical existential meaning at the core via compositional existential meaning at the close periphery all the way to ad hoc existential meaning imposed by the construction at the distant periphery, no lexical-semantic approach may fully capture the range of predicates and PredPs licensed in the EX S-pattern.

There is a difference, however, between being licensed and being conventionalized in the P1 order. The radial nature of the CC of existence also accounts for the conventionalized use of certain predicates in the EX S-pattern. The closer the predicate is to the core, the better is its chance to be routinely encoded in the EX S-pattern. The existential predicate *be* (the *lexical* verb *be*) in English is conventionalized in the P1 order, rendering its appearance in the S1 orders (*God is*; *the powers that be*) a highly marked option. It goes without saying that the Hebrew predicate *yeš*, which has been characterized as endemic to the EX S-pattern, appears only in this construction. *Yeš* does have a highly marked word order variant with the existent at the beginning (*memšala yeš, sarim en* 'a government there is, ministers there aren't'), but this word order cannot be viewed as an instance of any S1 S-pattern. Rather, it instantiates the marked existent-initial linearization of the EX S-pattern.

On the other hand, the peripheral verb *wait* is routinely encoded in the S1 order in the V S-pattern (*Mary waited for John*), while its use in the EX S-pattern

(*On the table, there waited for me a bottle of wine*) is highly marked and requires special pragmatic licensing conditions in the EX S-pattern.

A corpus based frequency count may reveal that certain predicates, or certain conventionalized expressions, should be moved up the hierarchy from peripheral to more central locations. Such expressions may prove closer to the core than expected in the present analysis, and may also turn out to be encoded more frequently in the P1 order. The sentences of (33) and (34) above, with cognate or tautological verbs, are good candidates for such a promotion. It is certainly obvious, even without corpus-based statistics, that sentences such as *hitmazel mazali* 'has lucked out my luck' appear almost exclusively in the P1 order.

The fact that the possessive sentence in Hebrew is a core existential sentence, merely using a transitive variant of the core predicate *yeš*, means that its primary encoding is in the P1 construction. It may also have marked word order variants, but again, these require specific discourse-pragmatic licensing conditions (for some details see Netz, & Kuzar 2011). The issue of the choice between S1 and P1 encoding will be further discussed in Chapter 8.

The CC of existence has been theorized based on the data of sentences in the EX S-pattern. Interestingly, however, it has broader validity than just for this S-pattern. The Locative Inversion (LI) S-pattern, which has not been discussed in this book, apparently has a similar scope of predicates as the EX S-pattern (see Nakajima 2001 for a taxonomy of LI predicates and comparison with EX predicates and Birner & Ward 1998: 187–194 for an information structure analysis). In other words, the two constructions share the same CC, different as they may be in other matters. Whether the overlap between the two constructions is total is still an open question. As a working hypothesis, it might be suggested that more similarity will be displayed near the core, and gradually growing variation will show up at the closer and more distant periphery.

A similar affinity may be established between the CC of existence and thetic sentences of the kind shown in (38). While in (38a) the word *car* appears in SMALL CAPS (in line with Lambrecht's practice to mark accent through small caps), the sentences of (38b–c) have regular CAPITALS, since they were spelled with capitals in the original attested form. These are rare cases, in which the speakers are aware of the prosodic prominence of the subject and express this awareness through capital letters.

(38) a. My CAR broke down (Lambrecht 1994: 14).
    b. A DISASTER is taking place and soon in Australia classical music will be almost non existent. (I)
    c. The end of the year is just around the corner and we thought A CHANGE is in order. (Email from department coordinator)

This construction does not have a name. In the spirit of the nomenclature used here, as in S1 and P1, it could be named the *accented subject initial* (AS1) construction. Clearly, there is no identity between the predicates of the CC of existence and the predicates of the AS1 construction. This is primarily a presentational construction, hence propositions with the core existential verb *be* may not be encoded in it. Lexically negative existential predicates, such as *break* are not licensed in the English EX S-pattern, but they are felicitous in the AS1 S-pattern, as can be clearly seen in (38a) above. The details of the relations between all these presentational and introductory constructions still await scholarship.

In the next chapter, the CC of evaluation is addressed.

CHAPTER 6

The conceptual category of evaluation

6.1 Preliminary discussion

The function of the EV S-pattern, as presented in 3.2.2, is repeated in (1) as a reminder.

(1) Through the use of the evaluative predicate, the EV S-pattern evaluates the evaluee. The evaluation is made relevant to an affectee, if present.

A frequent question during earlier oral presentations of this chapter has been: who needs a semantic characterization for this form? Why not just say that the predicates that are licensed in this construction select propositions (or events) in their argument structure, and that the evaluative meaning is epiphenomenal? In other words, evaluation is just what you would predicate on propositions and events. This challenge can be refuted by the analysis of the similarities and differences between the two sentences in (2).

(2) a. [Have a facial, pedicure, your hair colored, – they have a deal called "Day of Beauty."]
I think it will lift up your spirits to have some pampering! (I)
b. *I think it will lift up the panel to press the button.

The predicate *lift up* in the S1 V S-pattern is licensed to take many kinds of objects. If you *lift up your face*, no evaluative act is involved. The verb phrase becomes evaluative, when used in the EV S-pattern, provided that the context is supportive as well. the VP *lift up your spirits* gets its evaluative meaning compositionally from the verb *lift up* and the NP *spirits*, since it implies *be good for you*. As can be seen in the (attested) sentence of (2a), this sentence is indeed felicitously couched in its (attested) context. The event encoded in the InfP *to have some pampering* is evaluated as being *good for you*. In the case of (2b), however, *lift up the panel* does not have an evaluative meaning. It cannot mean *it is good/bad/recommended/worthy for you*, and this is the only reason that this sentence is uninterpretable, regardless of context.

A similar case would be a VP with the verb *make* in a resultative argument structure, as witnessed in the pair of sentences in (3).

(3) a. It makes them happy to do that sort of thing. (I)
    b. *It makes the smoke yellow to add sulfur to the mixture.

A VP with resultative *make* is licensed in this construction only if the whole VP may be construed as evaluative. The resultative adjectives *happy* and *yellow* are the elements that make the difference. The VP *makes them happy* implies *good for them*, whereas *makes the smoke yellow* does not have a similar implication. This shows that not the selectional properties of the predicate license an EV sentence but the semantic effect of its entire PredP.

Incidentally, predicates without evaluative meaning may acquire such a meaning in the course of diachronic change. The predicate in its new meaning is thus rendered fit to appear in the EV S-pattern. Colors, for example, do not usually occur as predicates of EV sentences, hence the constructed sentence of (4a) is unacceptable, but since *green* has acquired the meaning *beneficial to the environment*, implying it is *good*, it now has evaluative power, and the equivalent attested sentence of (4b) is felicitous.

(4) a. *It is yellow to abandon Middle East oil for coal liquification.
    b. Nobody will think it is green to abandon Middle East oil for coal liquification, even if it can be done competitively. (I)

A similar case involves the predicate *katan* 'small' in Hebrew. Haiim Rosén, who pioneered the identification of the Hebrew EV S-pattern in 1963, said (1977b: 221), in his discussion of evaluative predicates, that *katan* 'small' does not qualify as a predicate in this construction. Little did he know that *small* and *large* would develop evaluative meanings. Today, the phrase *katan al X* 'small on X' means "easy for X to handle", and *gadol al X* 'large on X' means "hard for X to handle". Since *easy/hard* are evaluative, so are the expressions that imply them. See the example in (5).

(5) *katan al-eha lehitra'ayen tox-kedey še-hi modedet bgadim.* (I)
    small on her to.be.interviewed amidst that she tries.on clothes
    'She can easily handle being interviewed while trying on clothes.'

To account for the semantics of evaluation as expressed in the EV S-pattern, it is suggested here that we view it as a conceptual category (CC), in the sense discussed earlier (Chapter 5) with regard to the CC of existence.

The CC of evaluation is, however, somewhat different from the CC of existence. The first difference concerns the nature of the core of this CC. In the EX S-pattern, the core has been shown to have a single existential predicate (*be* in English, *yeš* in Hebrew), whose unmarkedness represents a wide range of existential and presentational meanings. In the case of the EV S-pattern, no single predicate plays the same role. In the EX S-pattern, what constituted the first ring of periphery was inherently-existential predicates. In the case of the EV S-pattern, it is the core that consists of inherently-modal predicates. The core, then, is shared by a number of modal/evaluative predicates.

Modality has been extensively discussed in linguistic and philosophical literature, and the current study does not attempt to make a contribution to its further elaboration (see Nuyts 2005 for a state-of-the-art report on modality). For the sake of simplicity, the domain of modality has been divided here into four quite commonly accepted subcategories: deontic, attitudinal, evidential, and epistemic modality.

These modalities are very different from one another. They do not boil down to a single concept. This means that at the core of the EV S-pattern, there are a host of modal predicates, conveying four sets of meanings. The question arises, then: can we still maintain the claim that the relation between the core and the periphery is such that the meaning of a peripheral predicate or PredP implies the meaning of the core?

Granted the multiplicity of meanings in the core, the relation between core and periphery follows the same principle of implication, mutatis mutandis, as in the CC of existence. A predicate or PredP is peripheral to the CC of evaluation if its meaning implies the meaning of *one* of the core predicates. Hence, the PredP *lift up your spirits* does count as a peripheral member of the CC of evaluation, since its meaning implies *good for you*, with *good* being a core attitudinal predicate of this CC.

The EV S-pattern has been shown to have sub-patterns. These sub-patterns have been described above, but the full justification for considering them as separate patterns, rather than peripheral meanings of the EV S-patterns, has not been fully elaborated. Now the criterion should be clear: even though the sub-patterns may have a meaning that could express some attitude, its predicates may not imply modal meaning of the core of the CC of evaluation.

For example, the VP of the Cost S-pattern cannot be replaced by a modal predicate. The VP of (6a) does not imply any of the meanings of (6b).

(6) a. It often takes me three hours to write a letter.
    b. It is often good/bad/recommended/obvious for/to me to write a letter.
    c. The writing of a letter often takes me three hours.

The Cost S-pattern has a separate function that is only loosely connected to the function of the EV S-pattern, namely that the announcement of the cost of something usually also involves an evaluation of that cost. Without the evaluative edge, the same proposition is often encoded in the S1 V S-pattern, as shown in (6c).

Similarly, the VP *koev l-i* 'hurts to me' in the Body-part-condition sentence of (7) does not boil down to some evaluative meaning such as *my head is good* or *necessary*, although the whole situation *is* evaluated as a sorry state.

(7) *ko'ev li ha-roš.*
    hurts to me the head
    'My head hurts.'

In both cases the separate constructions, the Cost and the Body-part-condition S-patterns, are related to the EV S-pattern as daughter constructions (sub-patterns), but their predicates or PredPs may not be viewed as being in the periphery of the CC of evaluation.

In the rest of this chapter, the core and periphery of the CC of evaluation will be presented in detail, first in English, then in Hebrew.

6.2 Core and periphery of the conceptual category of evaluation in English

6.2.1 The core of the conceptual category of evaluation in English

The core of the CC of evaluation contains inherently-modal predicates of the deontic, attitudinal, evidential, and epistemic kind. Some of these verbs are presented in the following passages in these four groups of modality.

Through deontic modality, the speaker commits himself (or another participant of the event) to different degrees and kinds of permission or obligation towards the event encoded in the evaluee. Predicates such as *necessary*, *forbidden*, and some senses of *possible*, instantiate deontic modality, as in (8).

(8) a. First it is necessary to stand on your own two feet. (I)
    b. In France, it is forbidden to call a pig Napoleon. (I)
    c. It is possible to survive without coffee. (I)

Through attitudinal modality, the speaker expresses his (or some other participant's) attitude towards the event encoded in the evaluee. In (9), the predicates *fun*, *disgusting*, and *annoying* exemplify attitudinal modality.

(9) a. It is fun riding home with a lot of your friends. (I)
    b. It is disgusting that people waste food this way. (I)
    c. It is annoying to click a thread and have it take forever to load. (I)

Nuyts (2005: 12) mentions this modality (also known as boulomaic modality) under the heading of "categories on the margins of modality" and says:

Why this category has not been systematically analyzed in the work on modal notions is unclear. Maybe it is because this meaning is hardly present in the system of modal auxiliaries in the West European languages, which has strongly dominated the analysis of modality.

Indeed, modality deserves to be analyzed at levels other than individual modal verb behavior, in our case, at the level of sentential syntax. Once modality is viewed from the point of view of sentential constructions, English as well as Hebrew turn out to plentifully encode attitudinal modality, most prominently in the EV S-pattern.

The third type of modality is evidential modality. Through evidential modality, the speaker provides evidence for the event (or the statement) encoded in the evaluee. Such evidence is often the source of the statement. Predicates such as *be rumored*, *evident*, and *be decided* represent evidential modality, as in (10).

(10) a. It has been rumored that Ford will discontinue the Taurus X. (I)
    b. From this experiment it is evident that ice by friction is converted into water. (I)
    c. Then it was decided to also spray on a few coats of clear lacquer. (I)

Nuyts (2005: 10) refers to this kind of modality as marginal as well. "The category of evidentiality has traditionally been defined to cover only grammatical expressions of these meanings. English has hardly any such forms". Nuyts then discusses the auxiliary *must* as "a possible, though not uncontroversial exception". But again, from a constructional perspective, the inclusion of this modal meaning in the EV S-pattern, especially in reportative sentences (*reportative* being a subcategory of *evidential* Nuyts 2005: 10), makes English and Hebrew a central locus of syntactic (hence grammatical) encoding of this modality.

Fourth comes epistemic modality. Through epistemic modality, the speaker evaluates his or her certainty about the reality of the event or the truth condition of the statement encoded in the evaluee. The predicates *the case*, *true*, and *certain* represent epistemic modality in (11).

(11) a. It is not the case that simple clear questions have simple clear answers. (I)
    b. It is true that tacit knowledge is very difficult to tame. (I)
    c. It is certain that climate science has enormous room for improvement. (I)

In the working definitions of the types of modality given above, deontic and attitudinal modality have been associated with the *event* encoded in the evaluee, while evidential and epistemic modalities have been related to either the *event* or the *statement* encoded in the evaluee (see Palmer 2001 on *event* and *propositional* modalities). This distinction, which requires further exploration, seems often to be blurred in actual discourse. For example, (10a) would not be used merely to assert that the *statement* in the evaluee *that*-clause is a rumor, but more forcefully also to render the *event* newsworthy, albeit with some reservation about its source.

Naturally, the diversity of predicates at the core is not adequately represented by the three examples given above for each kind. There are dozens, if not hundreds, of such predicates. Furthermore, to enhance clear presentation, all the examples above have been single-word bare predicates. But the same predicates may also serve as heads of phrases (PredPs). Instead of *it is fun* we may have *it is a lot of fun*, instead of *it is true* we may find *it is so painfully true*, etc. What counts for inclusion in the *core* of the CC of evaluation is the presence of a clear modal meaning in the predicate itself, be it bare or the head of a PredP.

Since the core of the CC of evaluation does not have a single prototypical predicate in it, it is similar to the first ring of the CC of existence, rather than to its core, as it accommodates a variety of meanings. Consequently, the number of rings around the core amounts to only two rings, compared to the three rings of the CC of existence.

6.2.2 The first ring of the conceptual category of evaluation in English

Around the core of inherently-evaluative predicates, we find the first ring, which hosts PredPs whose head is not evaluative, yet the PredP as a whole gets its evaluative meaning compositionally from a modifier or a complement of the predicate. The nouns *thing*, *matter*, or *idea*, for example, do not by themselves have any modal force, and they cannot be bare predicates in an EV sentence. What make the whole NP around these nouns modal is the modifier of the head noun, namely the adjectives *bad*, *great*, or the PP *of routine* (in this case they are all attitudinal), as shown in (12).

(12) a. It's a bad idea to threaten bloggers. (I)
      b. It is not a great thing to work for weapons companies. (I)
      c. It is a matter of routine that one empties his or her pockets of all metal before going through a metal detector. (I)

VPs Also exhibit similar behavior. For example, the verb *make* in itself has no evaluative power, but when combined with resultative adjectives such as *sad, happy, angry*, etc., these VPs are rendered evaluative, as shown in (13).

(13) a. It really makes me sad to think of people acting this way. (I)
      b. It makes them happy to do that sort of thing. (I)
      c. Has it made some people angry that I've done some things differently? (I)

The examples above, which have all been of the attitudinal type, may leave the impression that PredPs whose meaning is compositionally construed are specific to one type of modality, but they are not. To complete the picture, the set of examples in (14) below has sentences with deontic (14a), evidential (14b), and epistemic (14c) modalities:

(14) a. It is a necessary thing to acquire at least one of the books relating to this approach. (I)
b. It has been brought to my attention that ear muffs are not cool. (I)
c. It strikes me as untrue that the media has been slack on climate change. (I)

The predicates alone – *thing*, *be brought* and *strike* – are not inherently-modal, yet compositionally *a necessary thing* has deontic force, *be brought to X's attention* provides the evidence for the subsequent statement, and *strike X as untrue* carries epistemic force. Here too, the modifiers endow the PredP with modal force, while the heads themselves are not modal.

The fact that the predicate itself, namely the head of the PredP, is not in itself modal, poses a challenge to a strictly lexical approach to the licensing conditions for predicates in the EV S-pattern.

6.2.3 The second ring of the conceptual category of evaluation in English

Keeping a comparative eye on the parallel CC of existence, we should expect the second ring of the CC of evaluation to be similar to the third ring of the CC of existence, namely to be populated by PredPs whose components have no inherent evaluative meaning, but thanks to the evaluative force of the construction, the evaluative meaning is imposed on them.

In some cases, none of the components carry evaluative meaning, but the whole phrase is conventionalized as an evaluative idiom. Formally, these cases may belong here, but if idioms are viewed holistically as complex lexical entries, these examples may need to be promoted closer to the core. One idiomatic group involves chunked PPs, such as *out of the question*, *at one's discretion*, and *on the agenda*, as in (15).

(15) a. It is out of the question to remain here if war breaks out. (I)
b. It is at your discretion to negotiate the payment. (I)
c. It is on our agenda to launch a future contract on carbon emissions. (I)

A second group of idiomatic predicate expressions in this ring consists of VPs in which neither the verb alone nor its complement/adjunct alone have any evaluative meaning, thus the VP is not understood compositionally as evaluative. For example, in (16a), neither the verb *go* nor the adjunct *without saying* have any literal evaluative sense. Together, though, the meaning of the idiomatic expression *goes without saying* amounts to *is obvious*, a clearly evaluative sense. The same goes for idiomatic VPs such as *leave one speechless, curdle one's blood*, and all other VPs in (16).

(16) a. It goes without saying that preparation is the key to any negotiation. (I)
 b. It leaves me speechless to think that this can be true. (I)
 c. It curdles my blood to think that there are women willing to live this way. (I)
 d. It moves me that you can tackle these obstacles with the stress you're under. (I)
 e. It weighs on me that I'm not doing more about this massacre besides marching and donating to antiwar organizations. (I)
 f. If it is not in the cards to give a gift on that day, a congratulatory phone call is expected. (I)
 g. It made my day to see this on the cover. (I)
 h. It drives her crazy that I tell people she's actually older than I am. (I)
 i. It fries our brains to think about getting that into a short paragraph. (I)
 j. It soothed my ego to see him go out of his way to connect with me. (I)
 k. It will open the gates of hell to let you out. (I)
 l. It kindles my interest to learn from one whose life exuded spiritual reality. (I)

These idiom VPs may be used also in S1 sentences in the same evaluative sense, (e.g. *your behavior left me speechless*), a point which proves that it is not the construction that gives the expression its evaluative force, but rather the expression itself. One example that is clearly different is given in (17).

(17) It stands to reason that pregnancy hormones may be responsible, at least in part, in causing your pregnancy headaches. (I)

The VP *stand to reason* is also an idiomatic expression, but unlike the example above, it is not used in the V S-pattern (the BNC has thirty occurrences of this idiom, all in the EV S-pattern, none in the V S-pattern). There are, then, idiomatic VPs that are endemic to the EV S-pattern. In this case, then, it is plausible that the consolidation of this expression as evaluative has been boosted by the force of the evaluative meaning of the construction. Only systematic quantitative usage-based research will reveal to what extent the existence of a second ring in the CC of evaluation is supported by more data.

This concludes the discussion of the CC of evaluation in English. The next section will be devoted to showing that the CC of evaluation in Hebrew is identical to that of English, a fact which enhances the cross-linguistic validity of this CC and the general cognitive basis for the emergence of an evaluative sentential construction which in this typological group is encoded as a P1 S-pattern.

6.3 Core and periphery of the conceptual category of evaluation in Hebrew

6.3.1 The core of the conceptual category of evaluation in Hebrew

In Hebrew, as in English, the core of the CC of evaluation hosts numerous predicates. Some of them are the unique endemic predicates discussed in Section 6.3.1, but they are only a fraction of the whole set. A predicate in the core of this CC passes the test of membership if it has clear modal meaning in one of the four types of modality discussed in 6.2.

Where things are very similar to English, as is the case at the core, the discussion of the Hebrew examples will be more parsimonious. Accordingly, the four types of modality – deontic, attitudinal, evidential, and epistemic – are respectively instantiated by the four sentences of (18).

(18) a. *carix leha'avir et ha-pacua le-maxleket ha-trauma.* (I)
    necessary to.transfer the wounded to the.department.of trauma.
    'The wounded man has to be transferred to the trauma ward.'

   b. *xaval še-ha-saxkanim ha-ce'irim lo mekablim dakot.* (I)
    too.bad that the players the young not get minutes.
    'It's too bad that the young players don't get some minutes of play time.'

   c. *huxlat le'ašer et ha-toxnit.* (I)
    was.decided to ratify ACC the plan.
    'It was decided to ratify the plan.'

   d. *naxon še-ha-menacxim zaxu be-prasim yafim.* (I)
    true that the winners won in prizes nice.
    'It is true that the winners won nice prizes.'

The meanings of the predicates of these sentences, and many other variants of these meanings in the four types of modality, are the core meanings that are implied in the meanings of predicates farther away from the core.

6.3.2 The first ring of the conceptual category of evaluation in Hebrew

The first ring around the core of the CC of evaluation is populated by predicate phrases whose head is not evaluative, but the predicate phrase as a whole gets its meaning compositionally from a modifier or a complement of the predicate. The sentence in (19) has an NP with the non-evaluative head noun *ra'ayon* 'idea' accompanied by the attributive adjective *mavrik* 'brilliant'.

(19) *ra'ayon mavrik la'asot xulcot k-a-ele.* (I)
idea brilliant to.make shirts like.the.these
'It is a brilliant idea to make such shirts.'

It is the attribute *mavrik* 'brilliant', rather than the head noun *ra'ayon* 'idea', that renders the whole PredP evaluative. In this case, the PredP holistically conveys attitudinal modality.

The same goes for VPs. The sentence in (20) instantiates evidential modality. It has a VP whose head verb *ala* 'arise' is not evaluative, but the PP complement *me-ha-xakira* 'from the interrogation' reveals the source of the information conveyed in the *that*-clause. In this case, the VP holistically conveys evidential modality.

(20) a. *od ole me-ha-xakira ki b-a-monit yašvu šnei nos'im me'al ha-mutar.* (I)
further arises from the interrogation that in the cab sat two passengers above the allowed.
'It further arises from the interrogation that the cab had two passengers beyond the permitted limit.'

Similar to the parallel discussion in English, here too, the encoding of evaluative meaning in the modifier rather than the head of the PredP poses a challenge to a purely lexicalist attempt to characterize the licensing conditions of predicates in the EV S-pattern.

6.3.3 The second ring of the conceptual category of evaluation in Hebrew

If Hebrew follows the pattern of English, then the second ring should have PredPs whose components have no inherent evaluative meaning, but thanks to the evaluative force of the construction, the evaluative meaning is imposed on them. Here, as was the case in English, the examples are not one-time combinations, but rather idiomatic chunks whose evaluative meaning inheres in them holistically, as in (21).

(21) a. *kana oti še-lo hitnapalta alay.* (Interviewee to interviewer, on the radio)
bought me that not you.attacked on.me.
'You won me over by not attacking me.'

b. *mevi l-i et ha-se'if še-hu xotex li šurot lif'amim.* (I)
brings to me ACC the clause that it [=my mailer] cuts me lines sometimes
'It drives me crazy that my mailer sometimes cuts lines on me.'

The verb *kana* 'buy' in (21a), accompanied by a direct object with a human referent means inter alia "win over", hence *kana oti* literally means "bought me", but idiomatically says "won me over", implying the attitudinal core meaning "pleased me". The expression *mevi l-i et ha-se'if* 'brings to me the clause' is shorthand for "activates in me the psychological condition cited in clause so-and-so of my medical record", in other words "drives me crazy". These expressions may also be used in S1 sentences, and they still have the same evaluative meaning. No genuine examples of ad hoc combinations have been found where only the force of the construction renders the PredP evaluative.

6.4 Summary and conclusion of Chapter 6

This chapter has been devoted to the CC of evaluation. The CC of evaluation, like the CC of existence in the preceding chapter, is a prototype-based radial category, which licenses predicates and PredPs to appear in the EV S-pattern. This CC has a core and at least one ring of periphery around it, perhaps even two. The periphery is related to the core by the fact that the meaning of a peripheral predicate or PredP implies a core meaning. In the CC of evaluation, unlike the CC of existence, there are multiple meanings at the core in four types of modality. The peripheral predicate or PredP implies *one* of the modal meanings of the core.

In the CC of evaluation, there are fewer rings than in the CC of existence. The core of the CC of evaluation, containing the inherently-evaluative predicates, is equivalent to the first ring in the CC of existence, which accommodates the inherently-existential predicates. The first ring of the CC of evaluation, then, is equivalent to the second ring in the CC of existence, containing predicates that are not evaluative, but the PredP acquires evaluative meaning compositionally, from a modifier inside the PredP. For example, the noun *idea* is modified by *bad*, to form the PredP *a bad idea*.

The second ring has conventionalized expressions, such as *goes without saying* which is construed as meaning *obvious*, i.e. it implies a modal core meaning. Unlike the expressions in the CC of existence, here some expressions, such as *stands to reason* are not in use in the S1 word order. It would make sense then to consider the force of the construction as a factor in their conventionalization as such.

The existence of expressions of the kind *AP idea* or *makes one AP/NP* renders a purely lexical approach to licensing the predicates of the CC of evaluation very problematic. Not only are the slots around the head N or V above open to a vast number of modifiers, but also the *hosting* expressions are multiple. Other shell nouns besides *idea* may be used, such as *thought, thinking, thing, matter, tendency, trend*, etc. A simple enumeration of such expressions would be inelegant, if not impossible. The prototype based licensing mechanism suggested here is lexical–semantic near the core, but requires pragmatic considerations at the outer periphery. Expressions have to amount to an evaluative construal, or else they fail to be felicitous.

Besides licensing, there is also the question of preferred encoding in S1 or P1 S-patterns. Clearly, Hebrew has some predicates that are endemic to the EV S-pattern. But many others, such as *tov* 'good', *madhim* 'amazing', *me'anyen* 'interesting', appear both in S1 and in P1 S-patterns. In English, the division of labor is more straightforward: when the evaluee is a noun, it can only be encoded in the S1 S-pattern (*The book is good* versus the ungrammaticality of **it's good the book*), while in the case of an evaluee in the form of a nominal, the P1 order is unmarked (*it's good to see you*), whereas the S1 order (*to see you is good*) is highly marked, requiring special pragmatic licensing conditions.

In Hebrew there is a real choice, since evaluative sentences may have NPs – in addition to nominals – in the role of evaluee (discussed in Section 3.3.3). Yet some predicates tend to get encoded in a P1 construction more than in an S1 construction. Even without frequency data, *daruš* 'needed', for example, can be safely classified as being encoded both in the EV S-pattern (*daruš moxer* 'needed a salesperson') and in the S1 order (*hasefer daruš l-i l-a-avoda* 'The book is needed by me for work'. A frequency count may reveal which of the two is more habitual, and whether the meanings are different or nuanced, when in the S1 or P1 order.

Some aspects of these issues will be further discussed in Chapter 8. Others will have to wait for a quantitative corpus-based study, comparing the distribution of these (and similar) predicates in S1 vs. P1 constructions.

CHAPTER 7

The conceptual category of environmental conditions

7.1 Preliminary discussion

The CC of environmental conditions has the same basic structure as the other aforementioned CCs. Here too, one may not assume only lexical licensing conditions for all the predicates populating the ENV S-pattern. While the core hosts predicates that have a clear lexical–semantic profile, namely indicating environmental conditions, the environmental meaning in the periphery can only be accounted for compositionally or pragmatically.

The three semantic domains covered by environmental predicates are weather, time, and ecological well-being. Each domain is correlated with only one or two parts of speech. Weather predicates are verbs and adjectives (*rain, cloudy*), time predicates are nouns (*evening, Sunday*), and ecological predicates are adjectives (*crowded, dark*).

Since there is no difference between the behavior of English and Hebrew predicates of environmental conditions, and since the data are fewer, the two will not be treated in separate sections, as has been the case with the CCs of existence and evaluation, but together in each of the following sections.

7.2 The core of the conceptual category of environmental conditions

The core of the CC of environmental conditions consists of predicates that inherently convey environmental conditions. The environment may be defined as what the speaker experiences as "the world", or it may be a more limited space, explicitly stated by the speaker or just implied. The English examples are in (1), the Hebrew ones in (2).

(1) a. It was snowing all across the country. (I)
    b. In the afternoon it got cloudy. (I)
    c. If it's Tuesday, this must be Belgium. (Title of a film)
    d. Brrr. It's winter, alright. (I)
    e. I have seen two reviews saying it is crowded at Fihalhohi. (I)

(2) a. *gešem yarad bemešex kol ha-layla, ax b-a-boker hitbaher.* (I)
rain descended during all the night, but in the morning cleared.up
'Rain was pouring all night, but in the morning it cleared up.'

b. *haya nora xam. hu hizia betox xulcat ha-diyolen šelo.* (I)
was terribly hot. he sweated inside the.shirt.of the Diolen of.his
'It was terribly hot. He sweated inside his Polyester shirt.'

c. *mazal še-kayic ve-ani yexola livroax haxuca midey pa'am.* (I)
lucky that summer and I can to.escape outside every once
'Luckily it's summer and I can sneak outside once in a while.'

In the English translation of (2a), the pronoun *it* may be understood as a regular pronoun, but it should in fact be read as an expletive. In other words, *hitbaher* 'cleared up' should not be construed as referring to *gešem* 'rain', since in Hebrew rain does not "clear up". The predicates of the core do not pose any problem to a purely lexicalist view.

7.3 The first ring of the conceptual category of environmental conditions

In the first ring of the periphery, the head of the predicate phrase is not environmental, but it is accompanied by a complement that is an environmental term. These are mostly partitive or quantifying head words, such as *middle of*, *sof* 'end of', *me'al* 'over', whose complements are the semantic nucleus of the expression, e.g. *summer*, *aviv* 'spring' etc., as in (3) and (4).

(3) a. It was the middle of the summer here and the heat was unbearable. (I)
b. It is the first of May today, a national holiday in France. (I)
c. It's on the verge of snowing again outside right now. (I)
d. It's like 16 degrees without the wind chill factor. (I)

(4) a. *kvar sof ha-aviv ve-rak etmol haya šarav.* (I)
already end.of the spring and only yesterday was a.heat.wave
'It is already the end of spring and just yesterday there was a heat wave.'

b. *me'al arba'im ma'alot. hexlatnu lehistovev be-makom im mazgan.* (I)
above forty degrees. we.decided to.walk.around in a.place with an.airconditioner
'It's above forty degrees. We decided to walk around in an airconditioned place.'

These PredPs present a challenge to a lexicalist taxonomy of predicates in the ENV S-pattern. However, since partitive and quantifying expressions are lexically identifiable, a lexico-syntactic mechanism may be able to include partitive and quantified phrases that take environmental predicates as complements as appropriate environmental PredPs. As we move further into the periphery, the criteria of inclusion in the CC of environmental conditions become progressively more pragmatic.

7.4 The second ring of the conceptual category of environmental conditions

In the second ring, no conventionalized environmental lexeme is mentioned. Instead, ad hoc expressions are used, local to a certain circumstance, such as a season defined ad hoc: *the VCD days* in (5a), *cherry picking season* in (5b), *exams* in (5c). Another example involves the adjective *green*, which does not canonically serve to define the environment, but in the given contexts of (5e), is construed as being stated in the general context of (but not directly referring to) the surrounding sea. The adjective *forested* in (5f) serves to define the environment 'here" in an ad hoc way. Especially striking is the use of the noun *desert* as an environmental predicate in this construction in (5g).

(5)   a.   It was the height of the VCD days.   (I)
       b.   It was cherry-picking season again.   (I)
       c.   Well, it is exams here at Briercrest, and everyone is busy, busy, busy. (I)
       d.   It's just the beginning of the revolution, arm yourself with invaluable knowledge.   (I)
       e.   I swam with my eyes open and it was green and dark
                                                         (Hemingway 1968: 87).
       f.   As you can see, it is quite forested here.   (I)
       g.   Since coming down from the Andes onto the coastal lowlands it's been desert all the way.   (I)

In the Hebrew examples of (6), we have *tkufat bxinot* 'exam period' as an ad hoc characterization of the temporal environment in (6a). Exceptional ecological conditions in a specific local setting (*eclaxem* 'at your whereabouts', *po* 'here') are declared to be *mafxid* 'frightening', *mavxil* 'nauseating', and *asuk* 'busy' in (6b–d).

(6)   a.   *ani yodea še-tkufat bxinot, ve-kaved ve-kaše le-kulanu.*   (I)
            I know that season.of exams, and heavy and hard to all.of.us
            'I know it's exam season, and it's heavy and hard on us all.'
       b.   *šma, mafxid exlaxem. ani šokel laxzor le-yerušalayim.*   (I)
            listen. frightening at.yours. I consider to.return to Jerusalem
            'Listen, it's frightening at your whereabouts. I'm considering going back to Jerusalem.'

c. *xa-xa lo dani, ani lo mesugelet, mavxil po.* (I)
   ha-ha no Danny, I not able, nauseating here
   'Ha-ha no Danny, I can't, it's nauseating here.'

d. *asuk po. nedaber axar-kax.* (text message from my son)
   busy here. we.will.talk later.
   'It's busy here. Let's talk later.'

Note that these Hebrew expressions are sentences, not interjections, as discussed in Section 3.3.4. In all these English and Hebrew examples, the environmental PredP is not inherently environmental through some lexical component canonically defined as such, yet the environmental construal is coerced by the context and by the constructional force of the ENV S-pattern.

7.5 The third ring of the conceptual category of environmental conditions

Some predicates that appear in the ENV S-pattern are even less prototypical, since they combine inner and outer space. On the one hand, they convey affective inner states. These affective states, however, are construed as publicly prevailing in some location, hence they are environmental. Such predicates always require some indication of space, either implicitly or through a locative adjunct, otherwise they cannot have the general, environmental effect. Compare (7a–b) to (7c–d). The sentences of (7a–b), which display the mental state predicates *sad* and *boring*, cannot be acceptable with the reading of *it* as an expletive. With the addition of a locative adjunct, however, as is the case in (7c–d), they become generalized as a public property of the whole environment indicated by the adjunct, and *it* is naturally perceived as an expletive.

(7) a. It was very sad.
    b. It's so boring.
    c. It was very sad at the meeting when they announced the changes. (I)
    d. It's so boring here, we're listening to Japanese music and playing snake on our cell phones. (I)

Similar Hebrew examples are given in (8). The mental state predicate *mešaʾamem* 'boring' is a public characterization of the space defined by *po* 'here', referring to some Internet forum. Similarly, *acuv* 'sad' is the public mood prevailing *kan* 'here', and triggered by the absence of *ha-yona* 'The Dove', an alias of one of the regular participants of that forum.

(8) a. *ma kore, xaverim. mamaš mešaʼamem po.* (I)
what happens, friends. utterly boring here
'What's happening, guys? It's boring like hell here.'

b. *acuv nora kan bli ha-yona.* (I)
sad terribly here without the dove
'It is terribly sad here without The Dove.'

In the third ring, then, the shift from personal to public experience in a specific environment is effected, given the right context, by the constructional power of the ENV S-pattern. No finite list of such expressions may be provided lexically. Hence, the characterization of predicates and PredPs licensed in the ENV S-patterns is best done through the prototype based CC of environmental conditions, which is lexically defined at the core, but pragmatically defined in its periphery. Peripheral PredPs are construed as environmental, thanks to the constructional force of the ENV S-pattern itself.

7.6 Summary and conclusion of Chapter 7

The CC of environmental conditions is more loosely organized than the two CCs previously discussed. The CC of existence has been shown to have a single predicate at its core, which is implied by every predicate in the periphery. The CC of evaluation has been shown to be looser in structure. It has multiple predicates at the core, organized in four modality groups. Every predicate in the periphery has an equivalent predicate implied at the core. Finally, the CC of environmental conditions is the loosest in structure. Not every peripheral predicate has the kind of implication relation with a core predicate observed in the CCs of existence and evaluation. Here only one thing is implied, namely that the meaning is construable as environmental.

The inherently-environmental predicates are at the core. The first ring has the environmental indication in a modifier, rather than the head of the PredP. The second ring is only contextually understood as environmental, a meaning that is facilitated by the constructional force of the ENV S-pattern.

The third ring requires a place adjunct, along with the force of the construction, in order to facilitate the environmental meaning. A comparison with the PredP-alone S-pattern, which is a sub-pattern of the EV S-pattern, will clarify the difference between the third ring of the ENV S-pattern and the PredP-alone sub-pattern. As a reminder, some examples of the PredP-alone sub-pattern are repeated here in (9).

(9) *mešaʿamem/kar/xam/car l-i.*
boring/cold/hot/distressful to me
'I am bored/cold/hot/sorry.'

The PredP-alone S-pattern is a separate construction, since its meaning is not environmental but personal. It has been linked to the ENV S-pattern, because in terms of form, just like the ENV S-pattern, it does not have the final component (existent, evaluee, etc.) that is always present in the EX and EV S-patterns and sub-patterns.

If we look at predicates that are shared by The PredP-alone S-pattern and the third ring of the ENV S-pattern, the difference becomes clear, as is shown in (10).

(10) a. *mešaʿamem l-i.*
boring to me

b. *mešaʿamem po.*
boring here

c. *mešaʿamem l-i po.*
boring to me here

Example (10a) is a PredP-alone sentence. It conveys the affectee's personal experience. Sentence (10b) belongs to the third ring of the CC of environmental conditions. This is a non-environmental predicate whose environmental meaning is imposed by the construction in the domain indicated by the place adjunct *po* 'here'. Boredom is not associated with an affectee. This shows that this is not an affectee's personal experience, but the experience publicly felt in the specified location.

Note, however, that this is not the case in (10c), which is a PredP-alone sentence with an added locative adjunct. Here the experience remains personal, even though a location is specified, limiting the experience to that place, hence the translation *I am bored here*. The adjunct does not have the generalizing role that it has in the third ring of the CC of environmental conditions. When used in the ENV S-pattern, the PredP is made to prevail publicly through the constructional force of the ENV S-pattern. It is therefore justified to keep the meanings of the third ring of the CC of environmental conditions within the ENV S-pattern, rather than assign it a separate sub-pattern.

In a conclusion of the three chapters on CCs, it has been shown that the P1 S-patterns are semantically associated with corresponding CCs, which are radial categories that represent the lexical strength of the predicate in relation to its S-pattern. The CCs have been shown to have both a lexical–semantic dimension at and near the core and a pragmatic dimension in the more distant periphery. The CCs of the P1 S-patterns are similar to the argument structure constructions *within* the V S-pattern in that these S-patterns, just like argument structure constructions, are able to host predicates not inherently associated with them by way of constructional imposition.

CHAPTER 8

Situation types and information structure

8.1 The non-arbitrary nature of the S1 and P1 word orders

Information structure has accompanied our discussion at various junctures in this book, but its interaction with S-patterns has not been under focus. In this chapter, the relation between the two mechanisms of information structure and S-patterns will be explored. Two types of motivation for the S1 and P1 orders will be presented. One has to do with the difference between bipartite and monopartite sentence structure, the other with the linearization of predicate–argument structure in the sentence.

Narration is a basic need in human communication, both in its reportative and in its fictional mode. (The centrality of narration in the current study has been briefly discussed in Section 2.3). Much of our verbal activity involves providing factual reports and telling stories. Two basic facets of narration are manifest in a report or a story. One is the set of actions and events foregrounded in the unfolding storyline, the other is the set of auxiliary statements interlaced in the storyline at various points.

The foregrounded actions of a storyline are encoded in English within a categorical judgment that has a bipartite subject–predicate sentence form (Lambrecht 1994), instantiating the V S-pattern. The V sentence of the storyline is accompanied by the unmarked prosodic construction of predicate focus. This is then a prototypical topic–comment information structure construction.

Auxiliary statements may be of different kinds. In some cases, background information needs to be provided regarding entities already active in the storyline. To the extent that the background information amounts to states, they are often encoded in the COP S-pattern, which has the form of a categorical judgment encoded in a bipartite subject–predicate sentence form. As such, the COP S-pattern has the same bipartite structure as the V S-pattern. Both the V and the COP S-patterns are S1 constructions that have a prototypical canonical subject.

Another type of auxiliary statement is the introduction of a new entity into the discourse. This is often done through the EX S-pattern. Other interruptions of the storyline involve evaluation of situations in the EV S-pattern, and statements about the surrounding environment in the ENV S-pattern. All of these auxiliary statements in the EX, EV, and ENV S-patterns are thetic constructions lacking a prototypical subject. Needless to say, these auxiliary functions may also be carried out by V sentences, since the V S-pattern, as the unmarked S-pattern, is capable of expressing all semantic contents.

The two groups of S-patterns – S1 and P1 – are bilaterally symmetrical in some ways, but also asymmetrical in others. Let us look at the V S-pattern and the EX S-pattern for a start. Some bilateral symmetry may be evident in their form. The V S-pattern has the general form [NP VP], while the EX S-pattern has the general form [PredP NP]. This is true for both English and Hebrew (the English expletives *it* and *there* are ignored here).

The V S-pattern, then, has an NP (the subject) on the left, the EX S-pattern an NP (the existent) on the right. The specific grammatical dimensions of these NPs are prototypically opposite: the subject of the V S-pattern is primarily pronominal (Lambrecht 1994: 172–184), or at least definite lexical, while the existent of the EX S-pattern is mostly indefinite. In terms of the activation states (Chafe 1994: 53–56) of these NPs, the subject of the V S-pattern is prototypically active in the consciousness of the hearer, whereas the existent of the EX S-pattern is prototypically inactive. These features, then, are bilaterally asymmetrical.

With regard to the information structure constructions these NPs participate in, the subject of the V S-pattern usually serves as topic, while the existent of the EX S-pattern is usually the most salient element (the *rheme proper* Firbas 1957; 1975) of its focus domain.

Despite apparent symmetry here as well, the two information structure patterns are, in fact, very different in their basic organization. The bipartite sequence [NP VP] of the V S-pattern is translated into a *bipartite structure of topic and comment*, with the focus domain being the comment, and the most salient focal element being placed and accented at, or towards the end of the comment. On the other hand, the bipartite sequence [PredP NP] of the EX S-pattern is translated into a *single (monopartite) ascending scale of new information flow* that culminates with the most salient focal element being the final component, the accented NP, namely the existent.

This difference may be generalized *mutatis mutandis* to the other S1 and P1 S-patterns. In its most typical behavior, the COP S-pattern shows similarity to the V S-pattern in that its bipartite form translates into a parallel bipartite topic–comment information structure with focus within the comment, while the EV S-pattern in its most typical behavior resembles the EX S-pattern in forming an ascending scale of its sentential focus domain, with the focus accent falling within its final component, the nominal representing the evaluee. The ENV S-pattern is monopartite even in its form, and it lines up with the other P1 constructions in that it is all new, lacking any additional initial or final component slot altogether.

A motivation may, then, be formulated regarding the correspondence between situation type and sentence form on the one hand, and information structure on the other. If the situation type is an action or a background state involving referents active in the storyline, it will be hinged on a topic in a topic–comment information structure, i.e. an S1 S-pattern. If, on the other hand, the situation type involves existence, evaluation, or environmental conditions, it will not be hinged on a topic and will be encoded in a thetic all-new ascending focus structure, i.e. a P1 S-pattern.

The S1 and P1 orders in English and Hebrew are also motivated from another perspective: the internal linearization of the predicate–argument structure in the sentence. This is a cognitive motivation, which has been comprehensively studied in 1844 by Henri Weil ([1844] 1887). Weil's is a fascinating book, with many observations that have maintained their freshness to this day. His model is guided by a cognitive principle that he considers universal. "There is a progression of thought", says Weil ([1844] 1887: 28), "which differs from that of syntax, because it is independent thereof, and because it remains the same amid the diverse transformations of the sentence, and even when we translate into a foreign tongue."

This progression of thought, which Weil also calls the "march of ideas" ([1844] 1887: 28), came into being, according to Weil, after man had passed the phylogenetic stage of one-word deictic exclamations and moved on to reporting past events.

> It was in the first place necessary that this other personage, with whom it was desired to communicate, should be placed at the same point of view with the speaker; it was necessary that a word of introduction should precede the remark which it was intended to utter; it was necessary to lean on something present and known, in order to reach out to something less present, nearer, or unknown. There is then a point of departure, an initial notion which is equally present to him who speaks and to him who hears, which forms, as it were, the ground upon which the two intelligences meet; and another part of discourse which forms the statement [...]. This division is found in almost all we say (Weil [1844] 1887: 29).

In Weil's view, then, the topic–comment word order is based on natural cognitive motivation. At the same time, Weil is aware of the fact that not *all* statements have this form.

> There are two conditions under which they follow each other in the reverse order from that indicated above, and there are other cases in which the initial notion is wholly wanting (Weil [1844] 1887: 43).

When the "initial notion" is wanting, the sentence is without a "point of departure", without a topic. This observation precedes Brentano's (1874) philosophical distinction between categorical and thetic judgments by thirty years, and unlike

Brentano's, it was made in linguistics proper. However, beyond making this principled distinction, Weil also suggests that this principle has consequences in the linearization of the sentence, namely that the topic has to be in the initial position, since this is "the movement of the human mind itself".

This view has found its most ardent following in Halliday's (1967) framework, in which *any* initial element is the topic, including the auxiliary verb in interrogative sentences, or the expletive elements *it* and *there* in EV and EX sentences. Halliday's is a minority view in linguistics, since most linguists only consider lexical (not grammatical) words as topics. The first position of the sentence has also been an object of extensive deliberation in the Prague school of Functional Sentence Perspective (FSP).

An important constraint on the generality of the initial position as topic was offered by Lambrecht, who identified a "universal ordering tendency" (Lambrecht 1994: 202) to use the initial position for *marked* topics (such as fronted or left-dislocated components). After all, unmarked topics are in many languages simply the unmarked subjects, and their position in the linearization of the sentence is determined by the syntax of each language. For example, in VSO languages, such as Biblical Hebrew and Classical Arabic, the subject slot in a regular declarative V sentence is in the second position, following the initial verb.

Given that subjects may occupy various positions in the linearization of sentences, it may be asked whether the initial position of the subject in the S1 S-patterns of SVO languages such as English and Hebrew is merely incidental. Does the subject happen to be in the initial position just as it happens to be in the second position in VSO languages, or is it motivated there?

In English and Hebrew, and indeed in a wide range of languages, the V and COP S-patterns are S1. In these languages, then, the universal tendency to place the *marked* topic in the initial position has been generalized to cover the *unmarked* topic as well. Consequently, in this language type, the initial position hosts both the unmarked and the marked topic.

There seems to be a cognitive advantage to this linearization. A *marked* topic, such as a left dislocated argument or a fronted object or adjunct, occupies the initial position not only because it is first in an iconic "sequential-order principle" (Givón 2001a: 35–36). Beyond the simple ordering advantage of being first, this position also has a special status in terms of the management of argument structure in speech. When filled by an NP, this NP is cognitively suspended for the hearer, since it has not yet been assigned a semantic (theta) role. Only when the predicate is encountered by the hearer, does the initial NP receive its semantic role and come out of suspension.

The state of suspension of initial NP referents is universal by definition. In languages such as English and Hebrew, this suspension is generalized to the initial *unmarked* subject (in addition to other marked initial components). Even though the unmarked subject NP is not external to the sentence, the way left-dislocated components are, it is still cognitively suspended, since it lacks its semantic role (for empirical evidence for the "memory cost" of this suspended position see Gibson 1998). The hearer is able to assign an argument role to the initial NP only retroactively, once the predicate has been encountered and its argument structure revealed. This moment in the unfolding of the sentence is the moment of *sentence initiation* (Kuzar 1992b).

There is, then, a state of iconic relation (Haiman 1985) between the suspension of the subject in terms of its semantic role assignment and the pragmatic suspension of its referent as the topic of the sentence. This cognitive suspension is utilized by the speaker to present to the hearer "the ground upon which the two intelligences meet", the "point of departure" (Weil [1844] 1887: 28), "what the sentence is about" Strawson 1964: 97, "the peg on which the message is hung" (Halliday 1967: 212), the "hitching post" (Chafe 1976: 43–45), for the rest of the utterance. This way, the unmarked sentences of the V S-pattern obtain a bipartite categorical information structure.

It is, of course, not claimed here that this suspension is borne out in each and every utterance of a V sentence. "English SVO word order displays functional over-generalization, or *overkill*: it is there even when you don't need it", says Durie (1995: 278) about a different aspect of this order, but his assertion is valid here as well. Sentences such as MY CAR *broke down*, for example, have the same SVO structure, but they override their default information structure by having a deviant prosodic structure.

Following the logic of sentence initiation, the P1 S-patterns used for statements that are all new, all comment, or in Lambrecht's terms, have the focus structure of "sentence focus", also have a linear structure iconically signaled by the word order. When a sentence starts with the verb, or with any other predicate, the semantic roles of the arguments are revealed to the hearer at once and are ready to be assigned *before* the first argument is encountered. Hence, no argument is in suspension. When the arguments are uttered, they already have semantic roles waiting to accommodate them. Lacking a suspended element, such a sentence is informationally monopartite. Note that in both S1 and P1 sentences, Bolinger's (1952) principle of linear modification applies, namely the most salient, focal element appears at the end, or as close to it as grammatically and pragmatically feasible.

Through the use of two groups of S-patterns with two cognitively motivated linearizations, the major situation types that feature prominently in discourse conveniently fall into two corresponding groups. The foregrounded actions of a storyline naturally need a sentential topic which is part of the topical skeleton, the aboutness chain, of the storyline, to which comments are attached as the storyline unfolds. Hence, the V S-pattern, which hosts these actions, belongs to the S1group, in which the suspended initial subject is the topic. Background information is also typically associated with actors already active in the storyline, hence the COP S-pattern is also S1, hinging the new background comment onto the suspended subject–topic.

On the other hand, the introduction of new participants into the storyline is typically not hinged on an existing participant. An EX sentence, which has no suspended position in it, is motivated in the P1 order, having the existential predicate in initial position and the existent NP in final prominent focal position.

Evaluative statements typically have a similar organization. The focus in such sentences is typically within the evaluee, which is in final position, while the evaluative predicate only paints the evaluated situation encoded in the evaluee in some evaluative color. Put in the P1 order, the evaluative predicate leads to the situation described in the evaluee, which again is well motivated to be in final focal position.

If these major situation types are so well motivated to be encoded in S1 and P1 linearizations, as the case may be, the question arises: why do all the languages in the world not do so? The answer lies in the different prioritization of mechanisms grammaticalized in language as a multifactorial system. This iconic relation between the linear ordering of predicate–argument structure and the encoding of information structure is *one* cognitive option for signaling topicality or its absence. The S1 and P1 structures are, therefore, motivated in the sense of being a plausible cognitive option, materialized cross-linguistically, but not universally.

In VSO languages, priority has been set in a different way. The advantage of having a verb at the beginning of the sentence is obvious: no cognitive suspension of elements takes place, thus lesser interpretive effort is exerted. Preferring this advantage over the advantage of suspending an argument as topic may be the reason that VSO languages, such as Biblical Hebrew and Classical or Modern Standard Arabic, place the verb initially both in the narrative sentence pattern and in the existential and evaluative ones. In the narrative V S-pattern, the unmarked topical subject appears only in second position, namely as the *first* argument mentioned, *after* argument structure has been revealed. "Languages choose one option or they choose the other. Which choice it is may be arbitrary indeed", says Ariel (2008: 131) on a different issue (the choice between accusative vs. ergative case encoding systems described in Du Bois 1987), but the arbitrariness of choice may similarly apply here as well.

Some self-criticism is due at this point. The iconic isomorphism between the grammatical and pragmatic suspension of the subject as topic was described in my dissertation (Kuzar 1989: 60 in Hebrew), and then in two articles (Kuzar 1992b; 1992a in English). But I made two mistakes in those studies. One, as a devout structuralist at that time, I distanced myself from any cognitive interpretation, claiming that "my description of this mechanism is intra-disciplinary, in that it is not based on and does not imply parallel mental processes". Gladly, I have learned a thing or two about cognition and language since then. Two, I have not recognized the non-universal nature of these mechanisms. Consequently I attempted to describe Biblical Hebrew and Modern Standard Arabic (VSO languages) as languages with no unmarked topic (Kuzar 1989: 310), a position that seems cognitively untenable. With the tools of cognitive linguistics at hand, a typological, rather than universal characterization of this iconic relation makes much more sense.

Is, then, the subject that appears in the second position of a narrative sentence in a VSO language a topic? And if it is, is it the same kind of topic as the subject of a narrative sentence in an SVO language? Do speakers of both languages experience them in the same way? If the assignment of the topic role and the formation of a topical progression ("thematic progression" Daneš 1974) in the narrative is a universal need, do the two different means of producing a topic in S1 and P1 language types amount to the same conceptual experience? These should all be research questions, not a priori assumptions. Li & Thompson (1976), in their characterization of languages as topic-prominent and subject-prominent, have taken a stand in favor of the non-universal character of the concepts subject and topic. Further research is needed here.

Since the motivations for using S1 and P1 word orders are shared by English and Hebrew, one might suggest that there should be no word order differences between them. This, however, is not at all the case. In English and Hebrew, the motivation for the S1 and P1 word orders is the same only with regard to the central meanings of each construction. This is precisely what defines the typological group at hand: using the S1 order for foreground and background information on the storyline and the P1 order for existential statements, modal evaluations, and statements on environmental conditions. These are the major situation types of this typology, but there are many other situation types beside them.

One such situation type is the expression of possession. As described previously (Section 3.3.1.2), possession in Hebrew is conceptualized in terms of existence, whereas in English a dedicated verb in the V S-pattern is used for this task. The encoding of the possessor as a subject in English is well in line with the strong tendency of English to encode the human participant, regardless of its agency level, in the subject role. Through this cognitive tendency, the human agent as subject is generalized towards the human participant as subject. And since it is generally agreed that the prototypical possessor in possessive constructions is a human being (Seiler 1983: 4; Taylor 1989: 202–203; Heine 1997: 39), the affiliation of the possessor with the subject position of the V S-pattern in a possessive statement in English is well motivated by this principle.

Incidentally, the complexity of the V S-pattern as being both designated (marked) for actions and open to non-agentive situation types (unmarked) such as possession was observed by Weil ([1844] 1887: 24) a long time ago:

> We should not be surprised [...] to find in sensible [perceptible, concrete – RK] action the prototype of the proposition. [...] Of course, it is not always a sensible action, often it is not an action at all that we express. We say [...] "this man has talent" exactly as we say "the lion has torn his prey".

Hebrew, on the other hand, tends to encode human agents in the subject role, but non-agentive human participants in an oblique syntactic role. The encoding of the possessor, a non-agentive human role, in a *le-* 'to/for' PP within a P1 S-pattern is, therefore, well motivated in Hebrew.

The choice between these two ways of expressing possession is totally unrelated to the two motivations for S1 and P1 word orders described above. Mathesius (1943: 188, in Firbas's 1966: 239 translation) once proposed that "English differs from Czech in being so little susceptible to the requirements of FSP [Functional Sentence Perspective = Information Structure – RK] as to frequently disregard them altogether". Despite Firbas's (1966: 253) criticism of Mathesius's statement, it seems to have some truth in it. Information structure is not the only player in the field. It cannot explain all the facts of linear sentence forms and the choice between diverse sentence forms. Information structure interacts and competes with other mechanisms that determine the shape of the sentence. And in English, it is often the case that other mechanisms have the upper hand, leaving information structure to operate within more confined limits. Scholars that expect word order to operate under universal principles are dismayed by the unpredictability of word order:

> If different word order principles apply to different languages in an ad hoc way, it would pose a challenge to developing a universal account of language as a human cognitive process (Komagata 2003: 191).

The different default linearizations of the possessive constructions in English and Hebrew, which arise out of two different sets of motivations, are also associated with two different default information structures. Thus two prototypical possessive sentences in English and Hebrew are only partly equivalent, an outcome which is to be expected in a multi-factorial system.

in English, the possessor is a prototypical subject, hence a *primary topic* (Lambrecht 1994: 147), or what Gundel (1985: 86) calls a *syntactic topic*, namely a constituent "in a syntactic position reserved for topics". Most subjects of S1 declarative sentences in English are pronominal (91% in Michaelis & Francis 2007: 9), and the possessors of possessive sentences are no exception. In other words, being pronominal (or at least definite lexical) these possessors are well designed to serve as topics. How, then, can they not be topics in Hebrew?

Hebrew encodes possession in a monopartite thetic construction, in which the affectee-turned-possessor is an optional oblique object (without it the sentence has regular existential reading). Yet 86% of declarative possessive sentences in spoken Hebrew have been found to have pronominal possessors (Netz & Kuzar 2011). The possessor, then, is a good candidate to be a topic, but in the EX S-pattern it is not a primary but a *secondary topic* (Lambrecht 1994: 147). It is a referent whose topicality is not established as part of the prototypical instantiation of the primary topic in a syntactic construction, namely subjecthood, but rather as a participant, whose information status is calculated by the hearer in real time. The hearer comprehends the speaker's communicative intentions on the basis of accessibility considerations and other pragmatic clues.

In example (1), parallel texts from the English and Hebrew Internet editions of the daily Haaretz (24.6.2009) are compared. It is the exact same text in both languages, so the context prior to the possessive sentence is given in English only. The English possessive statement appears in (1a), the Hebrew one in (1b).

(1) [On a number of occasions Netanyahu has said that he is in a position to take action to improve the day-to-day life of Palestinians in the West Bank in a way that would significantly better the economic conditions in the area. Both Netanyahu and Barak believe that ultimately]
    a. they will have no choice but [...]
    b. *lo tihye l-ahem brera ela* [...]
       not will.be to them choice but

In our case here, the possessor is the referent of *they* in English and *l-ahem* 'to them' in Hebrew, namely Netanyahu and Barak. In English, *they* is a primary topic, the subject of a V sentence. In Hebrew *l-ahem* 'to them' is a secondary topic, whose topicality is established by the hearer from the context, supported by the prototypical pronominal nature of the possessor slot.

Though different in the nature of their topicality, still the two kinds of topics in the two languages functionally achieve a similar effect and are therefore sufficiently compatible renditions of each other. This does not mean, however, that the *choice of forms* in which these sentences are encoded in English or Hebrew is motivated by information structure. Such a claim would amount to saying that the identical context and the speaker's communicative intention actually motivate the choice of a topic–comment information structure construction in English, but a thetic one in Hebrew. Given the oneness of the situation represented in the two sentences, this would be a preposterous claim. The choice to encode a possessive sentence in an S1 S-pattern in English and a P1 S-pattern in Hebrew is motivated by the *situation type*, not by considerations of information structure. Information structure needs are accommodated within the selected forms as best as can be done.

What has been said with regard to possessive statements may be claimed, mutatis mutandis, with regard to other marginal situation types. Three of these are given in (2) in English and in (3) in Hebrew.

(2) a. She lost her wallet.
    b. He was stung by a bee.
    c. We are sure to be late.

(3) a. *avad l-a ha-arnak.*
       got.lost to her the wallet.
    b. *akca oto dvora.*
       bit him a.bee
    c. *batuax še-anaxnu ne'axer.*
       sure that we will.be.late

To be sure, some of these situation types may be phrased in Hebrew S1 constructions as well, but the P1 order is well conventionalized. The opposite is certainly not true for English. We see, then, that the situation type of losing an object is encoded in English (2a) in the V S-pattern with the human non-agent in subject position. In Hebrew (3a), this situation type is viewed as a negative existential statement, encoded in the EX S-pattern, with the loser being encoded as the affectee-turned-possessor. The situation type of an animal negatively affecting a person is encoded in English (2b) in the passive form of the V S-pattern, a way of encoding which puts the human being in the preferred subject position. Hebrew has its own P1 S-pattern for this purpose (3b), the Animal-induced-condition S-pattern, which is a sub-pattern of the EV S-pattern. In it, the affected person is syntactically encoded as object. Finally, the modal evaluation of an event is favorably expressed in English either by augmenting the verbal complex with a modal verb, or by using a raising predicate, such as *sure* in (2c). This practice culminates in the human argument being placed in the subject position of the S1 sentence, while in Hebrew, modality is favorably expressed in the EV S-pattern, a P1 construction, as in (3c), and the human argument is relegated to the subject slot of the subordinate clause.

The choice of S-patterns has been argued here to be motivated by situation types, not by considerations of information structure. It is now time to look at information structure options within these S-patterns.

8.2 Information structure within and across sentence patterns

In order to sort out the information structure options within and across S-patterns, the issue of markedness needs to be revisited. It has been suggested (Section 1.8), and assumed throughout this book, that when all S-patterns are taken as a set, as a category of S-patterns, the V S-pattern is unmarked, whereas all others are marked. This statement, however, has been said to be related to the functional roles of the S-patterns; namely, all S-patterns other than the V S-pattern have designated functions, associated with specific situation types, while the V S-pattern may be home to sentences expressing all the situation types expressible in the others (in addition to its designated function of expressing agentive events).

Markedness, then, is not an absolute, but rather a relative property of linguistic forms. Linguistic forms are always marked or unmarked *with regard to* some functional category.

In the following discussion, it will be said that all S-patterns have unmarked and marked word orders (linearizations), which are used for the organization of information structure. It should be clear, then, that the unmarkedness of a specific linearization of a specific S-pattern with regard to information structure is not in contradiction with the markedness status of its S-pattern in conveying a specific situation type, and vice versa.

All S-patterns have an unmarked linearization, which is the one used in earlier chapters as the model of its formula. Take the N COP S-pattern as an example, instantiated by (4).

(4) The area was a battleground. (I)

The formula of the N COP S-pattern is NP COP NP (simplified for our discussion here; the full formula appears in Section 2.4.1). Sentence (4) instantiates the unmarked word order of this S-pattern. As such, it conveys the designated (marked) function of the N COP S-pattern to assign equivalence between the basis subject and the predicate NP. it does so without any additional twists.

However, if the predicate NP is placed initially, we get a marked linearization NP NP COP, as in (5a–b). In addition to its S-pattern function, the sentence in this linearization now also conveys a marked linearization function in the field of information structure. The AP predicate of an A COP S-pattern may similarly be fronted, as in (5c). Here too, the marked information structure function is added *on top of* the marked S-pattern function (which is to assign attribution of a property to a basis subject).

(5) a. A battleground it was (Birner & Ward 1998: 60).
    b. Einstein he is not (Birner & Ward 1998: 75).
    c. Unfortunately, it is a feeling John will never know, for clever he is not. (I)

The exact characterization of the actual information structure function of this linearization need not concern us here (e.g. "scalar affirmation" and "proposition denial" (Birner & Ward 1998: 57, 65) or "contrastive topic" Lambrecht 1994: 291–295; Rafajlovičová 2010: 33). In fact, some of the functions of word order are in the field of discourse organization, which may or may not be included under the umbrella term "information structure". What matters at this point is the distinction that must be drawn between the S-pattern functions of the various S-patterns as hosts of situation types and the information structure functions of the various linearizations of each S-pattern.

This distinction is crucial with regard to the P1 S-patterns. It has been noted in Section 8.1 that within the typological group of languages discussed here, the S1 and P1 S-patterns are cognitively motivated to be linearized in their respective NP PredP and PredP NP word orders, and that this choice gets manifested in the occurrence or absence of a sentence-initial suspended argument. It has further been noted above that the choice of using the S1 or P1 S-patterns is primarily a matter of the situation types represented. The P1 S-patterns have designated (marked) functions. Prototypically, they represent the existence of an existent, the evaluation of an evaluee, and the environmental conditions prevailing in the world.

In addition to their default linearizations, each of the P1 S-patterns has other linearizations, which are marked with regard to information structure. Take, for instance, the EX sentence *change there is* in (6).

(6) It is at the conferences of Labour, the party that killed the grammar schools, that you see one fruit of that enlightened policy, which is that many of the younger delegates are incoherently illiterate. But change there is. 'Make the change', and Labour is a party on the make.   (BNC A2J.130)

It is not our task here to precisely define the function that the linearization of this sentence instantiates, be it a sentential information structure function or a different discourse function, or both. However here too, the function that ensues from this linearization is added on top of the S-pattern function, which in (6) is to express existence.

Listing the different linearizations of each S-pattern in each language is a laborious task, which raises practical and theoretical questions that cannot be gone into here in any exhaustive way. One such question, for example, regards the status of expletives in the linearizations. The example in (6) shows us that the expletive *there* persists in the marked linearization, namely the initially placed existent does not replace it as a subject (hence it is not a "displaced subject" Huddleston & Pullum 2002: 1391). This is, then, a true alternate linearization of the unmarked word order. Similarly, sentence (7) instantiates a marked linearization of the ENV S-pattern with the predicate placed initially. Here too the expletive *it* stays in place.

(7) Summer it is!!! (I)

Equivalent sentences without the expletive are ungrammatical, as is evident in (8).

(8) a. *Change is.
    b. *Summer is.

On the other hand, the expletive *it* does not appear in (9a), which is often (Quirk, Greenbaum, Leech & Svartvik 1985: 1392; Haegeman & Guéron 1999: 114–115) held to be an alternate linearization of (9b). The same sentence with an expletive is ungrammatical, as is evident in (9c).

(9) a. To hear him say that surprised me
        (Quirk, Greenbaum, Leech & Svartvik 1985: 1392).
    b. It surprised me to hear him say that
        (Quirk, Greenbaum, Leech & Svartvik 1985: 1392).
    c. *To hear him say that it surprised me.

These details of expletive behavior suggest that (9a) is not an alternate linearization of (9b) within the same S-pattern, but rather it represents a selection of a different S-pattern for the same proposition (the same argument structure and the same lexical semantic materials) in the V S-pattern, linearized in its unmarked S1 (SVO) linearization.

The term *linearization* might be misleading, in that it implies plain reordering. It should be clear, however, that besides plain linearizations, S-patterns may also be instantiated in more complex renditions, which involve the addition of various variables or constants. Left dislocation and right dislocation require a coreferential (resumptive) pronoun, and different cleft constructions provide pseudo-copular syntactic frames (*it was X that...*) which single out components for different types of prominence. Within Construction Grammar, the treatment of the *right-detached comme-N construction* (Lambrect 2004) is especially relevant here, since it creates a pronounced linkage between a subset of the A COP S-pattern, having the constant *c'est* and the variables [*un(e)* N, AP], and the right-detached *comme*-N construction with the same constant and the variables [AP] [*comme* N]. The former is an instance of the informationally unmarked A COP S-pattern, while the latter has a designated information structure function.

Furthermore, the right-detached *comme*-N construction belongs to a general syntactic template, the Right-Dislocation construction (Lambrecht's "right detachment"), which in Lambrecht's (2004: 192–193) view is specifically motivated in French, which prefers no lexical arguments in the kernel clause. This explains the prevalence of this construction in French, but not, for example, in English or German, though its formation in these languages is structurally feasible.

The list of acceptable linearizations of all the S-patterns (along with linearization that employ additional components, as well as other linearization-sensitive mechanisms, such as passivization) falls into intersecting subsets of sentences, each subset constituting a category (a substitution table) of all the truth-conditionally equivalent encoding options of a proposition.

For example, sentences (2a) (English) and (3a) (Hebrew) above, repeated here as (10a) and (11a), are unmarked within their respective S-patterns.

(10) a. She lost her wallet.
b. Her wallet she lost.
c. Her wallet got lost

(11) a. *avad l-a ha-arnak.*
got.lost to her the wallet

b. *ha-arnak avad l-a*
the wallet got.lost to her

c. *l-a avad ha-arnak.*
to her got.lost the wallet

d. *l-a ha-arnak avad.*
to her the wallet got.lost

e. *hi ibda et ha-arnak.*
she lost ACC the wallet

f. *et ha-arnak hi ibda.*
ACC the wallet she lost

Assuming a spontaneous, non-agentive event (not intentionally losing one's wallet), the English sentence will be encoded in the V S-pattern (10a) and the Hebrew one in the EX S-pattern (11a). But they may also have marked linearizations, less so in English, which has strict word order constraints, much more so in Hebrew, which is a fairly free word order language. Hebrew has more designated ways to respond to various discourse conditions, for which English has fewer forms.

For example, the unmarked English sentence in (10a) may also alternate with the marked object fronting form of (10b), given the right discourse conditions. In (10c) the sentence may appear with a reduced argument, incorporated as the possessor of *wallet*. These are all the options, and they are all within the V S-pattern.

In Hebrew, the options spread over two S-patterns: the V and the EX S-patterns. The list of options in (11) is not even exhaustive, but long enough to make the point. Sentence (11a) instantiates the unmarked linearization of the EX S-pattern, with some alternate linearizations in (11b–d). These forms also alternate with the unmarked V sentence in (11e) and its marked linearization in (11f).

The motivation for choices that speakers make between sentences instantiating various S-patterns and various linearizations of these patterns is again multifactorial. Situation types, narrative needs, text segmentation, and information structure are only some of these factors. An open eye to both the structural organization and the functional options should lead to a more accurate and nuanced description than taking just one aspect into consideration. Examples of such one-sided treatments and their flaws have been extensively discussed in the context of the EX S-pattern in English (Section 3.2.1), and need not be repeated here.

8.3 Summary and conclusion of Chapter 8

Sentence linearization has been shown to operate in the typological group of English and Hebrew at two levels. At the primordial level, the linearization of the predicate and its arguments is hinged on the process of sentence initiation, an event which takes place when the predicate is uttered (by the speaker) or encountered (by the hearer). In the S1 S-patterns, sentence initiation occurs after the suspended subject has been uttered or encountered. In the prototypical case, the sentence would then be construed as having a bipartite (subject–PredP) categorical (topic–comment) structure. In the P1 S-patterns, sentence initiation occurs initially, thus no argument is suspended, and the sentence is construed as having a monopartite thetic structure (constituting an ascending scale of new information). Additionally, since the V S-pattern is the unmarked S-pattern, thetic contents may be expressed in it as well, despite its bipartite appearance.

The choice between initial and non-initial sentence initiation in the S1 and P1 S-patterns renders them suitable for the encoding of different major situation types. The bipartite S1 S-patterns encode situation types that typically make use of the topic position, either for agentive actions developing the storyline via the V S-pattern or for providing background information in the COP S-pattern. The monopartite P1 S-patterns prototypically encode existential, evaluative or environmental statements in the EX, EV, and ENV S-patterns.

While the S-patterns are thus motivated at large, they are also home to marginal situation types. Hence, it may not be claimed that information structure directly motivates every S1 or P1 sentence instantiation. Hebrew has many less central situation types that have designated P1 S-patterns to express them. To the extent that they have a human participant, it is encoded as a secondary topic in an object position. English, on the other hand, favors the S1 S-patterns for these situation types, placing the human participant as a prototypical subject, i.e. a primary topic.

When different linearizations within each S-pattern – unmarked and marked – are added to the game, a large repertoire of actual sentence forms becomes available. Different subsets of this stock get organized as categories (substitution tables) available to the speaker to choose from at each junction of text production.

However, English and Hebrew differ in the number of sentential options available (S-patterns and their linearizations), because Hebrew is a free word order language to a much greater extent than English.

The situation type to be encoded as a sentence, the role of the sentence in the storyline, the place of the sentence in a well segmented text, and the information flow in the sentence – all these are only some of the decisions to be taken in the multifactorial system of form and function within sentential syntax.

CHAPTER 9

Non-canonical expletive behavior

9.1 Over- and under-grammaticalization in expletive behavior

The two English expletive elements *there* and *it* have developed from an earlier stage of English, which lacked expletives. The expletive *there* underwent grammaticalization in the thirteenth century (Williams 2000: 164), and the expletive *it* in the fifteenth century (Fischer, Koopman, Van Kemenade & van der Wurff 2000: 71). In Modern English, the expletive *there* in the EX S-pattern is used at all times, but the expletive *it* in the EV S-pattern is sometimes omitted in spoken contemporary English, as shown in (1). We might therefore say that when an English EV sentence lacks an expletive, it has an *under-grammaticalized* form.

(1) Good to See You Again, Alice Cooper. (Title of a film)

In standard Hebrew, expletives are not required, but Hebrew has developed an expletive element *ze*, which originates from the demonstrative pronoun *ze* 'this'. The only place in Hebrew where the expletive *ze* is obligatory is in the *it*-cleft sentence, a sentential construction directly borrowed from the substrate European languages at the time of the emergence of Israeli Hebrew. The Hebrew cleft sentence is instantiated in (2).

(2) ze haya legamre be-mikre še-ha-rakevet [...] hufneta le-ostriya. (I)
    this was totally in accident that-the train [...] was.directed to Austria
    'It was totally by accident that the train [...] was redirected to Austria.'

In the EX S-pattern, the use of expletive *ze* 'this' is totally ungrammatical, see the ungrammaticality of (3a). In the EV S-pattern *ze* is not required, but is nevertheless sometimes used, as demonstrated in (3b). The sentence would be just as grammatical without the expletive *ze*.

(3) a. *ze yeš kesef b-a-bank.
       this EXIST money in-the-bank.
       'There is money in the bank.'

    b. ze mamaš me'ule še-hu meruce mimeni axšav. (I)
       this really great that-he satisfied from.me now
       'It is really great that he is happy with me now.'

Since expletives are not regularly used in Hebrew, the cases where the expletive *ze* 'this' is used may be characterized as case of over-grammaticalization.

In the following sections of this chapter, cases of under-grammaticalization in English and cases of over-grammaticalization in Hebrew will be presented and discussed. They will be shown to be contrarily motivated by one principle.

9.2 Expletive reduction in English

The omission of expletives in English happens mostly in speech and in a colloquial writing style, such as personal letters, email messages, and blogs on the Internet. Some examples of under-grammaticalized EV sentences with predicates that take a *that*-clause evaluee are given in (4). An interesting concomitant feature in these examples is the omission of the complementizer *that*. The fact that the *that*-clauses tend to appear with a zero complementizer is part of the under-grammaticalized nature of these sentences.

(4) a. Pity the need to know overwhelms the ability to tell. (colleague, by email)
 b. Funny you should ask. (colleague, by email)
 c. Shame I couldn't attend this year. (I)
 d. Lucky we did some drainage work last summer. (I)
 e. Turns out Carly will be in Lod during the time we are there. (Friend, by email)
 f. Good job they're [cat and ferret] mates, otherwise the ferret would've won. (I)
 g. Good thing you don't put down any of your personal details at the end of your email messages. (Friend, by email)
 h. Seems we can look forward to a new Linksys VoIP handset by next week. (I)
 i. Small wonder that we all loved him exceedingly (Jespersen 1924: 122).

Similar examples of under-grammaticalized EV sentences with verbs that take an InfP or GrdP evaluee are given in (5).

(5) a. Time to go back (I)
 b. Fancy meeting you here. (colleague, at the toilet).

The predicates used in the sentences of (5), are endemic (Section 3.3.1.1) to the EV S-pattern. *Fancy* only has a modal–evaluative meaning in this construction. When used as a predicate in the COP S-pattern, the adjective *fancy* has a descriptive, not an evaluative meaning, as is evident in (6). The noun *time* (in its bare form) is never used as a predicate in the COP S-pattern.

(6) DIY styrofoam turntable is fancy in design and build. (I)

Neither do the nouns *pity* and *shame* in their bare form (used in (4) above) serve as predicates in the COP S-pattern. This behavior instantiates a more general point, namely that the predicates that may form EV sentences without expletives come from the stock of the core and the first ring of the CC of evaluation, not from the more distant periphery.

However, not all predicates of the core and the first ring show this ability. For example, *despicable* is an adjective from the core of the CC of evaluation, as it directly expresses modal meaning. It may easily serve as the predicate of a canonical EV sentence, as shown in (7a). Yet *despicable* may not serve as a predicate in the under-grammaticalized variant of this S-pattern, as is evident in (7b).

(7) a. It is despicable that you are taking advantage of hurting people . (I)
    b. *Despicable (that) you are taking advantage of hurting people.

Similarly, *good thing* is a predicate from the first ring of the CC of evaluation. Trying to replace the adjective *good*, as an attribute of *thing* (used above in (4g) and repeated here as (8a)), with other adjectives such as *interesting, important, exciting*, etc. would yield an unacceptable sentence, as shown in (8b–d).

(8) a. Good thing you don't put down any of your personal details at the end of your email messages. (Friend, by email)
    b. *Interesting thing you don't put down any of your personal details [...]
    c. *Important thing you don't put down any of your personal details [...]
    d. *Exciting thing you don't put down any of your personal details [...]

Some variations of the EV S-pattern have not been discussed in this book, for example those that employ complementizers other than *that*, such as *if, whether*, or *like*. If we add these to our discussion here, some more under-grammaticalized forms may be given, as in (9).

(9) a. Looks like the weather may not be too bad. Who's going? (I)
    b. Seems like the books are selling pretty well on Amazon. (I)

In other words, for predicates to be licensed in the under-grammaticalized version of the EV S-pattern, it is not enough that they belong to the core (or near it). Additionally, they have to be "lexically strong" (Bybee 1985: 117) or "entrenched" (Langacker 1987: 59) in this reduced syntactic construction. The identification of such forms by the hearer as evaluative predicates is so immediate that the beginning of the canonical construction, which usually signals the onset of the EV S-pattern – namely the expletive *it* along with the verb *be* – is felt redundant and is therefore reduced as part of its entrenchment process.

The relevance of the core (and close periphery) to the licensing of predicates in the under-grammaticalized variant of the EV S-pattern in English adds empirical support to the cognitive viability of this CC.

The over-grammaticalized EV sentences in Hebrew, to be discussed in the next section, displays complementary behavior to its English counterpart. Here too, the behavior of the expletive *ze* 'this' will be shown to be related to the structure of the CC of evaluation.

9.3 Expletive addition in Hebrew

The Hebrew expletive *ze* 'this' is used in the EV S-pattern with two distinct functions. The first function has to do with information structure. The second function is related to the structure of the CC of evaluation.

As for the first function, we may recall (Section 8.1) that the informationally unmarked form of the EV S-pattern usually has the focus accent in the evaluee, which in Hebrew would be either an InfP or a *that*-clause. In many other syntactic constructions, nominals often encode presupposed information active or accessible from previous context. EV sentences, on the other hand, usually put the content of the evaluee nominal under focus, in order to *assert* it, while the modal–evaluative perspective merely frames this assertion. Sentence (10) instantiates this default usage.

(10) *muvan še-ha-meida ragiš* ME'OD, *ve-laxen [...]*
  clear that the information is sensitive very, and therefore [...]
  'Clearly this information is very sensitive, and therefore [...]'

The preceding context of sentence (10) discusses the Social Security database of personal information about all citizens, and the subsequent conclusion is that access to this information has to be limited to authorized personnel. The text comes from an online newspaper and the prosodic interpretation can only be guessed, but the context is obvious enough to render its suggested prosody appropriate. The sentence intends to inform the reader that "the information is VERY sensitive", framing this statement in the modal perspective of being "clear".

Other prosodic options make the EV sentence informationally marked. In one case, the speaker intends to make the evaluation itself the most salient part of the sentence, in which case the nominal merely encodes presupposed information and serves as a secondary topic. In such cases, the predicate is accented and carries narrow focus, and the evaluee *that*-clause or InfP is just a long prosodic coda. To express this unusual focality of the evaluative predicate, the expletive *ze* is used in addition to prosodic marking. Often such predicates are also accompanied by quantifiers that maximize the effect, such as *me'od* 'very' and *mamaš* 'truly', as is shown in (11) (*ze* is represented in the gloss as THIS in small caps.)

(11) a. *ze* XAVAL ME'OD *še-ata lo yaxol lehitxaber l-a-internet me-ha-PS3*. (I)
THIS UNFORTUNATE VERY that you not can to.connect to the Internet from the PS3.
'It's VERY UNFORTUNATE that you can't connect to the Internet through the PS3.'

b. *ze mamaš* MEFAGER *laxšov kaxa*. (I)
THIS truly RETARDED to think thus
'It is truly RETARDED to think that way.'

Sentence (11a) is an Internet-forum reply to a question on how to transfer files when the PS3 is in the living room and cannot be connected to the Internet. Hence, the evaluee *that*-clause is a presupposed secondary topic, and the evaluative predicate expression itself is placed under narrow focus. The infinitival evaluee *laxšov kaxa* 'to think that way' in (11b) obviously encodes presupposed information.

A second marked prosodic structure divides the sentence into two intonation units, hence both the evaluative predicate and the evaluee are prominent and informative. Sentence (12) is a spoken example, said to me by a colleague, thus its accent marking represents authentic prosody.

(12) *ze* XAVAL *še-universita'ot b-a-aretz be-macav kol-kax* GARUA *še-lo yexolot lehacia misra le-yisraelim še-rocim* LAXZOR.
THIS UNFORTUNATE that universities in the country in a.situation so-much DEFECTIVE that not able to.offer a.position to Israelis that want TO.RETURN.
'It is UNFORTUNATE that universities in this country are in such bad SHAPE that they are unable to offer a job to Israelis wishing to RETURN.'

This is a long sentence with several prosodic peaks, each encoding the prominent part of their respective information units. One of the accented components is the predicate *xaval* 'unfortunate'/'too bad'. Both in (11) and in (12), then, we have marked prosody which puts informational prominence on the predicate.

In this function of highlighting the informationally prominent element, the use of the expletive *ze* is not constrained by the semantics of the predicate. Any kind of evaluative predicate may be thus accented, across the board of the CC of evaluation, core and periphery alike. This use of the expletive *ze* has been discussed here merely for the sake of giving a complete account of expletive usage in the EV S-pattern. Now, let us look at the usage of the expletive *ze* which is relevant to the CC of evaluation.

The expletive *ze* is often used when the head of a predicate phrase is not a *core* predicate, namely, when it is not inherently modal, or if it is questionably modal. In such cases, we may recall, the modal meaning arises compositionally, supported by the meaning of the construction. This is the case in (13), where the verb *moci* 'takes out' is not modal, but along with *oti mi-da'ati* 'me from my mind' it compositionally means "drives me crazy"/"drives me out of my mind".

(13) *ze moci oti mi-da'ati še-at lo po'elet be-ezešehi misgeret šel herkev.*   (I)
THIS takes.out me from my.mind that you not act in some framework of ensemble.
'It drives me crazy that you aren't active in some ensemble.'

Apparently, the cognitive task of identifying the initial expression as an evaluative predicate incurs a heavier cost on the hearer, when the predicate is not readily recognizable as evaluative. This cognitive load is however alleviated by the use of an over-grammaticalized version of the EV S-pattern with the expletive *ze*.

Sometimes, the predicate does have evaluative meaning, but is not in habitual use in the EV S-pattern. Being infrequently used, it is not entrenched enough in the role of an evaluative predicate. Its identification as such is enhanced by the use of the over-grammaticalized construction. One such example is the adjective *xolani* 'sickening/pathological' in (14).

(14) *ze xolani be-eynay še-šoftim yakelu al av še-ose ma'asim ka'ele b-a-yalda ha-xoreget šelo.*   (I)
THIS sickening in my.eyes that judges lighten on a.father that does deeds such in the girl step of.his
'It is sickening in my opinion that judges are lenient with a father that does such things to his step-daughter.'

To be sure, *xolani* 'sickening' appears frequently as the predicate of COP sentences (*their behavior is sickening*) or as an attribute of a noun (*sickening behavior*), but it is less frequent in EV sentences (*it is sickening to behave like this*). As such, the use of the evaluative predicate *xolani* imposes a cognitive load on processing. By adding the expletive *ze* in front of it, the speaker makes the construction more distinct at its very outset, thus making processing easier. Upon encountering the expletive, the hearer gets a signal to expect an EV S-pattern, hence the subsequent expression is identified as the evaluative predicate

The expletive *ze* is not likely to be used, though, with entrenched core predicates, unless they are put under narrow focus, as discuss in (11) and (12).

We see, then, that although Hebrew does not require expletives in the canonical form of the EV S-pattern, expletives are nevertheless used as a means towards improving the visibility of the construction by further grammaticalizing it. Without the expletive, a Hebrew EV sentence is identified as evaluative only in the process of its unfolding. This process may be visualized in the following way: first the hearer encounters the predicate. If it is inherently modal, the EV S-pattern is immediately identified. If the predicate is not inherently modal, identification is suspended till more semantic material is encountered or till the syntactic structure is unequivocally recognized as an instance of the EV S-pattern. This kind of identification process imposes an extra cognitive load on the hearer. In the over-grammaticalized variant of the EV S-pattern, where the expletive is added, processing is made easier, since an EV sentence is readily identified when a sequence of the expletive *ze* plus an element which is potentially a predicate starts to unfold.

We see that besides the behavior of the expletive *ze* to make predicates informationally prominent, it is also used to enhance the identification of semantically weak predicates or PredPs as components of the EV S-pattern. Semantically weak predicates and PredPs appear at the more distant periphery of the CC of evaluation, hence this CC is relevant to the decision of the speaker to use an over-grammaticalized variant of the EV S-pattern, a point which strengthens again the viability of the CC of evaluation as a theoretical construct.

9.4 Summary and conclusion of Chapter 9

The non-canonical behavior of expletives, namely their reduction in English and their addition in Hebrew, is based on common logic, which has two parts: (a) at the very core of the CC of evaluation, and especially with evaluative predicates entrenched in the EV S-pattern, the identification of the intended use of the construction is readily available by the very use of the evaluative predicate, thus less constructional support is needed; (b) when the predicate to be used in the EV S-pattern is not readily recognizable as evaluative, it needs further constructional support.

Part (a) of this logic is responsible for the reduction of the canonical expletive in English, while part (b) is responsible for the addition of the non-canonical expletive in Hebrew. The non-canonical behavior of expletives in English and Hebrew provides further support to the cognitive viability of the radial nature (core and periphery) of the CC of evaluation in these languages.

An MA thesis, completed at the University of Haifa (Aghion 2009), provides some empirical support for the account of expletive behavior in Hebrew offered here. The study was based on a statistical analysis. It asked questions which did not directly address the questions raised here. However, an analysis of the results and the detailed distribution facts of Appendix 1 (Aghion 2009: 57) seem to support the suggestions made here. The total number of sentences collected in Aghion's (2009) study is 450, of which I identified 152 occurrences of 11 predicates endemic to the EV S-pattern, and 298 occurrences of 86 predicates non-endemic to the EV S-pattern.

Seven of the endemic predicates are also morphologically unique: *xaval* 'too bad', *carix* 'necessary', *yitaxen* 'possible', *ixpat* 'matter', *efšar* 'possible', *keday* 'worthwhile', and *mutav* 'had better'. Another four predicates are not morphologically unique but are nevertheless endemic to the EV S-pattern in their evaluative sense: *xaser* 'had better not', *nidme* 'seem', *nitan* 'possible', and *car* 'distressing (be sorry)'.

The distribution of endemic and non-endemic predicates among canonical and over-grammaticalized (using *ze*) variants of the EV S-pattern in Aghion's corpus is given in Table (2).

Out of a total of 152 endemic predicates, 148 (97.5%) have been found in the canonical EV S-pattern, and only 4 (2.5%) in the over-grammaticalized variant of this construction. All other predicates, the non-endemic predicates, which have not been further classified along the periphery scale, show a very different distribution. 188 (63%) are used in the canonical construction and 110 (37%) in the extended construction.

As we may recall, some of the extended forms in both the endemic and the non-endemic groups might have been motivated by considerations of information structure (to signal focality or informational prominence) rather than by the peripheral status of the predicate, but these should constitute a small minority, and I have not been able to identify them and separate them from the total number of extended forms.

It is nevertheless quite clear, that endemic predicates of the EV S-pattern, which are core members of the CC of evaluation, on the whole (97.5%) do not tolerate the use of the expletive *ze*, whereas non-endemic predicates appear in the over-grammaticalized construction in 37% of the cases. This behavior pattern is predicted by the cognitive model of the CC of evaluation offered here.

Table 2. Endemic/non-endemic predicates among canonical/extended EV sentences

	Endemic predicates	**non-endemic predicates**
Canonical	148 (97.5%)	188 (63%)
Extended	4 (2.5%)	110 (37%)
Total	152 (100%)	298 (100%)

CHAPTER 10

Patterning revisited

10.1 Preliminary discussion

Patterning has been suggested in Section 2.4.4 as a mechanism of sentence formation which usually accompanies predication, but sometimes operates alone. The need for postulating patterning in addition to predication as a mechanism of sentence formation arises when the word expected to be the predicate in a certain sentence is awkward, attenuated, or entirely missing, yet the sentence is still grammatical. In the latter case, i.e. when the predicate is absent altogether, the arguments seem to get inserted correctly into their S-pattern slots, even though no predicate has directed them to do so. The grammaticality of such sentences originates, then, from the S-pattern itself, not from the defective or missing predicate.

Patterning has been shown in Section 2.4.6 to interact with predication in the formation of the COP S-pattern.

Patterning is also clearly at work in minor S-patterns, instantiated by the sentences of (1), which lack an element worthy of the name predicate.

(1) a. The sooner, the better.
    b. Once a priest, always a priest.
    c. Like father, like son.
    d. So far, so good.

In Chapters 5–7, we have seen predicates in the distant peripheral ring of their respective CC get their meaning primarily from the S-pattern. If we take it as a premise that patterning is *always* at work, not only where predication is difficult or impossible, but also where predication is smoothly active, then we have a systemic explanation why S-patterns can impose meaning. This behavior is part of the ongoing interplay between predication and patterning.

Let us look now at patterning in some additional cases not previously discussed. To start, three cases of major S-patterns will be discussed: the English EX S-pattern with the verb *be*, the Hebrew variant of the EX S-pattern without *yeš* (both in Section 10.2), and a variant of the EV S-pattern with no predicate both in Hebrew and in English in Section 10.3. The discussion of patterning will be concluded with the case of a minor S-pattern in Hebrew in Section 10.4.

10.2 Patterning in the EX S-pattern

In English, the EX S-pattern is an ideal candidate for basing its formation on patterning *rather than* predication. Recall that linguists have had difficulties in identifying the predicate of EX sentences. Over the years, the expletive *there*, the verb *be*, the two of them combined, as well as the existent, have all been proposed as predicates (Section 5.1). In other words, all parts of the construction have been suggested for the task. This indicates that no part of the construction truly stands out as a natural, unequivocal candidate for being predicate.

In the treatment of the EX S-pattern in the current study (Section 3.2), the verb *be* has been taken as the predicate, based inter alia on the similarity between *be* and *yeš* in the two parallel S-patterns. The predicate *yeš* is a genuine existential predicate. But as will become clear in the second case of patterning to be discussed next, *yeš* is not compulsory under certain discourse conditions, in which case patterning would be the only constitutive mechanism in the formation of an existential sentence.

If we view the verb *be* in the EX S-pattern as a grammatical rather than lexical verb, the anomaly of its double behavior (lexical in the EX S-pattern, grammatical as auxiliary or copula) is eliminated. This is certainly a more elegant state of affairs, if it can be defended. In Table 3, the two views are schematically summarized.

In the predication view, *were* appears in the same slot as the verbal existential predicate *appeared*, as shown in the upper part of Table 3. In contrast, in the patterning view, *were* is positioned in the COP slot, where it is placed when accompanying an adjectival existential predicate such as *extant*, as shown in the lower part of Table 3. In the lower part of Table 3, the lexical predicate is absent, and it is the existential construction at large, rather than some questionable act of predication, that renders the string *there were two manuscripts in our collection* a sentence. Out of all the predication views, the one that comes closest to the patterning view presented here is McNally's (1998) proposal to view *there-be* as a predicate. This view recognizes the difficulty in assigning the constitutive act of sentence formation to

Table 3. Viewing the verb *be* as positioned in the predicate versus copula slot

	Expletive		Verbal EX Pred.	Existent	Adjunct
Be in pred. slot	There		appeared	two manuscripts	in our collection.
	There		*were*	two manuscripts	in our collection.
	Expletive	COP	Adjectival EX pred.	Existent	Adjunct
Be in gramm. slot	There	were	extant	two manuscripts	in our collection.
	There	were	–	two manuscripts	in our collection.

one component and tries to assign the task to a combination of components. It does not, however, capture the different *nature* of patterning rather than predication as the constitutive act of sentence formation.

The second case of patterning to be presented here involves the EX S-pattern in Hebrew. This S-pattern has a variant in which the predicate *yeš* is absent. This variant is distributionally constrained (one detailed, albeit controversial, formulation of these constraints appeared in Rosén 1977b: 212–213). Not in every EX sentence in Hebrew can *yeš* be freely dropped. But where ellipsis is permitted, such a sentence nevertheless instantiates a variant of the EX S-pattern, not a different construction, since the form without the predicate *yeš* is always replaceable by the canonical variant (short of some fixed idioms), and since the constructional meaning is the same. An example of the variant without *yeš* is given in (1a) with the equivalent full form in (1b).

(1) a. [The research is financed by the Ministry of Labor and Welfare]
 ve-l-o šaloš matarot. (I)
 and to it three targets
 'and it has three objectives.'

 b. *ve-yeš l-o šaloš matarot.*
 and EXIST to it three targets
 'and it has three objectives.'

The view that (1a) is a variant of (1b) is commonly accepted lore. Besides Rosén's (1977b: 212–213) view referred to above, Rubinstein (1968: 204) also views the form without *yeš* as a "short *bicua* 'execution/performance'" of the full form. Azar (1995: 90) also holds that the full and shorter forms are constructional variants in Mishnaic Hebrew. These and other authors do not ask, however, how such a sentence is constituted, given that it is missing the predicate. The idea of patterning as developed here provides the answer to this question.

The two sentence forms, instantiating two variants of the same construction, show us that constructions indeed behave like any other linguistic sign. A construction may have variants, free or distributionally constrained, just as do the smaller and more familiar units of phonology and morphology.

In the case of the English EX S-pattern with the verb *be*, the formation of the *whole* S-pattern has been proposed in this section to be based solely on patterning. In the case of the Hebrew EX S-pattern, a *variant* of the S-pattern has been proposed to exist, whose formation is based on patterning alone. In the next section, it will be shown how certain sentence forms, lacking an evaluative predicate, are to be interpreted as belonging to the EV S-pattern and as getting their evaluative meaning directly from the construction.

10.3 Patterning in the EV S-pattern

In the Hebrew EV S-pattern, the predicate position, as we might recall (Section 3.2.2), may be filled by words of any part of speech, even morphologically unique words, so long as they are semantically compatible with one of the core modal–evaluative meanings of this S-pattern. These meanings may, then, be viewed as the polysemous constructional meaning of the S-pattern. The sentence in (2a) is a regular EV sentence with the N predicate *xova* 'duty'. Its variant sentence form in (2b) has no predicate at all, yet its meaning is similar to that of (2a).

(2) a. *xova al xevrat bituax lišloax mumxe az'akot le'axar divuax al prica.* (I)
    duty on company.of insurance to.send an.expert.of alarms after a report on burglary.
    'It is incumbent on an insurance agency to send an alarm expert after a reported burglary.'

 b. *lefi ha-xok, al xevrat ha-bituax lehacig l-a-mevutax kol tašlum.* (I)
    according.to the law, on the.company.of the insurance to.present to the insured every payment.
    'According to the law, it is incumbent on the insurance agency to present all payments to the insured.'

Evidently, the predicate *xova* 'duty' may be omitted, as long as the the preposition *al* 'on' is used with the affectee and the nominal is an InfP. This way, the shape of the sentence is distinctive enough to be recognizable as an instantiation of the EV S-pattern even without a predicate. The evaluative meaning of (2a) and (2b) is the same, whether or not the predicate is there. Aware of the problematic nature of sentences such as (2b), Rosén (1977a: 211) suggested that "the class IMPERS + *le-* includes (as a portmanteau morpheme) the preposition *al*". Technically, this is a clever solution, but it glosses over the fact that the P *al* 'on' here heads the PP containing the affectee. This is a separate functional role in the EV S-pattern.

The EV S-pattern is quite distinct from other S-patterns in its slot structure even without the predicate. Therefore, a reduced variant of this S-pattern, in which the predicate is absent, does not impair the classification of such a sentence as a proper instantiation of the EV S-pattern. Theoretically, several modal meanings could be restored for the absent predicate. The reduced form, however, has been conventionalized to have one particular modal meaning, that of obligation, and the P *al* 'on' echoes the specific transitive behavior of *xova* 'duty'.

English displays similar behavior in (3).

(3) a. It is incumbent on all of us to preserve these assets. (I)
 b. it is up to Georgia to protect its citizens. (I)

c. It is on you to decide how long you will watch clips. (I)
d. It is not in me to give up. (I)

In these sentences, we see a gradual reduction of the predicates from a fully lexical form in (3a), via a light predicate (the preposition *up*) in (3b), all the way to no predicate at all in (3c–d). In (3a), *incumbent* has the deontic meaning of obligation. In (3b), the preposition gets its deontic meaning metaphorically: "having control or force is up" (Lakoff & Johnson 1980: 15). In (3c–d), there are no predicates at all. The construction itself gives modal meanings to the sentences. Here, however, in contradistinction to Hebrew, English has conventionalized *two* reduced sentence forms, distinguishable in their meaning through the use of two different prepositions in the affectee role: the form with *on* expresses obligation, the one with *in* potentiality. The prepositions themselves cannot be considered predicates, since the PP slot is necessary for representing the affectee, just as it does in any canonical EV sentence. The two forms of (3c–d) are different from (3b) where the preposition *up* is the predicate. The sequence *up to* is *not* one complex preposition, as would be the case in *this room may contain up to 100 seats*, but two distinct ones. Note that the complex preposition *up to* has no modal–evaluative meaning. On the other hand, in (3b), *up* is the evaluative predicate and *to* introduces the affectee.

In a conclusion of this section, it is suggested that even if the core meaning of a construction is polysemous, as is the case in the EV S-pattern, a variant form of the construction with an omitted predicate is possible. What enables this state of affairs is the P of the affectee PP, which has been routinized in one particular meaning.

In the next section, patterning in a minor Hebrew S-pattern will be presented.

10.4 Patterning in a minor Hebrew S-pattern

The case to be discussed now is a minor S-pattern, which means that it is a stand alone (unlinked) S-pattern. Further elaboration may render this S-pattern a sub-pattern, but if this is the case, it is a very complex one, since it may need to be based on double inheritance from both the EX and the EV S-pattern. Until further elaboration is carried out, it will remain unlinked. This is the Existential–modal S-pattern. Sentence (4) is an example of this minor S-pattern.

(4) *yeš bi-yexolto levate kešet šlema šel regašot.* (I)
    EXIST in his ability to.express a.rainbow complete of feelings
    'He is able to express a wide range of feelings.'

The Existential–modal S-pattern uses the existential predicate *yeš* 'EXIST' (including its regular allomorphs: negative *en* 'NOT.EXIST' and future and past forms based on the verb *haya* 'be') as a constant of the construction. In other words, no other existential predicate may replace *yeš*.

The existential predicate *yeš* is followed in this construction by an obligatory adjunct PP headed by the P *be-* 'in'. The NP complement slot inside this PP may be filled by a handful of nouns expressing states of ability, possibility, and intention, such as *yexolet* 'ability' (used in (4) above), *racon* 'wish', *efšarut* 'possibility', *yad* 'hand' (metaphorically symbolizing 'power', 'potential'), *koax* 'power', and *kavana* 'intention' (the latter being used in (5) below). Other, more or less synonymous nouns may not be used in this construction. The nouns licensed in this construction are obligatorily associated with a possessor. In most cases they have pronominal possessive endings. To a lesser extent, they may be followed by a possessor NP. The sequence *yeš bi-yexolto* is glossed as EXIST in his.ability (*yexolto=yexolet + o* possibility + his) and will be translated as "He is able". The final component is an InfP expressing the action to be carried out. The function of this S-pattern, then, is to express the capability/wish/intention of a human being to carry out an action.

What makes this S-pattern relevant to our discussion is the fact that it has a variant form lacking the predicate *yeš*, exemplified in (5), which has the exact same meaning.

(5) *romario hodia ki be-xavanato lifroš be-karov mi-kaduregel.* (I)
Romario announced that in his.intention to retire in near from football
'Romario announced that he intends to retire from football soon.'

The occurrence of the fuller form *yeš be-xavanato* 'EXIST in his intention' or the reduced form *be-xavanato* 'in his intention' makes no difference and is identical in meaning. Since the slots of this S-pattern are distinctive enough even without the predicate, the shorter form has been grammaticalized as an instantiation of a variant of the Existential–modal S-pattern, signaling the same meaning.

10.5 Summary and conclusion of Chapter 10

Predication and patterning are related to each other in an inverted ratio of the information – structural and functional – contributed by each mechanism to the formation of a sentence. Five typical cases arise, to be summarized here in a decreasing order of predication and an increasing order of patterning.

High on the scale of predication is the V S-pattern, a mere recipient of the predicate and its argument choices. Predication is the dominant mechanism of sentence formation in the V S-pattern. The contribution of patterning amounts to linearizing the slots hosting the components of the predicate–argument structure. Since the S-pattern interacts with the argument structure construction, not with each verb's individual profile, it is blind to the level of matching between the verb's participant roles and its hosting argument structure roles. A V sentence whose predicate fully matches its target argument structure construction, is shown in (6a). When there is a mismatch between participant roles and argument roles, as in (6b), the discrepancy is handled by the argument structure construction, not by the S-pattern. Either way, the contribution of the S-pattern to the formation of the sentence is only linearization.

(6) a. Linda broke the window.
    b. Sam sneezed the napkin off the table.

Further down the scale of predication and up the scale of patterning we find non-prototypical predicates from the distant periphery of the CC of P1 S-patterns. In this case the sentence gets some of its meaning, its constructional meaning, directly from the S-pattern, as in (7).

(7) *nišdad snif bank be-ako.* (I)
    was.robed a.branch.of bank in Acre
    'There was a bank robbery at a branch in Acre.'

As we may recall, the EX S-pattern in Hebrew does not have an expletive subject; thus if it is verbal, its components are identical to those instantiated by its counterpart in the V S-pattern. The difference between them is only in word order. Whether a sentence is encoded in the V S-pattern or the EX S-pattern depends on the communicative intention of the speaker. Now, since the verb *nišdad* 'be robbed' is not a prototypical verb of existence or presentation, the presentational meaning that is part of the meaning of this sentence is not lexically encoded by the predicate, but is contributed by the construction. In this case, then, patterning contributes both presentational meaning and, as always, linearization.

Further up the scale of patterning, we find sentences with additional components, which are not related to the semantics of the predicate. These can be grammatical elements, such as the *it* and *there* expletives in the English EV and EX S-patterns, as in (8a–b), but they can also be adjuncts, such as the obligatory locative phrase in the locative inversion (LI) S-pattern in (8c).

(8) a. It is good to see you.
    b. There was some noise in the living room.
    c. On the horizon awaited more chaos and confusion. (I)

The locative phrase *on the horizon* in (8c) is not required by the verb *await*. It is an adjunct, namely an optional element in terms of predicate–argument structure, but it is obligatory, if a LI S-pattern is intended. The sentence has a presentational meaning with a flavor of "visual impact" (Breivik 1981: 12) added to it. This meaning is contributed to the sentence by the construction. The proportional contribution of patterning here is greater than in the first two cases. Patterning is responsible for the inclusion of a locative phrase, for the presentational meaning of the sentence at large, and – as always – for the linearization of the sentence.

The fourth case is even more radical in terms of the increased role of patterning and decreased role of predication. It involves a variant instantiation of an S-pattern, which has a canonical predicate slot, with null realization of the predicate. The components of the sentence, which normally would have been arguments of a predicate, are inserted into their S-pattern slots by the force of the construction alone, as in (9a). The fuller variant, with a lexical predicate, is shown in (9b).

(9) a. It is on you to decide how long you will watch clips. (I)
    b. It is incumbent on you to decide how much to trust the information you have received. (I)

Despite this seemingly catastrophic absence of a predicate in (9a), the sentence fares quite well. This is so, since the S-patterns instantiated by these two sentences have an array of non-predicate slots distinctive enough in their nature (form and function) to endow the sentence with the constructional meaning otherwise matched with the meaning of the predicate. Theoretically, more than one meaning could have been assigned to such a "defective" sentence, but this does not happen, since one meaning has been conventionalized by usage.

It seems as if in this case, patterning is the exclusive mechanism of sentence formation. However, even though the predicate in (9a) is absent, its spirit still hovers over the construction, since the S-pattern has a designated predicate slot, which is usually filled in the more prototypical instantiations of the construction.

A truly exclusive case of sentence formation by patterning is the fifth case, where there is no predicate slot at all in the S-pattern. This is the case of minor S-patterns such as the Comparative–Correlative S-pattern shown in (10).

(10) The sooner, the better.

The process of sentence formation, then, involves (a) specifying the number of components of an S-pattern, (b) naming the form and function of its components, (c) declaring its function at large, and (d) linearizing it. The mechanism of patterning carries out all these functions, either in tandem with the mechanism of predication or without it. Clearly, then, patterning proves to be a major factor in sentence formation.

CHAPTER 11

Noun incorporation

11.1 Preliminary discussion

Noun incorporation is described in the literature as taking place when "a noun stem is compounded with a verb stem to yield a larger, derived verb stem" (Mithun 1984: 847). A classic example of noun incorporation (in Southern Tiwa) is given in (1), where (1a) shows the object noun as a regular verb complement, while in (1b), the object is compounded with the verb.

(1) a. seuanide ti-mū-ban.
 man 1s:A-see-PAST
 'I saw the/a man.' (Example 13 in Allen, Gardiner & Frantz 1984: 295)
 b. ti-seuan-mū-ban.
 1s:A-man-see-PAST
 'I saw the/a man.' (Example 12 in Allen, Gardiner & Frantz 1984: 294)

Two paraphrases of the same proposition, one with the object in its canonical position and the other with an incorporated object, are usually motivated in such a way that one of them is marked for a more specific meaning.

Mithun observed that only nouns bearing patient, location, or instrument roles may be incorporated (Mithun 1984: 848, 875), whereas Baker, from a transformational perspective, claims that all these cases may be generalized as being "structural objects" (Baker 1988: 83).

Object incorporation has also been shown to be in operation in Hungarian (Kiefer 1990–1991). It is often, but not always, the case in Hungarian that the form with the free object designates an event in which the object represents a specific referent, e.g. "read a/the book", while the form with the incorporated object designates an activity in which the incorporated object is a generic term modifying the meaning of the verb, e.g. "do book-reading". This division of labor may be found in many languages (Mithun 1984: 856).

However, there are also cases of lexicalization which display incorporation without having a free-object counterpart (Kiefer 1990–1991: 154), something like the English verb *babysit*.

This short survey of the literature on incorporation indicates that incorporation always involves a verb. However, incorporation into the verb complex is only a special case of incorporation. Two other cases to be discuss below are incorporation into a non-verbal predicate (N and Unq) and incorporation of an argument into another argument.

English and Hebrew do not have a productive mechanism of incorporation. They do, however, display some cases of incorporation limited to certain non-verbal predicates in the EV S-pattern. In these cases, the slot of one of the arguments of the evaluative predicate is not a complement of the N or Unq evaluative predicate, as is normally the case, but rather its possessor. Where such a form has a non-incorporated counterpart, the pair of incorporated and unincorporated variants does not display the specific–generic functional distribution typical of the cases discussed in the literature on incorporation. The EV predicates that do display incorporation will be discussed in Section 11.2.

An entirely different type of incorporation in the Hebrew EX S-pattern, one that involves incorporation of an argument into another argument, will be discussed in Section 11.3.

11.2 Incorporation in the EV S-pattern

Let us look at the sentence in (2).

(2) It is my/John's turn to be the designated driver.

The nominal predicate *turn* expresses deontic modality (obligation) and like any EV sentence, it has two semantic roles in its argument structure: the person affected by the obligation, i.e. the affectee, and the situation which this obligation involves, i.e. the evaluee. The sentences of (3) are close enough semantically to serves as an almost-minimal pair.

(3) a. It is time for me to be the designated driver. (I)
 b. It is my turn to be the designated driver. (I)

The evaluative predicates are the nouns *time* in (3a) and *turn* in (3b). The evaluee is in both cases the InfP *to be the designated driver*. The affectee PP *for me* is in its canonical position in (3a). Its counterpart in (3b) is the possessive pronoun *my* serving as the determiner of the predicate noun *turn*. Sentence (3a) is an instantiation of the canonical variant of the EV S-pattern, whereas (3b) is an instantiation of its non-canonical counterpart, with the affectee incorporated into the predicate N as its possessive determiner.

The two N predicates *time* and *turn* differ in their requirements for an affectee. In the case of *time*, if the affectee is understood from the context, it may be absent (*it's time to go*). In the case of *turn*, however, the affectee is obligatory, as is clear from the ungrammaticality of (4a), where the possessive form is missing. Note that the canonical variant is not available with this predicate, as is evident in (4b).

(4) a. *It is turn to be the designated driver .
    b. *It is turn for me to be the designated driver.

Several nouns have been found to behave in a similar way, i.e. to serve as predicates of an EV sentence with a possessive expression inside the NP representing the affectee, such as *delight, duty, fate, intention, job, luck, place, practice, privilege, problem, right* and *task*. Some of these are shown in (5).

(5) a. It is the Government's duty to investigate those complaints. (I)
    b. It is your bad luck that your application was rejected on this ground. (I)
    c. It is my pleasure to once again welcome you to Montreal. (I)
    d. It is society's problem that so many kids think of sex as something to do when you're bored. (I)
    e. It is my right to ask the police if I am arrested or detained. (I)

These predicates do not necessarily require a possessive expression incorporated in them; they merely allow it. As can be seen in (6), the NP of the predicate *delight* may include a possessive expression, as in (6a). It may appear without one, having an article in the same position, as in (6b). Finally, it may have a canonical affectee with a *for*-phrase, as in (6c), or with a *to*-phrase, as in (6d).

(6) a. It is my delight to welcome you to the XXIX International Congress of Psychology. (I)
    b. It is a great delight to be in the presence of such promising biomedical scholars. (I)
    c. It is a great delight for me to share this exquisite music with Victoria audiences. (I)
    d. It is a great delight to me to see your face once more. (I)

The sentences of (6) only provide tangential support for noun incorporation. After all, the possessive pronoun that is the determiner of the predicate N is not obligatory, even if it is functionally equivalent to the canonical affectee. With predicates such as *turn*, however, which do not allow realizations without a possessive affectee, the affectee must be viewed as a required argument, hence possessive argument incorporation is the only explanatory option. This obligatory behavior is restricted to a handful of predicates such as *turn, business, fate, fault,* and *place*. Examples for *business* and *place* are given in (7).

(7) a. It is not your business to reform your roommate's sleep patterns. (I)

b. It is not the teacher's place to decide if the child will participate or not. (I)

The sentences of (7), with *business* and *place* as predicates, along with (3a), with *turn* as predicate, supply convincing evidence that these sentences are indeed structural variants of the EV S-pattern, differing from the canonical pattern only by their incorporation of the affectee as a possessive determiner of the NP headed by the predicate.

In Hebrew, the sentences of (8) display a similar behavior.

(8) a. *ha-šana lo tor-i le'areax, toda l-a-el.* (I)
the-year not turn my to.host, a.thank to the God
'This year it is not my turn to host [the holiday meals], thank God.'

b. *ha-šana tor ima šeli le'areax.* (I)
the-year the.turn.of mother mine to host.
'This year it is my mother's turn to host [the holiday meals].'

In sentence (8a), the noun *tor* 'turn' appears with the first person possessive suffix *-i* 'my', and in (8b), *tor* is in the *construct state*, followed by the possessor NP *ima šeli* 'my mother'. Hebrew has other predicates behaving in this way, but as was the case in English, there is only a handful of nominal predicates which *require* an incorporated possessive affectee, and may not appear without it. Two predicates of this kind are *ašma* 'fault' (with the construct state form *ašmat* 'fault.of') exemplified in (9).

(9) *ašmat-enu še-hem pi me'a yoter tovim mi-šar ha-xavarot?* (I)
fault our that they times hundred more good than the.rest.of the companies?
'Is it our fault that they are a hundred times better than all other companies?'

Besides nouns, Hebrew also displays this behavior with morphologically unique (Unq) (Section 3.3.1.1) predicates. One example is the word *day* 'enough'. On its own, this is an interjection. Besides being an interjection, it serves also as an evaluative predicate, as can be seen in (10a), where it happens to instantiate a sentence form without any affectee. Interestingly, though, it has acquired the ability to be conjugated for possessive suffixes as if it were a noun (already in Biblical Hebrew, and in the evaluative function since post-Biblical Hebrew). In other words, "our enough" means "enough for us", as in (10b). In addition, *day* may also take a canonical PP affectee headed by *le-* 'to', as in (10c).

(10) a. *day še-ha-memšala ha-falastinit timana mi-teror.* (I)
enough that the government Palestinian will.refrain from terrorism
'It would be sufficient if the Palestinian government refrained from terrorism.'

b. *day-enu še-yeš l-anu nivxeret kazot.* (I)
enough our that EXIST to us a.team such
'It is good enough for us that we have such a team.'

c. *day l-a-talmidim lehavin et divrey ha-paršanim.* (I)
enough for the students to.understand ACC the.words.of the commentators
'It is enough for the students to understand the words of the commentators.'

Forms of incorporation in the EV S-pattern date back to Biblical Hebrew. Example (11a–b) consists of Psalms 128: 1–2. All the English translations consulted have proven to be too liberal to count as appropriate renditions of the Hebrew original for our purposes here, so I have given my own gloss-oriented translation.

(11) a. *ashrey kol yere YHWH ha-holex bi-draxav.*
happiness.of every fearer.of YHWH the goer in his.ways
'[Let there be] happiness upon those who fear the Lord walking in His ways.'

b. *yegia kapexa ki toxel, ašre-xa ve-tov l-ax.*
the.labor.of your.hands when you.eat, happiness yours and good to you
'When you eat the labor of your hands, [let there be] happiness upon you and good for you.'

The stem of the noun at hand *ašre-* 'happiness' is a well established form in the Hebrew Bible, attested in forty four occurrences. The noun in its absolute state is not attested. In other words, it lost its independent form and usage already in Biblical times and has been grammaticalized specifically as a bound N predicate (in the plural or dual form) with either a pronominal possessive suffix, as in (11b) or with a possessive NP incorporated into its phrase, as in (11a). Its root ʔ.Š.R (ʔ=glottal stop), prevails in other words, having both the physical meaning of 'go straight/step forward' and the abstract meaning of 'happy'/'happiness', the two meanings being connected apparently by a metaphor of the kind "going straight is being happy".

Since *ašre-* in biblical Hebrew does not require a nominal (InfP or *that*-clause), this sentence is, strictly speaking, a manifestation of the PredP-alone S-pattern (Section 3.3.4.1), a sub-pattern of the EV S-pattern.

In (11b) we have a "synonymous parallelism" (Lowth [1753] 1787: Lecture 19), a typical form of Biblical poetic style, beginning with *ašre-xa* "your happiness" and ending with *tov l-ax* "good for you". The former is a noun phrase containing a possessive suffix, whereas the latter is a canonical manifestation of the PredP-alone S-pattern. An NP, then, is put in parallelism with a canonical PredP-alone sentence form. This clearly shows that this NP is indeed a sentence, a full predication of the predicate *ašre-* with an evaluee incorporated as its possessor.

While in Biblical Hebrew, these *ašre-* sentences do not have a nominal in them, the fuller form of the EV S-pattern with a *that*-clause developed in post-Biblical Hebrew, and is in regular use in Israeli Hebrew (for a full historical account and further justification for viewing such NPs as sentences see Kuzar 2000). Its currency across registers in Israeli Hebrew is evident from example (12), which is a talkback response to a news item reporting that some hacker demolished the Internet site praising Yigal Amir, the murderer of Prime Minister Yitzhak Rabin.

(12) *ašre-xa še-zaxita lehorid kaze atar.* (I)
happiness your that you.merited to.put.down such a.site
'Good for you that you had the privilege of knocking down such a site.'

It should be noted that the predicate *ašre-* can only be realized as the host of incorporation. It has no realization with a full affectee PP outside its own phrase. However, there are other predicates that may be realized either in their canonical EV S-pattern form or in the incorporation variant, such as *day* 'enough' (exemplified in (10) above), and others, in which the occurrence of an evaluee is optional, as is the case with *mazal* 'luck', *zxut* 'right', and *xova* 'duty', to name just a few. These are exemplified in (13). The (i) examples have no affectee, the (ii) examples have an affectee incorporated into the predicate phrase, and the (iii) examples (where relevant) give a canonical form with the affectee PP in its regular place.

(13) a. (i) *mazal še-necigey irgun ha-bri'ut lo legamre metumtamim.* (I)
luck that the.representatives.of the.organization.of the health not completely idiots
'It is a good thing that the representatives of WHO are not complete idiots.'

(ii) *mazal-i še-lo nafal po til.* (I)
luck my that not fell here a.missile
'It is my luck that no missile fell here.'

b. (i) *zxut gdola lihyot xelek me-asiya mevorexet kazo.* (I)
   privilege great to.be part from activity blessed such
   'It is a great privilege to be part of such a blessed venture.'

   (ii) *zxut-xem la'azov et ha-'arec.* (I)
   right your to.leave ACC the country
   'It is your right to leave the country.'

   (iii) *zxut gdola l-i levarex etxem im ptixat šnat ha-limudim 6569.* (I)
   right great to me to.bless you with the.opening.of the.year.of the
   studies [Jewish calendar] 6569
   'It is a great privilege for me to bless you upon the opening of the school year 2009.'

c. (i) *xova lehagiš et ha-tvi'a tox tiš'im yom.* (I)
   Duty to.submit ACC the suit within ninety day
   'It is obligatory to submit the law suit within ninety days.'

   (ii) *xovat ha-šofet lišrok be-macav ze.*
   the.duty.of the referee to.whistle in situation this
   'It is the referee's duty to blow his whistle in this situation.'

   (iii) *xova al kol student le-mišpatim lilmod retorika.*
   duty on every student for laws to.study rhetoric
   'It is a must for every law student to study rhetoric.'

In sum, the seeming possessor inside the NP/UnqP headed by an N/Unq predicate of the EV S-pattern is in fact an incorporated affectee. Some of these predicates obligatorily incorporate the affectee, others alternate between an incorporated NP and an external PP affectee. When the two options exist, the incorporated and the external affectee have the same semantic role, though the two forms may differ in register, style, or information structure.

This analysis expands the idea of incorporation the way it has been used in the literature in two ways. Firstly, so far, only verbal predicates have been shown to incorporate arguments. Here N and Unq predicates have been shown to do this. Secondly, while Mithun (1984: 848, 875) identified only the incorporation of nouns bearing patient, location, or instrument roles, this notion is extended here to the incorporation of an affectee as well.

Let us now look at incorporation data in the EX S-pattern in Biblical Hebrew.

11.3 Incorporation in the possessive EX S-pattern in Biblical Hebrew

Possession is expressed via existence in all historical stages of Hebrew. In Biblical Hebrew, possession may be expressed either by predication, but quite often by patterning; namely, the existential predicate *yeš* 'EXIST' is absent, leaving only the two arguments, namely the existent-turned-possessed and the affectee-turned-possessor. The two sentences of (14) exemplify this option in Biblical Hebrew. Sentence (14a) is the fuller form, with *yeš*, while in (14b) *yeš* is absent. Both of them equally convey possessive statements. Differences may have to do with register, style, or information structure considerations, but this is not our concern here.

(14) a. *yeš l-i tikva.* (Ruth 1: 12)
EXIST to me hope
'I have hope.'

b. *le-(e)lohim pitronim.* (Genesis 40:8)
to God interpretations
'God has interpretations.'

Equipped with this piece of knowledge, we may now approach Psalms 115: 5–7 in (15). This is a poetic passage that compares "our God in heaven" with the idols of the other nations. It contains a list of six possessive statements in a row. The first four (15a–d) have the reduced possessive sentence form, lacking the predicate *yeš*, while the last two (15e–f) are even more reduced, having a possessor NP incorporated inside the NP of the possessed. So instead of saying "[there are] hands/feet to them" all we have is just the NP "their feet".

(15) a. *pe lahem – ve-lo yedaberu.*
a.mouth to.them – and not they.speak
'They have mouths – but they do not speak.'

b. *eynayim lahem – ve-lo yir'u.*
eyes to.them – and not they.see
'They have eyes – but they do not see.'

c. *oznayim lahem – ve-lo yišma'u.*
ears to.them – and not they.hear
'They have ears – but they do not hear.'

d. *af lahem – ve-lo yerixun.*
a.nose to.them – and not they.smell
'They have a nose – but they do not smell.'

e. *yedeyhem – ve-lo yemišun.*
their.hands – and not they.feel
'They have hands – but they do not feel.'

f. *ragleyhem – ve-lo yehalexu.*
their.feet – and not they.walk
'They have feet – but they do not walk.'

Brockelmann (1913: 40) correctly identified this NP as a sentence form, followed later by Loewenstamm (1983: 149). Both, however, incorrectly view the suffix as the predicate, although this is a problematic solution, since the possessor and the possessed are *arguments* in a possessive statement, not predicates. The lack of an obvious predicate and the feeling that one needs to be present have led to this forced solution.

In the first four sentences (15a–d), patterning is facilitated – as it usually is – by the fact that the construction is distinctive and recognizable even without the predicate. In possessive statements, the form *to-NP NP* suffices for it to be identified as a variant of the possessive sentence, even though the initial *yeš* is absent (the full form being *yeš to-NP NP*). But when the form *to-NP NP* is further reduced into a single NP (*possessor's possessed*), how is the reader expected to identify what kind of sentence it is?

The answer lies in the fact that this is a poetic ad hoc formation, in which the constructional interpretation is not provided by the sentential phrase itself, but rather by the context of the four previous sentences. The whole passage is doubly structured. First of all, it has six sentences in the same form. Secondly, each of the six sentences has the same internal structure of a concessive statement, saying that "even though they have X, they don't Y", with X being a sensory organ and Y being the sense associated with it. Only under such tightly structured poetic context could a form like this have sentential interpretation.

Since the sentence forms here lack predicates – being based on patterning alone – we cannot speak here of incorporation in the sense developed in the literature and also in the previous section. Not the *predicate* incorporates the affectee-turned-possessor but rather the *other argument*, namely the existent-turned-possessed. This is, then, in some sense the opposite of the phenomenon known in the literature as *external possession* (Payne & Barshi 1999) or in relational-grammar terms *possessor ascension* (Bell 1983: 193). In external possession, a non-argument possessor does not appear in the "expected" position inside the NP headed by the possessed, but rather as a quasi-argument at the sentential level. In our case here, it is the other way round: an affectee-turned-possessor, i.e. an argument, does not appear at the sentential level, but rather inside the phrase headed by the possessed.

The Biblical Hebrew poetic form exemplified in (15e–f) is, then, reduced in two ways: first of all, it is missing the predicate *yeš* and is constituted through patterning. Secondly, it has one argument incorporated inside the other. While the combination of these two non-canonical behaviors is singular, the incorporation of an argument into another argument is not. Let us have a look at Hungarian. Hungarian is similar to Hebrew in that possession is expressed and conceptualized as "existence to someone". But there are some differences between Hebrew and Hungarian. While Hebrew has a unique predicate *yeš*, Hungarian simply uses the verb *lenni* 'be'. In languages of this kind, such as Latin, "I have money" may be expressed as "is to me money" (Lat. *est mihi pecunia* or with a lexical possessor *est viro pecunia* 'is to the man money'). This can also be done in Hungarian, but there is a difference: when the possessor is a lexical NP, it behaves like Latin, but when the possessor is an unstressed pronoun, it is incorporated into the NP of the possessed as a possessive suffix of the possessed noun stem, producing an expression that literally says "is my money", as in (16) (*van* 'is' = IIIsg. of *lenni* 'be').

(16) *van pénz-em*
    is money my (is my money)
    'I have money.'

This variation between lexical and pronominal possessors in Hungarian is a regular feature of Hungarian grammar. Biblical Hebrew does not support this incorporation in any regular way. Still, besides the poetic sentences of (15e–f) there is one sentence in Biblical Hebrew that displays this Hungarian behavior with a pronominal possessive suffix, as shown in (17).

(17) *lo tihye tifart-exa al ha-derex ašer ata holex.* (Judges 4,9)
    not will be glory your (your glory) on the way that you go
    'There will not be glory for you in the way that you are taking.'
    i.e. 'you will have no glory in the way that you are taking.'

This sentence displays predication, not patterning, since the verb *haya* 'be' here is not the grammatical copula, but rather the lexical future variant of *yeš*, the existential predicate (expressed via the verb *be*). Instead of "there is glory for you" the text reads "there is your glory". The Bible translations had difficulty with this sentence, interpreting the possessive phrase in diverse ways. The translation of the Jewish Publication Society interprets it in the manner presented here (following Brockelmann 1913: 263 and Loewenstamm 1983: 150 here as well), as can be seen in (18).

(18) There will be no glory for you in the course you are taking.
    (Judges 4,9; JPS)

With the exception of some additional dubious forms of this kind, the incorporation of the possessor into the NP headed by the possessed is, then, an ad hoc device in Biblical Hebrew. It demonstrates, however, that even when such processes are not on a grammaticalization trajectory, they can be accounted for as synchronic variants.

11.4 Summary and conclusion of Chapter 11

In the introductory section, the prevailing view of incorporation was presented. In this view, a sentence displaying incorporation instantiates a variant of a construction, in which one of the arguments has been included in the verb complex. However, incorporation into the verb complex is only a special case of incorporation into a predicate phrase. The case discussed in Section 11.2 involved non-verbal predicates, N and Unq, in the EV S-pattern. Incorporation is manifest in an NP (or an UnqP) headed by the predicate N (or Unq), with the affectee-turned-possessor NP incorporated into it.

In Section 11.3, sporadic incorporation in the Biblical Hebrew possessive form of the EX S-pattern has been discussed. In this case, incorporation has involved the inclusion of an argument in another argument, namely the possessor into the possessed.

The cases discussed in this chapter broaden and deepen the scope of phenomena classified under the rubric of incorporation.

CHAPTER 12

Conclusion

12.1 Preliminary discussion

In this book two concepts have been suggested as necessary ingredients in a constructional account of sentence structure: sentence patterns and patterning. I will start this concluding chapter by summarizing these two concepts in Section 12.2 and 12.3. I will then discuss the typological aspects of this study in Section 12.4. Finally, I will briefly mention some additional points in Section 12.5.

The text in this chapter is not interrupted by back references to the various relevant passages. Instead, key concepts will be italicized on a first appearance. The italicized concepts have detailed references in the index.

12.2 Sentence patterns

The first concept introduced in this book is the *sentence pattern* (S-pattern). S-patterns are not new to linguistic literature. Here they have been introduced as a separate type of construction in the framework of cognitive–constructional models of sentential syntax.

Among the various constructions that interact in the formation of a sentence, the S-pattern constitutes the mechanism that specifies the components of the S-pattern and their linearization. Each component is presented in its own slot in terms of its form and function.

For those sentences that have a predicate, the S-pattern serves as a linearization construction. In the verbal sentence, for instance, *Argument structure constructions* are needed for mapping participant roles onto argument roles, but the argument structure constructions themselves do not determine word order. This task is taken up by the S-pattern.

But many S-patterns have slots for components other than the predicate and its arguments, such as expletives, copulas, and certain kinds of adjuncts. The S-pattern specifies their form, function, and place in the linear sequence.

The S-pattern is a typical construction: it has its own form and function/meaning. The slots of the formulas of each S-pattern carry labels that represent the parts of the construction. To some extent, the parts of the construction are equivalent to *parts of speech*, but they are established in a *top down* motion by a division of the sentence into its constitutive parts based on distributional testing, rather than in a bottom up motion of combining parts of speech given in advance.

Staying still in the realm of its form, the formula of an S-pattern may contain constants (e.g. the expletive *there* or the predicate *yeš* EXIST), closed-class variables (e.g. copular verbs), and open-class variables (e.g. NPs). The Formula of the S-pattern contains the maximal number of slots assignable by the predicates instantiating it, allowing for different predicates to make use of less than the full pattern, according to their specific argument structures. The realization of objects, for example, varies across different predicates.

While the *subject initial* (S1) *Verbal* (V) S-pattern only has verbs as predicates, the *predicate initial* (P1) S-patterns are not specific to one predicate class, and are open, in addition, to V, N, A, and P predicates. The postulation of *multivariate predicate slots* (hosting multiple parts of speech) affords an elegant presentation of a many-to-one relation of form and function, which would otherwise require a network in which the same function would be stated in a highly redundant way.

As for the functional dimension, every S-pattern has its own meaning. The V S-pattern conveys agentive *actions*, but it also serves as the *unmarked* S-pattern, able to express all the functions that other S-patterns are marked for. The *copular* (COP) S-pattern conveys *states* of affairs, in which an Assigned term is presented as equivalent, attributed, or in relation with the Basis subject.

While in the subject initial (S1) S-patterns (V and COP) the name of the S-pattern does not refer to its functions, the predicate initial (P1) S-patterns have been given functional names that indicate their function. These are the *existential* (EX), the *evaluative* (EV), and the *environmental condition* (ENV) S-patterns. Similarly, the *sub-patterns* linked with them have been given functional names such as *Cost*, or *Body-part-condition*.

In the V S-pattern, sentence formation is a process in which (a) individual participant roles of a predicate are matched with argument roles of argument constructions; (b) argument roles are matched with S-pattern roles; and (c) S-patterns interact with other sentence-level constructions, such as prosodic constructions, *information structure* constructions, sentential mood constructions, and modality constructions.

The semantic profile of predicates licensed to appear in the P1 constructions is organized in a *conceptual category* (CC). Three CCs have been presented: the *CC of existence*, the *CC of evaluation*, and the *CC of environmental conditions*. They all share the same prototype-based radial structure: predicates at or near the *core* are lexically marked as belonging to the CC, that is, they have an inherent meaning of existence, evaluation, or environmental conditions respectively. In the medium *periphery*, the predicates are not inherently marked as having the meaning of the CC, but they get their meaning contextually, by interacting with other lexical items that have these meanings. This compositional meaning is enhanced by the constructional meaning of the S-pattern. Finally, at the distant periphery there are predicate phrases that only get the meaning of the CC by *imposition*, namely the S-pattern imposes existential, evaluative, or environmental meaning on the predicate phrase.

The postulation of CCs associated with S-patterns has several theoretical advantages. First of all, the existence of such CCs lends support to the cognitive linguistic claim that semantic information is patterned in the human mind according to a prototype-based organizing principle. Furthermore, it is suggested here that the imposition of constructional meaning on non-canonical predicates is at work not only where there are gaps between the argument roles of argument structure constructions and the participant roles of verbs inserted into them (*Sam sneezed the napkin off the table*), but also where no such gaps exist; but other gaps transpire between the prototypical meaning of a CC associated with an S-pattern and the non-prototypical meaning of predicates that are forced into this S-pattern (*there parked a car*). In the latter case, existential or presentational meaning is imposed by the EX S-pattern on the verb *park* due to the use of this predicate in an environment (the EX S-pattern) that constructionally encodes this meaning, even though this meaning is not inherently integral to this verb.

The S-patterns are organized in a partly ordered *field* of S-patterns. In English and Hebrew, the field of S-patterns contains two networks of *major S-patterns*: the Subject Initial (S1) network containing the V and COP S-patterns and the Predicate Initial (P1) Network, containing the EX, EV, and ENV S-patterns. The field also contains some *minor S-patterns* (such as *the sooner the better*). Within the P1 network, the three S-patterns (EX, EV, and ENV) have sub-patterns (Body-part-condition, Cost, etc.), which are related to them in form and meaning, but cannot be included in them. The primary test for inclusion in an S-pattern is that the meaning of the predicate (or predicate phrase) implies the core meaning (or one of the core meanings) of the CC associated with that S-pattern. If this is not the case, the sentence has to belong to a different S-pattern.

If the formation of sentences depended merely on predication, one might suggest that there is some overall, highly generalized construction, which is linked to all presumably unlinked S-pattern, the way the Subject–Predicate Construction heads Goldberg's (1995: 109) network of argument structure constructions. But if some S-patterns lack predicates and others lack subjects, not much is left from this generalization. This touches upon the very heart of the question: what is a sentence and what generalizations may be made over all sentences? If the only possible answer is that sentences are manifestations of S-patterns, then no top node is necessarily implied. Networks of S-patterns exist, but no connection needs to be obligatorily postulated among them or between a network and an isolated S-pattern.

12.3 Patterning

Sentential syntax has been largely based on the premise of *predication*, namely that the life-giving component of a sentence is its predicate. This has been so due to the centrality of the verbal sentence in literature on sentential syntax. A closer look at the verbal sentence, and a fresh look at copular sentences, as well as predicate-initial sentences, has made it clear that not all sentences instantiate a predicate–argument relation. Furthermore, some sentences contain constants and variables that are not part of the predicate–argument array, yet they need to be specified and allotted a slot in the linearization of the sentence. Finally, some sentences look like they instantiate a certain S-pattern, exhibiting most of the slots of that S-pattern, yet the predicate slot itself is empty.

Due to the premise of predication, the search for the predicate has often yielded controversial candidates exhibiting atypical predicate behavior. In the case of such failures of the predication premise, *patterning* has been suggested as a formative mechanism, either in addition to, or instead of predication.

The relation between predication and patterning has been described in terms of the relative proportion of information – structural and functional – contributed by each mechanism to the formation of a sentence. In the context of the sentences discussed in this book, five typical cases of proportions between predication and patterning have been described.

In the first case, most of the information is contributed by predication. Patterning only linearizes the slots hosting the predicate argument structure. In the second case, the predicate used in the S-pattern is non-prototypical. The sentence gets some of its meaning, its constructional meaning, directly from the S-pattern. In the third case, there are additional components in the sentence. These may be grammatical elements, such as the *it* and *there* expletives in the EV and EX S-patterns, but they can also be adjuncts. The fourth case has a null predicate, yet the S-pattern has a predicate slot which goes unfilled. The components of the sentence, which normally would have been arguments of a predicate, are inserted into their slots by the force of the construction alone. The fifth case has no predicate slot at all, the components of the sentence are not arguments, and patterning is the only mechanism at work. We see, then, that patterning is a major factor in sentence formation.

It might be tempting to view patterning in light of the debate around the need for phrasal constructions, and the arguments made in favor of such constructions within Construction Grammar in, for example, Fried & Östman (2004). But the literature on phrasal constructions has so far addressed only phrases with some dependency relations between them which are articulated outside the phrasal construction itself, such as argument structure constructions in sentences or determiner and noun relations in NPs.

I am not sure I know how to formulate the translatability between the device of patterning developed here and phrasal constructions of the type just mentioned. The independence of S-patterns from the grip of argument structure constructions is evident in the gradient between the pole of sentences leaning mostly on argument structure and the pole of sentences leaning exclusively on patterning. The latter pole might make this translatability a difficult challenge at this stage of theorizing.

12.4 Typological aspects

This book is about English and Hebrew. As such it is a contrastive study. It is, however, also a *typological* study. Not much has been said in this book about other languages, thus most of the typological perspective of this book has been left implicit. Yet many readers must have noticed that certain constructions described here are reminiscent of parallel constructions in other languages, certainly readers with a European linguistic background. This sense of familiarity is not incidental. To show that there is indeed a language typology here, the terms of the typology have to be stated explicitly.

The typology proposed in this study is based on the following criteria. The language has two types of unmarked word orders: S1 and P1. These word orders are defined by a calculus of the lexical components of the S-patterns, thus grammatical components such as expletives, auxiliaries, copulas, etc. are not counted in.

The S1 order in these languages is used to build up the *foreground* and the *background* of the *storyline* of a narrative. V sentences convey the actional skeleton of the storyline and COP sentences prevail in conveying the states of affairs at different points of the storyline. The P1 order in a language of this typology is used to make existential, evaluative, and environmental statements.

By and large, Hebrew and English maintain this basic word order, regardless of whether the NP slots are filled by lexical or by pronominal elements. Other languages to be included in this typology, e.g. French, may have variant word orders for sentences with pronominal versus lexical NPs. Such issues will have to be dealt with in the description of these languages.

Beyond the existence of a common typological ground, much variation may prevail between the languages of this typology. Possession, for example, is expressed in Hebrew in terms of existence, i.e. in the P1 order, while in English it is expressed by means of a possessive verb in the S1 order. Some differences have to do with the distribution of *situation types* that are included in the semantic scope of the P1 S-patterns. For example, the event of a person being negatively affected by the action of an animal is typically expressed in Hebrew in a P1 sub-pattern that is associated with the EV S-pattern (*akca oti dvora* 'stung me a bee'), while in English it is expressed in a passive S1 sentence (*I was stung by a bee*).

This typology also interacts with other typologies, such as the typology of languages that use *expletives* versus those that do not. Contrary to the Chomskyan view that expletive behavior is a *universal* parameter, *globally* set for each language, it has been shown here that expletive behavior is variable in both English and Hebrew. English has non-canonical reduced sentence forms in which the expletive is absent, while Hebrew has non-canonical forms with an added expletive. It has been shown that in both cases, these behaviors are determined by the prototype-based radial form of the CCs of the P1 S-patterns.

Many other similarities and differences may be associated with the basic defining properties of our typology both in the two languages of this study and in other languages of this typology. In certain respects, English and Hebrew occupy two poles in this typology, but this hypothesis awaits testing, as do all other aspects of this typology when applied to other languages.

12.5 Finally

Attention to detail has been a quality of both structuralist and constructional approaches, often frowned on by the generative universalist view. However, the understanding that in the constructional approach there are no extra-systemic details, but rather it is "constructions all the way down" (Goldberg 2003), has made us constructional linguists both eager and patient when it comes to dealing with details. This preoccupation concerns both description and exemplification.

This book indeed makes a point of exemplifying phenomena to quench this kind of thirst. Many details discussed throughout the book have not entered this concluding chapter. Such details involve discussions of *borderline* cases, of *markedness*, of *sub-patterns*, of *morphologically unique* and *endemic* predicates, of syntactic *syncretism* in word order, of *granularity* and *resolution* in viewing constructions, of the *motivated* nature of the S1 and P1 word orders, and of variants of S-patterns displaying *incorporation*, among others.

I hope this study has delineated an interesting research perspective. For me it certainly has, and hopefully it will prove to have done so for others too.

References

Aghion, Gallith 2009. Linguistic effects on the use of the evaluative pattern [ze + fossilized Pred. + Comp.] in informal Contemporary Hebrew. MA Thesis supervised by Irit Meir at the Department of Hebrew. Haifa: University of Haifa.

Alba-Salas, Josep 2004. Lexically selected expletives: Evidence from Basque and Romance. SKY Journal of Linguistics 17, 35–100.

Allen, Barbara J., Donna B. Gardiner & Donald G. Frantz 1984. Noun incorporation in Southern Tiwa. International Journal of American Linguistics 50(3), 292–311.

Allsopp, Fred W. 1992. Albert Pike A Biography. Kessinger Publishing, LLC.

Ariel, Mira 2008. Pragmatics and Grammar. Cambridge textbooks in linguistics. Cambridge: Cambridge University Press.

Azar, Moshe 1995. taxbir lešon hamišna [The Syntax of Mishnaic Hebrew]. Jerusalem & Haifa: The Academy of the Hebrew Language and University of Haifa Press.

Bain, Alexander 1871. English Composition and Rhetoric. A facsimile reproduction with an introduction by Charlotte Downey. American linguistics, 1700–1900 Scholars' Facsimiles & Reprints, vol. 497. New York: D. Appleton.

Baker, Mark C. 1988. Incorporation: A Theory of Grammatical Function Changing. Chicago: University of Chicago Press.

Bally, Charles 1922. Copule zéro et faits connexes. Bulletin de la Société de Linguistique de Paris 23.

Barri, Nimrod 1977. Clause Models in Antiphontean Greek. Munich: Wilhelm Fink.

Battistella, Edwin L. 1990. Markedness: The Evaluative Superstructure of Language. Albany: State University of New York Press.

Battistella, Edwin L. 1996. The Logic of Markedness. New York: Oxford University Press.

Beckner, Clay & Joan Bybee 2009. A usage-based account of constituency and reanalysis. Language Learning 59(Suppl. 1), 27–46.

Bell, Sarah J. 1983. Advancements and ascensions in cebuano. In D.M. Perlmutter (ed.), Studies in Relational Grammar 1 (143–218). Chicago: University of Chicago Press.

Bendavid, Abba 1958. kecad seder nose venasu [What is the order of subject and predicate]. Lešonenu La'am 87. Jerusalem: Academy of the Hebrew Language.

Bendavid, Abba 1971. lešon mikra ulešon xaxamim [Biblical Hebrew and Mishnaic Hebrew]. Volume II. Tel-Aviv: Dvir.

Benveniste, Emile [1950] 1971. The nominal sentence. In E. Benveniste (ed.), Problems in General Linguistics, translated by M.E. Meek (131–144). Coral Gables: University of Miami Press.

Benveniste, Emile [1960] 1971. The linguistic functions of 'to be' and 'to have'. In E. Benveniste (ed.), Problems in General Linguistics, translated by M.E. Meek (163–179). Coral Gables: University of Miami Press.

Bergs, Alexander & Gabriele Diewald (eds.) 2009. Contexts and Constructions. Constructional Approaches to Language 9. Amsterdam: John Benjamins.

Berman, Ruth A. 1980. The case of an (S)VO language: Subjectless constructions in Modern Hebrew. Language 56(4), 759–776.

Biber, Douglas, Stig Johansson, Geoffrey Leech, Susan Conrad, & Edward Finegan 1999. Longman Grammar of Spoken and Written English. London: Longman.

Birner, Betty J. & Gregory Ward 1998. Information Status and Noncanonical Word Order in English. Amsterdam: John Benjamins.

Bloomfield, Leonard 1933. Language. New York: Henry Holt.

Boas, Hans C. 2003. A Constructional Approach to Resultatives. Stanford, CA: CSLI Publications.

Boas, Hans C. 2008. Resolving form–meaning discrepancies in Construction Grammar. In Jaakko Leino (ed.), Constructional Reorganization, Constructional Approaches to Language 5. Amsterdam: John Benjamins.

Bolinger, Dwight L. 1952. Linear modification. Publications of the Modern Language Association of America 67, 1117–1144.

Bolinger, Dwight L. 1977. Meaning and Form. London: Longman.

Breivik, Leiv Egil 1981. On the interpretation of existential there. Language 57(1), 11–46.

Breivik, Leiv Egil 1999. On the rhetorical function of existential there. Nordlit 6, 3–14.

Brentano, Franz 1874. Psychologie vom empirischen Standpunkt. Leipzig: Duncker & Humblot.

Brockelmann, Carl 1913. Grundriß der vergleichenden Grammatik der semitischen Sprachen II. Berlin: Reuther. Reprinted 1961, Hildesheim: Georg Olms Verlag.

Brugman, Claudia & George Lakoff 1988. Cognitive topology and lexical networks. In S. Small, G. Cottrell & M. Tannenhaus (eds.), Lexical Ambiguity Resolution (477–507). San Mateo CA: Morgan Kaufman.

Buyssens, Eric 1987. The preposition for with an infinitive clause. English Studies 4, 336–347.

Bybee, Joan 1985. Morphology: A Study of the Relation between Meaning and Form. Amsterdam: John Benjamins.

Bybee, Joan 2006. From usage to grammar: the mind's response to repetition. Language 82(4), 711–733.

Bybee, Joan 2007. Frequency of Use and the Organization of Language. Oxford: Oxford University Press.

Byrd, Patricia 1997. English Grammar and Pedagogical Grammars. Http://www.gsu.edu/~eslhpb/grammar/Sentpart#Verb Types.

Carnie, Andrew 2002. Syntax: A Generative Introduction. Oxford: Blackwell.

Chafe, Wallace 1976. Givenness, contrastiveness, definiteness, subjects, topics, and points of view. In C.N. Li (ed.), Subject and Topic (25–55). New York: Academic Press.

Chafe, Wallace 1994. Discourse, Consciousness, and Time: The Flow and Displacement of Conscious Experience in Speaking and Writing. Chicago, London: University of Chicago Press.

Chomsky, Noam 1957. Syntactic Structures. The Hague & Paris: Mouton.

Chomsky, Noam [1981] 1993. Lectures on Government and Binding: The Pisa Lectures. Berlin: Mouton de Gruyter.

Chomsky, Noam 1995. Categories and transformations. In N. Chomsky (ed.), The Minimalist Program (219–394). Cambridge, MA: MIT Press.

Coffin, Edna Amir & Shmuel Bolozky 2005. A Reference Grammar of Modern Hebrew. Cambridge: Cambridge University Press.

Croft, William 2001. Radical Construction Grammar. Oxford: Oxford University Press.

Croft, William 2007. Logical and typological arguments for Radical Construction Grammar. In V. Evans, B. Bergen & J. Zinken (eds.), The Cognitive Linguistics Reader (638–673). London: Equinox.

Daneš, František 1974. Functional sentence perspective and the organization of the text. In F. Daneš (ed.), Papers on Functional Sentence Perspective (106–128). Prague & The Hague: Academia and Mouton.

Dori-Hacohen, Gonen 2007. Corpus of Hebrew Political Call-In Radio Programs. Compiled for Ph.D. Dissertation under the supervision of Tamar Katriel & Yael Maschler, University of Haifa.

Dowty, David 1991. Thematic proto-roles and argument selection. Language 67(3), 547–619.

Driver, Samuel Rolles 1874. A Treatise on the Uses of the Tenses in Hebrew. Oxford: Clarendon Press.

Du Bois, John W. 1987. The discourse basis of ergativity. Language 63(4), 805–855.

Durie, Mark 1995. Towards an understanding of linguistic evolution and the notion 'X has a function Y'. In W. Abraham, T. Givón & S.A. Thompson (eds.), Discourse Grammar and Typology: Papers in Honor of John W.M. Verhaar (275–308). Amsterdam: John Benjamins.

Emonds, Joseph E. 1976. Root and Structure-Preserving Transformations [MIT diss. 1970]. New York: Academic Press.

Erdmann, Peter 1990. Discourse and Grammar: Focussing and Defocussing in English. Tübingen: Max Niemeyer Verlag.

Fauconnier, Gilles & Mark Turner 2002. The Way We Think: Conceptual Blending and the Mind's Hidden Complexities. New York: Basic Books.

Fillmore, Charles J. 1985. Frames and the semantics of understanding. Quaderni di Semantica 6(2), 222–254. Proceedings of the Fourteenth Annual Meeting of the Berkeley Linguistics Society, vol. 6. Berkeley.

Fillmore, Charles J. 1999. Inversion and constructional inheritance. In G. Webelhuth, J.-P. Koenig & A. Kathol (eds.), Lexical and Constructional Aspects of Linguistic Explanation (113–128). Stanford: Center for the Study of Language and Information.

Fillmore, Charles J. 2006. The articulation of lexicon and constructicon. Plenary lecture. The Fourth International Conference on Construction Grammar (ICCG4). The University of Tokyo, Japan.

Fillmore, Charles J. Forth. Border conflicts: FrameNet meets Construction Grammar.

Fillmore, Charles J., Christopher R. Johnson, & Miriam R.L. Petruck 2003. Background to FrameNet. International Journal of Lexicography 16(3), 235–250.

Fillmore, Charles J., Paul. Kay, & Mary Catherine O'Connor 1988. Regularity and idiomaticity in grammatical constructions: The case of let alone. Language 64(3), 501–538.

Fillmore, Charles J. & Paul Kay 1993. Construction Grammar Coursebook. Berkeley: University of California [unpublished MS].

Firbas, Jan 1957. Some thoughts on the function of word-order in Old English and Modern English. Sborník Prací Filosofické Fakulty Brněnské University A5, 72–98.

Firbas, Jan 1966. Non-thematic subjects in Contemporary English. Travaux Linguistiques de Prague 2, 239–256.

Firbas, Jan 1975. On the thematic and the non-thematic section of the sentence. in H. Ringbome (ed.) Style and Text: Studies Presented to Nils Erik Enkvist (317–334). Turku & Stockholm: Åbo Akademi and Skriptor.

Fischer, Olga, Willem F. Koopman, Ans Van Kemenade & Wim van der Wurff 2000. The Syntax of Early English. Cambridge: Cambridge University Press.

Fried, Mirjam & Jan-Ola Östman 2004. Construction Grammar: A thumbnail sketch. In M. Fried & J.-O. Östman (eds.), Construction Grammar in Cross-Language Perspective (11–86). Constructional Approaches to Language 2. Amsterdam: John Benjamins.

Fries, Charles Carpenter 1952. The Structure of English: An Introduction to the Construction of English Sentences. New York: Hartcourt, Brace & World.

Gibson, Edward 1998. Linguistic complexity: Locality of syntactic dependencies. Cognition 68, 1–76.

Givón, T. 1983. Topic continuity in discourse: An introduction. In Talmi Givón (ed.), Topic Continuity in Discourse: A Quantitative Cross-Language Study Amsterdam: John Benjamins.

Givón, T. 1993. English Grammar: A Function-Based Introduction. Vol. II. Amsterdam: John Benjamins.

Givón, T. 2001a. Syntax: An Introduction. Vol. I. Amsterdam: John Benjamins.

Givón, T. 2001b. Syntax: An Introduction. Vol. II. Amsterdam: John Benjamins.

Glinert, Lewis 1989. The Grammar of Modern Hebrew. Cambridge: Cambridge University Press.

Goldberg, Adele E. 1991. It can't go up the chimney down: Paths and the English resultative. Berkeley Linguistic Society 17, 368–378.

Goldberg, Adele E. 1995. Constructions: A Construction Grammar Approach to Argument Structure. Chicago: University of Chicago Press.

Goldberg, Adele E. 2003. Constructions: A new theoretical approach to language. Trends in Cognitive Sciences 7, 219–224.

Goldberg, Adele E. 2006. Constructions at Work: The Nature of Generalization in Language. Oxford: Oxford University Press.

Goldberg, Adele E., Devin Casenhiser & Tiffani R. White 2007. Constructions as categories of language. New Ideas in Psychology 25, 70–86.

Goldberg, Adele E. & Alex Del Giudice 2005. Subject-Auxiliary Inversion: A Natural Category. Linguistic Review 22, 411–428.

Goldberg, Adele E. & Ray Jackendoff 2004. The English resultative as a family of constructions. Language 80, 532–567.

Goldenberg, Gideon [1985] 1998. On verbal structure and the Hebrew verb (English translation of 1985 Hebrew article). In G. Goldenberg, Studies in Semitic Linguistics (148–196). Jerusalem: Magnes Press of the Hebrew University.

Greenbaum, Sidney & Randolph Quirk 1990. A Student's Grammar of the English Language. Essex: Longman.

Gundel, Jeanette K. 1985. Shared knowledge and topicality. Journal of Pragmatics 9, 83–107.

Haegeman, Liliane & Jacqueline Guéron 1999. English Grammar: A Generative Persapective. Oxford: Blackwell.

Haiman, John, (ed.) 1985. Iconicity in Syntax: Proceedings of a Symposium on Iconicity in Syntax, Stanford, June 24–26, 1983. Amsterdam: John Benjamins.

Halliday, Michael A.K. 1967. Notes on transitivity and theme: Part 2. Journal of Linguistics 3, 199–244.

Halliday, Michael A.K. 1994. An Introduction to Functional Grammar. London: E. Arnold.

Hannay, Michael 1985. English Existentials in Functional Grammar. Dordrech: Foris Publications.

Harris, Zellig S. 1951. Methods in Structural Linguistics. Chicago: University of Chicago Press.

Hatcher, Anna Granville 1956. The existential sentence and inversion of the subject in Spanish. Supplement to Word Monograph No. 3, 5–24.

Hazout, Ilan 2004. The syntax of existential constructions. Linguistic Inquiry 35(3), 393–430.

Heine, Bernd 1997. Possession: Cognitive Sources, Forces, and Grammaticalization. Cambridge: Cambridge University Press.

Hemingway, Ernest 1968. The Old Man and The Sea. Worcester: Trinity Press.

Hetzron, Robert 1975. The presentative movement: Or why the ideal word order is V.S.O.P. In C.N. Li (ed.), Word order and Word Order Change (347–388). Austin: University of Texas Press.

Hjelmslev, Louis [1943] 1961. Prolegomena to a Theory of Language. 2nd revised English edition, translated by Francis J. Whitfield. Madison: University of Wisconsin Press.

Hoffmann, Sebastian 2005. Grammaticalization and English Complex Prepositions: A Corpus-Based Study. Routledge Advances in Corpus Linguistics. New York: Routledge.

Holt, Jim 1996. Beauty's truth: A defense of scientific elegance. Slate, 1996/7/24.

Hopper, Paul J. 1979. Aspect and foregrounding in discourse. Syntax and Semantics 12, 213–241.

Huddleston, Rodney 1984. Introduction to the Grammar of English. Cambridge: Cambridge University Press.

Huddleston, Rodney 2001. English Grammar: An Outline. Cambridge: Cambridge University Press.

Huddleston, Rodney & Geoffrey K. Pullum 2002. The Cambridge Grammar of the English Language. Cambridge: Cambridge University Press.

Jackendoff, Ray 1997. The Architecture of the Language Faculty. Linguistic Inquiry Monographs. Cambridge MA: MIT Press.

Jackson, Howard 1981. A Comparison of sentence patterns in English and German. Papers and Studies in Contrastive Linguistics 13, 69–81.

Jakobson, Roman [1932] 1984. The structure of the Russian verb. In L. Waugh & M. Halle (eds.), Russian and Slavic Grammar Studies, 1931–1981 (1–14). Berlin: Mouton.

Jespersen, Otto 1924. The Philosophy of Grammar. London: George Allen and Unwin.

Jespersen, Otto [1937] 1984. Analytic Syntax. Chicago: University of Chicago Press.

Jurafsky, Daniel 1992. An on-line computational model of human sentence interpretation. Technical Report: CSD-92-676. UC Berkely.

Kaltenböck, Günther 2000. It-extraposition and non-extraposition in English discourse. Corpus Linguistics and Linguistic Theory: Papers from the Twentieth International Conference on English Language Research on Computerized Corpora (ICAME 20).

Kautsch, Emil Friedrich & Arthur Ernest Cowley (eds.) 1910. Gesenius' Hebrew Grammar. Second English edition. Oxford: Clarendon Press.

Kay, Paul 2005. Argument structure constructions and the argument–adjunct distinction. In M. Fried and H.C. Boas (eds.), Grammatical Constructions: Back to the Roots (71–98). Constructional Approaches to Language 4. Amsterdam: John Benjamins.

Kay, Paul & Chad K. McDaniel 1978. The linguistic significance of the meanings of basic color terms. Language 54, 610–646.

Kidron, Yael & Ron Kuzar 2002. My face is paling against my will: Emotion and control in English and Hebrew. Special Issue: The Body in Description of Emotion. Edited by Nick. J Enfield & Anna Wierzbicka. Pragmatics and Cognition 10(1–2), 129–157.

Kiefer, Ferenc 1990–1991. Noun incorporation in Hungarian. Acta Linguistica Hungarica 40(1–2), 149–177.

Komagata, Nobo 2003. Contextual effects on word order: Information structure and information theory. Proceedings of Modeling and Using Context: 4th International and Interdisciplinary Conference, CONTEXT 2003, Stanford, CA, USA, June 23–25, 2003 (190–203). Berlin & Heidelberg, Springer.

Kuningas, Johanna & Jaakko Leino 2006. Word order and construction grammar. SKY Journal of Linguistics 19, 301–309: (Special supplement: A Man of Measure: Festschrift in Honour of Fred Karlsson on his 60th Birthday).

Kuno, Susumu 1971. The position of locatives in existential sentences. Linguistic Inquiry 2(3), 333–378.

Kuroda, Sige-Yuki 1972. The categorical and the thetic judgment (evidence from Japanese). Foundations of Language 9, 153–185.

Kuzar, Ron 1989. mivne hameser šel hamišpat be'ivrit isre'elit [Message Structure of the Sentence in Israeli Hebrew]. Ph.D. Dissertation. Jerusalem, Hebrew University.

Kuzar, Ron 1992a. Message structure of interrogatives. Lingua Posnaniensis 34, 35–46.

Kuzar, Ron 1992b. The unfolding of predicate valency in the sentence. Folia Linguistica 26(3–4), 305–331.

Kuzar, Ron 1993. haxagam: xelek dibur o emda taxbirit [The impersonal predicate: A part of speech or a syntactic position?]. Leshonenu 56(3), 241–248.

Kuzar, Ron 1996. lama miflacot nimšaxot le'avtipusim: iyun betorat ha'avtipusim babalšanut [Why freaks are attracted to prototypes: An inquiry into prototype theory in linguistics]. Proceedings of the Eleventh Annual Meeting of the Members of the Societas Linguistica Europaea in Israel, 69–73.

Kuzar, Ron 1997. Scientificity in linguistic practice: Structuralism. Semiotica 113(3–4), 223–256.

Kuzar, Ron 2000. ašrei hama'amin vetavniyot domot ba'ivrit al revadeha [ašrei hama'amin and other similar constructions in the different historical layers of Hebrew]. Balshanut Ivrit 46, 55–67.

Kuzar, Ron 2002. tavnit haxagam hapšuta balašon hameyuceget kimeduberet [The simple impersonal construction in texts represented as Colloquial Hebrew]. In S. Izre'el (ed.), medabrim ivrit: lexeker halašon hameduberet vehašonut halešonit beyisra'el [Speaking Hebrew: Studies in the Spoken Language and in Linguistic Variation in Israel] (=Teuda 18) (329–352). Tel-Aviv: Tel-Aviv University.

Kuzar, Ron 2006. tavnit mišpat hakiyum ketoremet lemašma'ut hakiyum [The existential sentence construction as a contributor to existential meaning]. mexkarim belašon [Language Studies] of the Hebrew University in Jerusalem 10, 101–112.

Kuzar, Ron 2007. digmei hamishpat shel ha'ivrit hayisre'elit al-pi Rosén [The sentence patterns of Israeli Hebrew according to Rosén]. ha'ivrit ve'axyoteha [Hebrew and its Sisters] 6–7, 269–294.

Lakoff, George 1987. Women, Fire, and Dangerous Things: What Caregories reveal about the Mind. Chicago: University of Chicago Press.

Lakoff, George & Mark Johnson 1980. Metaphors We Live By. Chicago: University of Chicago Press.

Lakoff, George & Mark Johnson 1999. Philosophy in the Flesh: The Embodied Mind and Its Challenge to Western Thought. New York: Basic Books.

Lambrecht, Knud 1994. Information Structure and Sentence Form: Topic, Focus and the Representation of Discourse Referents. Cambridge: Cambridge University Press.

Lambrecht, Knud 2000. When subjects behave like objects: An analysis of the merging of S and O in sentence focus constructions across languages. Studies in Language 24(3), 611–682.

Lambrect, Knud 2004. On the interaction of information structure and formal structure in constructions: The case of French right-detached comme-N. In Mirjam Fried & Jan-Ola Östman (eds.), Construction Grammar in cross-Language Perspective, Constructional Approaches to Language 2. Amsterdam: John Benjamins.

Langacker, Ronald W. 1987. Foundations of Cognitive Grammar: Volume I: Theoretical Prerequisites. Stanford: Stanford University Press.
Langacker, Ronald W. 1991. Foundations of Cognitive Grammar: Volume II: Descriptive Application. Stanford: Stanford University Press.
Langacker, Ronald W. 2000. Grammar and Conceptualization. Berlin: Mouton de Gruyter.
Leech, Geoffrey & Jan Svartvik 1975. A Communicative Grammar of English. Essex: Longman.
Levin, Beth 1993. English Verb Classes and Alternations: A Preliminary Investigation. Chicago and London: University of Chicago Press.
Levin, Beth & Malka Rappaport Hovav 2005. Argument Realization. Cambridge: Cambridge University Press.
Li, Charles N. & Sandra A. Thompson 1976. Subject and topic: A new typology of language. In C.N. Li (ed.) Subject and Topic (466–471). London: Academic Press.
Loewenstamm, Samuel E. 1983. hakinuy hadavuk šel hašem kenasu be'ivrit uve'ugaritit [The pronominal suffix of the noun as a predicate in Hebrew and in Ugaritic]. Leshonenu 47, 149–150.
Longacre, Robert E. 1987. The semantics of the storyline in East and West Africa. Journal of Semantics 5, 51–64.
Lowth, Robert [1753] 1787. Lectures on the Sacred Poetry of the Hebrews. Translated by Richard Gregory. London: J. Johnson.
Lumsden, Michael 1988. Existential Sentences: Their Structure and Meaning. London: Routledge.
Lyons, John 1969. Introduction to Theoretical Linguistics. Cambridge: Cambridge University Press.
Martinez Insua, Ana Elina 2001. Present Day English existential there-constructions and their pragmatics. Towards an integrated categorisation. Miscelánea: A Journal of English and American Studies 23, 29–56.
Mathesius, Vilém 1928. On linguistic characterology with illustrations from Modern English. Actes du premier congres international des linguiste, 56–63.
Mathesius, Vilém 1929. Zur Satzperspektive im Modernen Englisch [On sentence perspective in Modern English]. Archiv für das Studium der neueren Sprachen un Literaturen 84(155), 202–210.
Mathesius, Vilém 1943. Ze srovnávacich studií slovosledných [From comparative word order Studies]. Časopis pro moderní filologii 28, 181–190, 302–307.
Mathesius, Vilém [1961] 1975. A Functional Analysis of Present Day English on a General Linguistic Basis. In Josef Vachek (ed.), translated by Libuše Dušková. The Hague & Paris: Mouton.
Matushansky, Ora 2002. Tipping the scales: The syntax of scalarity in the complement of seem. Syntax 5(3), 219–276.
McCann, Hugh J. 1979. Nominals, facts, and two conceptions of events. Philosophical Studies 35, 129–149.
McNally, Louise 1998. Existential sentences without existential quantification. Linguistics and Philosophy 21(3), 353–392.
Melnik, Nurit 2002. Verb-Initial Constructions in Modern Hebrew. Ph.D. Dissertation. University of California at Berkely.
Melnik, Nurit 2006. A constructional approach to verb-initial constructions in Modern Hebrew. Cognitive Linguistics 17(2), 153–198.

Michaelis, Laura A. & Hartwell S. Francis 2007. Lexical subjects and the conflation strategy. In N. Hedberg & R. Zakharski (eds.) Topics in the Grammar-Pragmatics Interface: Papers in Honor of Jeanette K. Gundel (19–48). Amsterdam: John Benjamins.

Michaelis, Laura A. & Knud Lambrecht 1996a. The exclamative sentence type in English. In A. Goldberg (ed.), Conceptual Structure, Discourse and Language (375–389). Stanford: Center for the Study of Language and Information.

Michaelis, Laura A. 1996b. Toward a construction-based theory of language function: The case of nominal extraposition. Language 72(2), 215–247.

Miller, Philip 2001. Discourse constraints on (non)-extraposition from subject in English. Linguistics 39(4), 683–701.

Milsark, Gary Lee 1979. Existential Sentences in English. New York and London: Garland Publishing.

Mithun, Marianne 1984. The evolution of noun incorporation. Language 60(4), 847–894.

Moore, Farrell & John Ackerman 2001. Proto-Properties and Grammatical Encoding: A Correspondence Theory of Argument Selection. Stanford monographs in linguistics. Stanford: CSLI Publications.

Moravcsik, E. & J. Wirth 1986. Markedness – An Overview. In F. R. Eckman, E. Moravcsik & J.R. Wirth (eds.), Markedness New York: Plenum Press.

Moro, Andrea 1997. The Raising of Predicates. Cambridge: Cambridge University Press.

Nakajima, Heizo 2001. Verbs in locative constructions and the generative lexicon. The Linguistic Review 18, 43–67.

Nemoto, Noriko 2005. Verbal polysemy and Frame Semantics in Construction Grammar: Some observations on the locative alternation. In Mirjam Fried & Hans C. Boas (eds.), Grammatical Constructions: Back to the Roots, Constructional Approaches to Language 4. Amsterdam: John Benjamins.

Netz, Hadar & Ron. Kuzar 2011. Word order and discourse functions in Spoken Hebrew: A case study of possessive sentences. Studies in Language 35(1), 41–71.

Nida, Eugene A [1963] 1966. Synopsis of English Syntax (Janua Linguarum, Series Practica: No. 19) (second revised edition). The Hague: Mouton.

Nikiforidou, Kiki 2010. Discoursal categories and grammatical description: A constructional integration. ICCG-6 – International Conference on Construction Grammar 6. Prague.

Nuyts, Jan 2005. Modality: Overview and linguistic issues. In W. Frawley (ed.), E. Eschenroeder, S. Mills, & T. Nguyen (assist. eds.), The Expression of Modality (1–26). Berlin: Mouton de Gruyter.

Om Grammar 2008. Prepositional Phrases Commonly used. Http://www.ompersonal.com.ar/omgrammar/frasespreposicionales.htm.

Ornan, Uzzi 1979. ha-mišpat ha-pašut [The Simple Sentence]. Jerusalem: Academon.

Östman, Jan-Ola 2010. On external features in Construction Grammar: The case of the TatT-Construction. ICCG-6 – International Conference on Construction Grammar 6. Prague.

Paducheva, Elena V. 2007. Locative and existential meaning of the Russian Byt. Annual Meeting of the Slavic Cognitive Linguistics Association. Chicago.

Palmer, Frank Robert 2001. Mood and Modality^2. Cambridge: Cambridge Univesity Press.

Payne, Doris L. & Immanuel Barshi (eds.) 1999. External Possession. Amsterdam: John Bejamins.

Polotsky, Hans Jacob 1944. Étude de syntaxe copte. Cairo: Société d'Arxchéologie Copte. (Reprinted in Polotsky 1971).

Polotsky, Hans Jacob 1960. The Coptic conjugation system. Orientalia 29, 392–422. (Reprinted in Polotsky 1971.)

Polotsky, Hans Jacob 1971. Collected Papers. Jerusalem: Magnes Press.
Postal, Paul M. 1974. On Raising: One Rule of English Grammar and Its Theoretical Implications. Cambridge MA: MIT Press.
Quirk, Randolph, Sidney Greenbaum, Geoffrey Leech, & Jan Svartvik 1985. Comprehensive Grammar of the English Language. Harlow: Longman.
Radford, Andrew 1988. Transformational Grammar: A First Course. Cambridge: Cambridge University Press.
Radford, Andrew 2004. Minimalist Syntax: Exploring the Structure of English. Cambridge: Cambridge University Press.
Rafajlovičová, Rita 2010. Variation of clause patterns: Reordering the information in a message. In A. Kačmárová (ed.), English Matters: A collection of papers by the Department of English Language and Literature Faculty (30–36). Prešov: University of Prešov.
Rando, Emily & Donna Jo Napoli 1978. Definiteness in there-sentences. Language 54(2), 300–313.
Rappaport Hovav, Malka & Beth Levin 1998. Building verb meanings. In Miriam Butt & Wilhelm Geuder (eds.), The Projection of Arguments: Lexical and Compositional Factors (97–134). Stanford: CSLI Publications.
Reinhart, Tanya 2002. The theta system – An overview. Theoretical Linguistics 28(3), 229–290.
Richards, Jack, John Platt, & Heidi Platt 1992. Longman Dictionary of Language Teaching and Applied Linguistics. Essex: Longman.
Rosch, Eleanor & Carolyn B. Mervis 1975. Family resemblances: Studies in the internal structure of categories. Cognitive Psychology 7(1), 573–605.
Rosch, Eleanor 1978. Principles of categorization. In Eleanor Rosch & Barbara B. Lloyd (eds.), Cognition and Categorization (27–48). Hillsdale: Lawrence Erlbaum.
Rosenbaum, Peter S. 1967. The Grammar of English Predicate Complement Constructions. Cambridge, MA: MIT Press.
Rosén, Haiim B. 1966. ivrit tova: iyunim betaxbir[2] [Good Hebrew: Studies in Syntax]. Jerusalem: Kiryat Sepher.
Rosén, Haiim B. 1977a. Contemporary Hebrew. The Hague: Mouton.
Rosén, Haiim B. 1977b. ivrit tova: iyunim betaxbir[3] [Good Hebrew: Studies in Syntax]. Jerusalem: Kiryat Sepher.
Rubinstein, Eliezer 1968. hamišpat hašemani: iyunim betaxbir yameinu [The nominal Sentence: A Study in the Syntax of Contemporary Hebrew]. Tel-Aviv: Hakibbutz Hameuchad.
Ruppenhofer, Josef, Michael Ellsworth, Miriam R.L. Petruck, Christopher R. Johnson & Jan Scheffczyk 2006. FrameNet II: Extended Theory and Practice. Berkeley: International Computer Science Institute.
Ruwet, Nicolas 1991. Syntax and Human Experience. Translated by John Goldsmith. Chicago: University of Chicago Press.
Sag, Ivan A. 2010. Sign-based construction grammar: An informal synopsis. In Hans C. Boas and Ivan A. Sag (eds.), Sign-Based Construction Grammar (39–160). Stanford: Center for the Study of Language and Information. Http://lingo.stanford.edu/sag/papers/theo-syno.pdf. Accessed: September 18, 2010.
Sandra, Dominiek 1998. What linguists can and can't tell you about the human mind: A reply to Croft. Cognitive Linguistics 9(4), 361–478.
Sasaki, Miyuki 1991. An analysis of sentences with nonreferential there in Spoken American English. Word 42(2), 157–178.
Sasse, Hans-Jürgen 1987. The Thetic/categorical distinction revisited. Linguistics 25(2), 511–580.

Saussure, Ferdinand de [1916] 1959. Course in General Linguistics. In Charles Bally & Albert Sechehaye (ed.), translated by Wade Baskin. New York: Philosophical Library.

Schmid, Hans-Jörg 2000. English Abstract Nouns as Conceptual Shells: From Corpus to Cognition. Topics in English linguistics. Berlin, New York: Mouton de Gruyter.

Seiler, Hansjakob 1983. Possession as an Operational Dimension of Language. Tübingen: Gunter Narr Verlag.

Shlonsky, Ur 1997. Clause Structure and Word Order in Hebrew. Functional Grammar. London.

Siwierska, Anna 1991. Functionl Grammar. London: Routledge.

Smith, Carlota S. 2003. Modes of Discourse: The Local Structure of Texts. Cambridge: Cambridge University Press.

Strawson, Peter F. 1964. Identifying reference and truth values. Theoria 30, 96–118.

Tanada, Tomoyuki 2002. Synchronic and diachronic aspects of overt subjects raising in English. Lingna 112(8), 619–646.

Taylor, J. R. 1989. Linguistic Categorization: Prototypes in Linguistic Theory. Oxford: Clarendon.

Tomasello, Michael 2003. Constructing a Language: A Usage-Based Theory of Language Acquisition. Cambridge MA: Harvard University Press.

Traugott, Elizabeth Closs 2010. Contexts and grammatical constructionalization. ICCG-6 – International Conference on Construction Grammar 6. Prague.

Tyler, Andrea & Vyvyan Evans 2003. The Semantics of English Prepositions: Spatial Scenes, Embodied Meaning and Cognition. Cambridge: Cambridge University Press.

Van Linden, An & Kristin Davidse 2009. The clausal complementation of deontic-evaluative adjectives in extraposition constructions: A synchronic–diachronic approach. Folia Linguistica 43(1), 171–211.

Van Valin, Robert D. Jr. & Randy J. LaPolla 1997. Syntax: Structure, Meaning, and Function. Cambridge textbooks in linguistics. Cambridge: Cambridge University Press.

Weil, Henri [1844] 1887. The Order of Words in the Ancient Languages Compared with That of the Modern Languages. Charles W. Super (Trans.).Boston: Ginn & Company.

Whitney, William Dwight 1875. The Life and Growth of Language: An Outline of Linguistic Science. New York: D. Appleton.

Williams, Alexander 2000. Null subjects in Middle English existentials. In Susan Pintzuk, George Tsoulas & Anthony Warner (eds.). Diachronic Syntax: Models and Mechanisms (164–187). Oxford: Oxford University Press.

Wright, William 1933. A Grammar of the Arabic Language: Translated from the German of Caspari and Edited with Numerous Additions and Corrections[3]. In W. Robertson Smith & M. J. de Goeje (Rev.). Cambridge: Cambridge University Press.

Zewi, Tamar 2000. Is there a tripartite nominal sentence in Biblical Hebrew? Journal of Northwest Semitic Languages 26(2), 51–63.

Ziv, Yael 1976. On the reanalysis of grammatical terms in Hebrew possessive constructions. In Peter Cole (ed.), Studies in Modern Hebrew Syntax (129–152). Amsterdam: North Holland Publishing Company.

Ziv, Yael 1982. On so-called 'existentials': A typological problem. Lingua 56, 261–81.

Index of constructions

This index lists the figures that represent each construction in a box format. The discussion of each construction precedes and sometimes follows the box. The exact scope of discussion of each construction may be looked up in the detailed Table of Contents. All the occurrences of the names of the constructions are also listed in the Subject Index.

Figure 5.	Verbal S-pattern in English	17
Figure 6.	Argument structure construction mapped onto S-pattern via label matching	18
Figure 8.	Nominal Copular S-pattern in English	35
Figure 9.	Adjectival Copular S-pattern in English	36
Figure 10.	Prepositional Copular S-pattern in English	37
Figure 11.	Copular S-pattern in English (unified)	54
Figure 12.	Verbal S-pattern in Hebrew	55
Figure 13.	Copular S-pattern in Hebrew (unified)	59
Figure 14.	Existential S-pattern in English	67
Figure 15.	Existential S-pattern in English (detailed version)	67
Figure 16.	Evaluative S-pattern in English	79
Figure 17.	The Cost S-pattern in English	83
Figure 18.	The Environmental S-pattern in English	84
Figure 19.	Existential S-pattern in Hebrew	94
Figure 20.	The Deteriorating Entity S-pattern in Hebrew	103
Figure 21.	Evaluative S-pattern in Hebrew with a nominal as evaluee	104
Figure 22.	Unified P1 S-pattern in Hebrew	110
Figure 23.	The Cost S-pattern in Hebrew	114
Figure 24.	The Body-part-condition S-pattern in Hebrew	117
Figure 25.	The Animal-induced-condition S-pattern	118
Figure 26.	The Environmental S-pattern in Hebrew	123
Figure 27.	The PredP-alone S-pattern in Hebrew	126
Figure 28.	The field of S-patterns in English	134

Figure 29.	The S1 root node for English and Hebrew	135
Figure 30.	The COP node for English and Hebrew	135
Figure 31.	The P1 root node for English and Hebrew	135
Figure 32.	The P1 + FC node for English and Hebrew	136
Figure 33.	The field of S-patterns in Hebrew	136

Author index

A
Ackerman, John 18
Aghion, Gallith 209–210
Alba-Salas, Josep 83
Allen, Barbara J 219
Allsopp, Fred W. 25
Ariel, Mira 192
Azar, Moshe 213

B
Bain, Alexander 33
Baker, Mark C. 219
Bally, Charles 57
Barri, Nimrod 78
Barshi, Immanuel 227
Battistella, Edwin L. 22
Beckner, Clay 39
Bell, Sarah J. 227
Bendavid, Abba 155
Benveniste, Emile 57, 142
Bergs, Alexander 2
Berman, Ruth A. 119
Biber, Douglas 35
Birner, Betty 100, 167, 197–198
Bloomfield, Leonard 133
Boas, Hans C. xvii, 2
Bolinger, Dwight I. 74, 83, 144, 191
Bolozky, Shmuel 57, 119
Breivik, Leiv E. 66, 70, 142, 217
Brentano, Franz 134, 189–190
Brockelmann, Carl 227–228
Brugman, Claudia 144
Buyssens, Eric 78
Bybee, Joan xiv, 39, 205
Byrd, Patricia 42

C
Carnie, Andrew 2
Casenhiser, Devin 10
Chafe, Wallace 96, 188, 191
Chomsky, Noam xiii–xiv, xvi, 150
Coffin, Edna A. 57, 119
Cowley, Arthur E. 44

Croft, William xiv, 4, 11–12, 21, 29, 49

D
Daneš, František 193
Davidse, Kristin 73
Del Giudice, Alex 10
Diewald, Gabriele 2
Dori-Hacohen, Gonen 88
Dowty, David 18–19, 24
Driver, Samuel R. 44
Du Bois, John W. 192
Durie, Mark 191

E
Ellsworth, Michael 142
Emonds, Joseph F. 72
Erdmann, Peter 67, 71
Evans, Vyvyan 144

F
Fauconnier, Gilles xiv
Fillmore, Charles J. xiv, 1, 5, 19, 25, 50, 88, 107, 133
Firbas, Jan 188, 194
Francis, Hartwell S. 194
Frantz, Donald G. 219
Fried, Mirjam 1, 8, 235
Fries, Charles C. xv, 100

G
Gardiner, Donna B. 219
Gibson, Esward 191
Givón, T. xvii, 19, 46, 69, 78, 142–143, 190
Glinert, Lewis 57, 119
Goldberg, Adele xiv, 1–10, 15–19, 21, 25, 29, 42, 60, 63–64, 123, 126, 128, 133, 145, 233, 236
Goldenberg, Gideon 57
Greenbaum, Sidney 42, 143, 151, 199
Guéron, Jacqueline 83, 199
Gundel, Jeanette 194

H
Haegeman, Liliane 83, 199
Haiman, John 191
Halliday, Michael A.K. 21, 190–191
Harris, Zellig S. xv
Hatcher, Anna G. 144
Hazout, Ilan 142
Heine, Bernd 89–90
Hemingway, Ernest 183
Hetzron, Robert 69
Hjelmslev, Louis 11
Hoffmann, Sebastian 41
Holt, Jim 4–5
Hopper, Paul J. 33, 45
Huddleston, Rodney 35, 36, 38, 72–73, 76, 143, 198

J
Jackendoff, Ray 60, 145
Jackson, Howard xvi
Jakobson, Roman 22
Jespersen, Otto xiv, 38, 39, 45, 49, 69, 204
Johnson, Mark xiv, 137, 215
Johnson, Christopher R. 88, 142
Jurafsky, Daniel 5, 25

K
Kaltenböck, Günther 73
Kautsch, Emil F. 44
Kay, Paul xiv, 1–2, 19, 50, 110
Kemenade, Ans Van 203
Kidron, Yael 24
Kiefer, Ferenc 219
Komagata, Nobo 194
Koopman, Willem F. 203
Kuningas, Johanna 10
Kuno, Susumu 142
Kuroda, Sige-Yuki 134
Kuzar, Ron xvi, 12, 24, 75, 94, 107, 155, 167, 191–193, 195, 224

L
Lakoff, George xiv, 1, 25, 39, 43, 63, 71, 100, 137, 144–145, 215
Lambrecht, Knud 43–44, 69, 74, 96, 108, 135, 137, 167, 187–188, 190–191, 194–195, 198–199
Langacker, Ronald W. xiv, 11, 90, 205
LaPolla, Randy J. 2
Leech, Geoffrey 35, 42, 143, 151, 199
Leino, Jaakko 10
Levin, Beth 5, 19, 28, 52, 60, 83, 145
Li, Charles N. 193
Loewenstamm, Samuel E. 227–228
Longacre, Robert E. 33
Lowth, Robert 224
Lumsden, Michael 71
Lyons, John 143

M
Martinez Insua, Ana Elina 69
Mathesius, Vilém 24, 70, 194
Matushansky, Ora 53
McCann, Hugh J. 75
McNally, Louise 141, 212
Melnik, Nurit 100, 117, 141
Michaelis, Laura A. 74, 108, 194
Miller, Philip 73
Milsark, Gary L. 66–67, 70, 100, 141
Mithun, Marianne 219, 225
Moore, Farrell 18
Moravcsik, E. 145
Moro, Andrea 142

N
Nakajima, Heizo 167
Napoli, Donna J. 100
Nemoto, Noriko 2

Netz, Hadar 94, 157, 195
Nida, Eugene A. xv, 25, 27
Nikiforidou, Kiki 2
Nuyts, Jan 171–173

O
Ornan, Uzzi 121
Östman, Jan-Ola 1–2, 8, 235

P
Paducheva, Elana V. 143
Palmer, Frank R. 173
Payne, Doris L. 227
Petruck, Miriam R.L. 88, 142
Platt, Heidi 42
Platt, John 42
Polotsky, Hans J. xiv–xvi
Postal, Paul M. 77
Pullum, Geoffrey K. 35, 38, 78, 143, 198

Q
Quirk, Randolph 38, 42, 143, 151, 199

R
Radford, Andrew 83, 142
Rafajlovičová, Rita 198
Rando, Emily 100
Rappaport Hovav, Malka 5, 19, 28
Reinhart, Tanya 72
Richards, Jack 42
Rosch, Eleanor 137, 144
Rosén, Haiim B. xv–xvii, 57–58, 90, 93–94, 105, 119, 170, 213–214
Rosenbaum, Peter S. 72–73
Rubinstein, Eliezer xvi, 57–58, 119, 122, 213
Ruppenhofer, Josef 142
Ruwet, Nicolas 83

S
Sag, Ivan A. 2
Sandra, Dominiek 144
Sasaki, Miyuki 69
Sasse, Hans-Jürgen 135
Saussure, Ferdinand de 4, 10
Scheffczyk, Jan 142
Schmid, Hans-Jörg 109
Seiler, Hansjakob 193
Shlonsky, Ur 155
Siwierska, Anna
Smith, Carlota S. 33, 73
Strawson, Peter F. 191
Svartvik, Jan 42, 143, 151, 199

T
Tanada, Tomoyuki
Taylor, J.R. 193
Thompson, Sandra A. 193
Tomasello, Michael xiv
Traugott, Elizabeth C. 2
Tyler, Andrea 144

V
Van der Wurff, Wim 203
Van Linden, An 73
Van Valin, Robert D. Jr. 2

W
Ward, Gregory 100, 167, 197–198
Weil, Henri 189–191, 194
White, Tiffani R. 10
Whitney, William D. 57
Williams, Alexander 203
Wirth, J. 145
Wright, William 45

Z
Zewi, Tamar 57
Ziv, Yael 44, 101

Subject index

A

action
volitional (agentive event) 22–23, 33, 43–44, 56, 163, 187, 189, 191–192, 194, 200–201
of animals, 118–119
intrinsic 151, 161
affectee 50, 53–54, 65, 75–83, 87, 102, 107, 112, 114–115, 117–119, 123–124, 126–127, 129, 137, 186,
ad hoc (in English) 154
affectee-turned-possessor, 90, 100, 112, 129, 154, 162, 165–166, 195–196, 226–227, 229
incorporated 220–222, 224–227, 229
affecting pred(icate) 126
agentive event *see* action
animal's action pred(icate) 118
Animal-induced-condition S-pattern 117–118, 127, 129–130, 136–137, 196
argument structure construction 3–10, 16–20, 29, 31–32, 50, 60, 63–64, 133, 138, 216–217
assigned pred(icate) function, 135
assigned term, 45–47, 49–52, 54–55, 59, 61
assignment/assigner
of attribution (of property to a term) 21, 23–24, 36–37, 41, 44, 46, 49–51, 54–55, 135, 197
of equivalence (between two terms) 21, 35–36, 39, 41, 44, 46, 49–55, 135, 197
of relation (between two terms) 36–41, 44, 46, 49–51, 53–55, 59, 135
attribution *see* assignment/assigner

B

background (information) 43–45, 60, 69, 82, 85, 187, 189, 192–193, 201
see also foreground
basis subject 21, 24, 36–38, 40, 45–46, 49–50, 54–55, 59, 61, 135, 197
bipartite (sentence structure) 57, 86, 120, 134–135, 187–188, 191, 201
bodily process pred(icate) 117
bodily state 115–116, 129–130
body-part-condition S-pattern, 114, 116–117, 123, 125, 136, 172
borderline
between copular and lexical verbs 51, 53, 54
between evaluative and existential meaning 99, 108, 110–111, 113, 128, 131

C

categorial affiliation (part of speech) 14–15, 17, 20–21, 31, 35, 38, 64, 66, 74–75, 85, 87, 105–106, 119, 138, 181 55, 80, 85, 105–106, 214
CC (conceptual category) 130, 141–142, 144–145, 201, 217
of environmental conditions 85, 181–186
of evaluation 169–180, 205–210
of existence 141–168
circumstantial clause 44–45
comparative-correlative construction/S-pattern 1, 50, 218
composite category 110, 113, 131
composite preposition (PNP) 37, 39–41, 50, 54, 58–59, 61
conceptual category see CC
considered referent 135–136
constructicon 5, 25, 133, 139
COP(ular) S-pattern 16, 21, 187–188, 190, 192, 201, 204–205
A(djectival) COP S-pattern 21, 23–24, 34, 36–37, 45–46, 50, 105, 114, 134, 136, 197
N(ominal) COP S-pattern 21, 35–36, 39, 134, 136, 197
P(repositional) COP S-pattern 21, 37–38, 40–41, 45–46, 50, 134, 136
unified COP S-pattern 43, 54–55, 58–59, 61
copula 15, 34–35, 41, 46–51, 54–58, 61, 67–68, 86–87, 90, 105, 120, 142, 212, 228
copular verb 41–43, 47–48, 50–54, 60, 68, 80
core (of CC) 130, 144–146, 150, 153–155, 158, 166–168, 170–172, 174–175, 177, 179–182, 185–186, 205–210, 214–215
cost pred(icate)/verb 81–83, 114
Cost S-pattern, 80–83, 113–114, 117, 129, 134, 136, 171
cost verb *see* cost pred(icate)

D

deictic (expression, PP, pro-form, etc.) 38–39, 50, 58, 189
depictive (copula/copular verbs) 41–42, 45, 52, 58
Deteriorating-entity S-pattern, 102–103, 116
deterioration pred(icate), 103
disappearance *see* non-existence
discourse mode 33, 43, 70
see also narrative

E

endemic (predicate) 87, 92, 104–106, 158, 163, 166, 176–177, 180, 204, 210

environmental condition 28, 65, 69, 83–85, 122, 124, 130, 181–186, 189, 193, 198
see also environmental predicate
ENV(ironmental) pred(icate)/verb 16, 84, 85, 120, 123, 183, 186.
see also environmental conditions
ENV(ironmental) S-pattern 65–66 68, 83–86, 119, 122–124, 127–129, 134–136, 139, 181–188, 198, 201
equivalence *see* assignment/assigner
EV(aluative) S-pattern 14, 16, 25–26, 65–66, 72–83, 103–114, 119, 123, 128–131, 134–136, 169–173, 175–180, 185–188, 196, 203–211, 213–215, 220, 222–225
EV(aluative) pred(icate) 13, 21, 74, 79, 80, 104, 110, 124, 169, 192, 207–209, 213, 215, 220, 222
evaluee 21, 75, 78–80, 83, 86, 103–104, 106–110, 113–114, 123–124, 128, 131, 135, 169, 172–174, 180, 186, 188, 192, 198, 204, 206–207, 220, 224
EX S-pattern 23, 25, 27, 63–64, 66–72, 79–80, 84, 86–92, 94–95, 97–104, 111, 129, 131, 134, 136, 141–142, 144–145, 148–149, 152–154, 158, 160–168, 170–171, 187–188, 195–196, 200–201, 203, 211–213, 217, 220, 225, 229, 233
existent 21, 23, 39, 64, 66–68, 86, 90, 92–94, 97–101, 103, 109–110, 112–113, 115, 123, 128–129, 131, 135, 141–145, 147–153, 157, 160, 162–163, 166–167, 186, 188, 192, 198, 212, 226–227
existent-turned-possessed 90, 101, 226–227
EX(istential) pred(icate)/verb, 66–68, 87, 92, 94, 98, 103, 110, 128–129, 141–142, 145–146, 158, 166, 168, 170–171, 179, 192, 212, 215–216, 226, 228
existential verb *see* existential predicate

Existential-modal S-pattern, 28, 215–216
expletive 63, 86, 94–95, 114, 119–120, 182
addition 206
it 12–13, 15, 63, 79, 80, 83–84, 86, 120, 131, 190, 198–199
non-canonical behavior 203–210
reduction, 204
there 15, 63, 67, 131, 190, 198
ze 203–209

F
FC *see* final component
field (of S-patterns 133–139
Final component (FC) 44, 64, 66, 86, 110–111, 123, 131, 134–136, 186, 188, 216
focus, 9, 96, 153, 192, 206
narrow (argument) focus 96–97, 137, 207–208
predicate focus (focus in the comment/PredP) 27, 33, 36, 43, 85, 137, 187–188
sentence focus 97, 137, 188–189, 191
foreground (of storyline/narrative) 33, 45, 187, 191, 193
functional role
sentential (within the S-pattern) 14–18, 20–21, 31–32, 34–35, 75 197, 214
of the S-pattern *see* narrative function

G
generalizing node, 134–136
see also instantiated node, root node
global (over a single language) 11, 20–21, 27, 29, 44, 48, 61, 63
see also universal
grain size *see* granularity
granularity (grain size, resolution) 9, 14, 29, 64, 137–139

H
hierarchy/hierarchical network 7–9, 25, 134
constituent/phrase structure 50, 61

I
implied (core meaning by periphery) 145–146, 166, 177, 181, 185
impose/imposing (meaning by construction) 145–146, 150–151, 153, 166, 178, 186, 211
incorporation 219
of argument into non-verbal predicate 220–225
of argument into argument 227–229
information structure 15, 26–29, 33, 36, 43, 73–74, 97, 130, 135, 137, 164, 187–201
instantiated node, 134–135
see also generalizing node, root node
intrinsic (predicate/property) 84, 145, 150–153, 160–162, 166

L
lexical verb, 43, 51, 142, 166, 212
lexicalist (approach to/model of sentence formation) 3, 5, 29, 60, 178, 182
LI *see* locative inversion
linearization/linearized (word order) 2–5, 7–10, 13–15, 17, 19–20, 27, 29, 31, 33–34, 44–45, 48, 63–65, 73, 86, 95–97, 122, 128, 138, 153, 156–157, 166–167, 179, 187, 189–194, 197–202, 217–218
locative inversion (LI) 28, 142, 167, 217
logical predicate, 135
logical subject, 135

M
major S-pattern 1, 21, 27–29, 31, 33, 50, 64, 133–134, 139,
marked(ness)/unmarked(ness) 22, 196–197
actions/agentive events 23, 25, 194
as part of the storyline 33
information structure 27, 33, 43–45, 135, 137, 187, 190–193, 197–199, 206
lexical meaning at core/periphery 144–146, 155

linearization/word order 3, 10, 27, 96–97, 122, 166–167, 180, 197–200
S-pattern 21–25, 31, 33, 56, 95–97, 130, 197, 201
minor S-pattern, 28, 211, 215
modal(ity) 173
  modal evaluation/ judgment 69, 80, 204, 206, 215
  types of modality 81, 123, 171–175, 177–178, 220
  inherently modal (core) predicate/ meaning 171–172, 174–175, 177, 179, 205, 208–209, 214
monopartite (sentence structure) 135, 187–188, 191, 195, 201
  see also bipartite
morphologically unique predicate (Unq) 75, 87, 92, 94, 104–106, 110, 142, 210, 214, 220, 222, 225, 229
motivation/motivated
  choice of word order 3, 10, 187, 194–195, 198
  choice of S-patterns 10, 130, 193–194, 200–201
  choice of preposition 47
  choice between V S-pattern and EV S-pattern 73–74
  Choice of information structure construction 196
  development of evaluative meaning 128
  existential meaning 150–151
  situation type motivating sentence form 187–192
multivariate (predicate slot in P1 S-patterns) 13–14, 74

N
narrative (narration)
  narrative (n.) 33, 71–72, 85, 193
  see also storyline
  narration, 33, 69, 187
  narrative function 29, 31, 33, 44–45, 60, 69, 71, 85, 129, 197
  narrative discourse mode 33, 43
  see also storyline
  narration see narrative

negative existence see non-existence
network,
  of argument structure constructions 5, 7–8, 19, 63–64
  of S-patterns 27, 64, 133–138
nominal (n.)
  nominalized situation (as a cover term for InfP, GrdP, and *that*-clause) 16, 32, 66, 75, 79, 81, 83, 86, 94, 97, 99, 103–104, 106, 108–111, 113–114, 129, 131, 135, 180, 188, 206, 214, 224
nominal sentence 57
non-canonical expletive behavior 203–211
non-existence (negative existence, disappearance) (in existential sentences) 70–72, 95, 99–100, 102, 115, 129
noun incorporation see incorporation

O
over-grammaticalization/ grammaticalized (sentence structure) 204, 206, 208–210
  see also under-grammaticalization, non-canonical expletive behavior

P
P1 S-pattern 44, 63–66, 85–86, 115, 127–129, 131, 139, 180, 186, 188–189, 194–196, 198–201
  unified 110
part of speech see categorial affiliation
patterning xvii, 1, 15–16, 28–29, 34, 45, 50–51, 54, 58, 61, 65, 142, 211–218, 226–228
periphery (of CC) 144–146, 154, 158, 165–167, 171–172, 177, 179–186, 205–207, 209–210
PNP see composite preposition
polysemy/polysemous
  in constructional meaning 214–215
  in predicates 111–113, 128, 146, 148, 150
  in prepositions 39
possessed 93–94, 226–229

  see also existent-turned-possessed
possession 89, 130
  expressed via
    existence 90–91, 101, 129, 154, 193–195, 225
  external 227
  inalienable 102
possessor, 87, 90–92, 94, 97, 100, 110, 112, 129, 154, 159, 162, 165–166, 193–195, 200, 216, 220, 222, 224–229
predicate initial S-pattern see P1 S-pattern
predication xv, xvii, 15–16, 28–29, 34–41, 43, 45–47, 49–50, 55, 60–61, 65, 211–213, 216–218, 225, 228
  secondary 66, 70
pleonastic 86
PredP-alone S-pattern, 123–127, 136, 185–186, 224
property see attribution

R
relation see assignment/assigner
relation pred(icate) 37
resolution see granularity
resultative 23, 41–42, 45, 50, 52, 58, 60–61, 169–170, 174
root node 134–135
  see also instantiated node

S
S1 S-pattern 10, 31, 33–34, 43–44, 130, 155, 166, 180, 189, 195, 201
sentence initiation 191, 201
sentential functional role see functional role
situation type 24, 31, 56, 69, 74, 82, 87, 97, 100–102, 107, 114, 117, 119, 126, 127–130, 137–139, 189–202
stand-alone (unlinked) construction 131, 133
storyline, 33, 43–45, 56, 60, 85, 100, 157, 187, 189, 191–193, 201–202
  see also narrative (n.)
stylistic (triggered) inversion 155–157
subject initial S-pattern see S1 S-pattern

suspension (suspended argument), 190–192, 198, 201, 209

T
thetic, 27, 85, 97, 100, 135, 137, 167, 187, 189, 195, 201
top-down (analysis) 4, 10–11, 14, 20, 29, 35, 43–44, 48
topic-comment 26–27, 33, 36, 43, 85, 97, 135, 137, 187–189, 195
triggered inversion *see* stylistic inversion
typology/typological XIII, XVII, 22, 57, 64, 66, 129, 136, 139, 177, 193, 198, 201, 231, 235, 239, 246

U
under-grammaticalization/grammaticalized (sentence structure) 105, 203–206
see also over-grammaticalization, non-canonical expletive behavior
universal XIII, XVI, 5, 20, 22, 29, 44, 46, 48, 61, 89–90, 189–190, 192–194
see also global
unmarked(ness) *see* marked(ness)
unq *see* morphologically unique

V
V S-pattern 31–34, 55–56, *throughout*
verbal sentence pattern *see* V S-pattern

W
word order *see* linearization/linearized